INNOVATION
JAPANESE STYLE

INNOVATION
JAPANESE STYLE

A Cultural and Historical Perspective

Paul Herbig

Q

QUORUM BOOKS
Westport, Connecticut • London

Library of Congress Cataloging-in-Publication Data

Herbig, Paul A.
  Innovation Japanese style : a cultural and historical perspective
/ by Paul Herbig.
    p.   cm.
  Includes bibliographical references and index.
  ISBN 0–89930–968–2 (alk. paper)
  1. Technological innovations—Japan.   2. Organizational change—
Japan.   3. Research, Industrial—Japan.   4. Japan—Economic
conditions—1945–   5. National characteristics, Japanese.   6. Japan—
Civilization—20th century.   I. Title.
  HC465.T4H47   1995
  338′,064′0952—dc20   94–39343

British Library Cataloguing in Publication Data is available.

Library of Congress Catalog Card Number: 94–39343
ISBN: 0–89930–968–2

First published in 1995

Quorum Books, 88 Post Road West, Westport, CT 06881
An imprint of Greenwood Publishing Group, Inc.

Printed in the United States of America

The paper used in this book complies with the
Permanent Paper Standard issued by the National
Information Standards Organization (Z39.48–1984).

10 9 8 7 6 5 4 3 2 1

To John Milewicz, Jim Golden, Ken Day, Fred Palumbo, Alan Shao, Bob Milam, Hugh Kramer, Danny Butler, Brad O'Hara, Jim Gray, Bob Gulbro, Joe Miller, Kim Marshall, Arch Woodside, Carol Howard, Barry Carr, Stephanie and Henry Smith, Alain Genestre, Joel Greene, Steve Dunphy, George Trivoli, Dabney Narvaez, and Dean Khosrow Fatemi—all my friends and collaborators, without whose support and encouragement this project would not have been started or completed. Thank you.

Special thanks to Connie Gnatz and Linda McDill, who assisted me in making a book out of a manuscript; to Marcy Weiner and Elisabetta Linton at Greenwood Press for all their invaluable assistance; and, of course, to my inspirational and supportive wife, Rachel and our sons, Robert and William, whose love and encouragement maintained me during this long endeavor.

Contents

Illustrations

FIGURES

TABLES

Introduction

Today's globally competitive environment has made it impossible for management to conduct its activities in a conventional manner. Survival, let alone success, is only possible when companies foster innovation. Innovation has become a competitive tool which enables companies to avoid the inevitable decline that comes with complacency and maintenance of the status quo. Innovation has become the source of many a company's comparative advantage in the international market arena. Innovation is a catalyst to growth and can be divided into three types: organizational, product, and technological (Makino, 1987). Organizational innovation is achieved by streamlining the structure of the company or by reorganizing the distribution system. Product innovation involves the manufacture of goods that are adapted to changes in consumer spending. Technological innovation, the focus of this book, involves growth based upon the development of new technology as well as the reorganization of the production system. Without these innovation measures, it is unlikely that a business will survive in the long run. With the shrinking global marketplace, this timeframe can be extremely short (i.e., less than a decade).

What does innovation require? According to Jorde and Teece (1990), major factors which lead to innovation include:

- the availability of a labor force with the requisite technical skills;
- economic structures that permit considerable autonomy and entrepreneurship;
- economic systems that permit and encourage a variety of approaches to technological and market opportunities;
- easy access to venture capital (either from a firm's existing cash flow or from an external venture capital community);

- good connections between the scientific community (especially the universities and research institutions) and the technological community (particularly the private sector);
- good communications between users and developers of technology;
- strong protection of intellectual property rights; and
- the availability of strategies and structures to enable innovating firms to capture a return from their investment.

How does Japan as a nation and the Japanese as a people and a society rate versus these factors? Are they truly innovative and, if so, how?

Many observers of Japan believe the Japanese are exceptional innovators and have taken the technological lead from the United States. For example, the National Science Foundation in its *The Science and Technology Resources of Japan: A Comparison with the United States* (June 1988) evaluated the relative positions in twelve technological areas in terms of basic research, advanced development, and production and engineering abilities. Japan was judged to be ahead in seven areas whereas the United States was judged to be ahead in only three (the rest were tied). In advanced development, Japan was judged ahead in four areas, even in three, and behind in five others. In basic research, Japan led in three but was behind in the other nine. The study also determined that Japan was not only ahead but was also pulling further away in fiber optics, integrated circuits, mobile radio systems, automated factory assembly, compact disk technology, and computer design. The report indicated that Japan's major weakness was in basic science and research whereas its greatest strengths were in the production and engineering areas.

However, many skeptics question Japan's innovative abilities. Many observers using the same data derive different conclusions; they believe that Japan is still primarily a "copycat" culture whereas the United States is the world's technological leader and will continue to be so. Proponents of this view indicate that even the famous Japanese management techniques are adapted and improved versions of North American models. The quality circle (QC) concept was adapted from the Scanlon Plan, which the Japanese observed in the United States and modified for their own usage during the 1950s (Sakach, 1987). Many Japanese say the QC concept is an adaptation of a local *ringi* (consensus group) and of methods which evolved from rice paddy farming. Statistical quality control was introduced in Japan in the early 1950s by W. Edwards Deming, an American. Almost all Japanese management practices can be described as a Nipponization of something seen in the West and thus interpreted differently from the way a Westerner would (even *Karaoke*, the latest fad from Japan, is good old American lip-syncing with an added Japanese twist). A 1992 McKinsey study says that while Japan has pulled ahead of the United States in several heavy manufacturing industries including cars and machinery, it lags far behind in at least half of its manufacturing base. Even many Japanese believe Japanese "society has become optimized for standardized mass production and Japan is the largest and most competitive producer in an industry only when the given products—transistors, automobiles, calculators, semi-conductors—have entered the state of mass production" (Sakaiya, 1993, p. 53).

Which side is right? Both or neither? Is Japan a superb innovator or a copycat? The technological behavior of Japanese firms is oriented toward shorter development times, an effective identification and acquisition of external technology, a higher propensity to patent, high manufacturable designs, incremental product and process improvement, competitive matching, an innovation system dominated by large firms, a tendency to combine technologies, interfirm technical cooperation, and a much stronger role of technological planning within corporate strategy. (In the United States, research and development [R&D] organizations tend to be independent of production centers whereas those in Japan are integrated with the manufacturing divisions.)

American thinking about the innovation process focuses excessively upon the earliest stages—those kinds of new products or technologies that occasionally emerge out of basic research (sometimes called radical innovation—see the Appendix for definitions and differences between the types of innovation), those creative leaps that sometimes establish entirely new product lines, and the activities of the upstream inventor or scientist rather than the downstream engineer. The emphasis is on major innovations and pioneering efforts rather than sustained effort and small improvements (Rosenberg and Steinmueller, 1988). An example of this is the American invention of the solid-state transistor. In 1953, Western Electric licensed the technology to Sony, whereupon Sony made dramatic improvements on it and launched a host of high-quality consumer electronics products. In 1968, Unimation, an American company, was the pioneer behind robots. It then licensed Kawasaki Heavy Industries to make industrial robots; the American robotics industry never quite got off the ground whereas the Japanese quickly perfected the idea. These are but two of many possible examples over the last thirty years of the Japanese improving and marketing a superior product that was *first* invented and innovated in the United States. The Japanese literally have concentrated on application to a point at which many of their copies are superior to the American originals (Sakach, 1987). When we look at Japan, we tend to see more application than we do invention. Even the literal Japanese translation of "R&D"—*kenkyu   kaihatsu*—implicitly denotes commercialization.

Imitation and application has its advantages. New state-of-the-art technology tends to be like a ladder: climb it and you acquire new knowledge that confers a competitive advantage but only until your competitors learn the new technology; then you have to climb the ladder again. Process-oriented innovation has no beginning and no end; each turn of the wheel improves an existing product and its production methods. The company unveils not-entirely-new products that keep getting better, more reliable, and cheaper, but cumulatively the advantage adds up. In addition, with the soaring cost of doing leading-edge research, the quick-moving follower has certain advantages. For example, the next-generation chipmaking method will use X-rays instead of light to print circuit patterns on silicon. Nearly half a billion dollars will have to be spent by each potential competitor to upgrade to this new technology. The number of entrants decreases in each cycle as the ante keeps climbing (the emergence of international strategic alliances is tacit acceptance that no one company, not even a company the size of Texas Instruments or Siemens, can remain in this game at this level and for these stakes). The pioneers must continue to run even faster just to stay ahead. The follower, in contrast, can watch and wait, seeing which way the wind blows; if the product or technology appears to be a winner, the follower can jump in, having allowed the pioneer to pay all the expenses of market research and development. However, being a follower (even one as good as Japan has been) still implies severe disadvantages and major risks, which could well cause an end or a slowing down of the Japanese miracle: Once a developing country has caught up and reached the technological frontier, no obvious areas exist in which application of large-scale capital can produce certainty of rewards. This is where Japan now stands—at the crossroads between being a capable follower and an inexperienced, unfamiliar, uncertain pioneer.

Within the last two decades, the Japanese economic machine has developed into the leading economy in the world on a per capita income basis, second only to the United States in Gross Domestic Product (GDP). (However, the average per capita conceals the fact that Japan's real purchasing power is reduced by the high costs of food, consumer goods, land, and housing.) Japan has virtually conquered the American consumer electronics, semiconductor, and machine tool marketplace and, except for quotas, would have done the same for the automotive segment. The reasons this has been accomplished are many, and some say it is because of the Japanese ability to listen and serve their customers, to deliver quality merchandise at a lower price, and to be innovators. Yet the question remains: How truly innovative are the Japanese? In what ways do they innovatively prosper and struggle?

This book examines innovation, how it is accomplished in Japan and explores the positives and negatives of Japan's innovative patterns by examining Japanese culture and history as indicative of its innovative policies. This book also discusses what this means through comparisons with the United States and international competition, and it provides views into future scenarios for Japanese innovative strategies and capabilities.

Chapter 1

Creativity in Japan

CREATIVITY

Any innovation represents a new concept. Concepts are created by humans. Thus innovation presupposes creativity: the ability to see or imagine new perspectives. Creativity involves problem finding as well as problem solving, and it requires talent and skills. Creation of innovations may be considered production of knowledge, since the prime purpose is to create new and better solutions which will be appreciated and accepted by customers.

Creative thinking is unconventional in that it requires the modification or rejection of previously accepted ideas. Creative thinking normally feeds on high motivation and persistence and takes place either over a relatively long period of time—continuously or intermittently—or at very high levels of intensity. A problem that requires creative thinking is normally vague and ill defined, and a critical part of the task is to formulate the problem. The three major components necessary for a truly creative individual performance are:

- domain-relevant skills (knowledge, skills, and talents from which any performance must proceed);
- creativity-relevant skills (cognitive style favorable to taking new perspectives on problems); and
- task motivation (motivational variables that determine an individual's approach to a given task).

Personality characteristics which endow creative individuals include risk-taking, curiosity, complexity, imagination, fluency, flexibility, and originality. A creative person generally has the following abilities:

- accepts conflict by tolerating bipolarity and integrating opposites;
- has a capacity to be puzzled, is able to accept tentativeness and uncertainty and is not frightened by the unknown and ambiguous;
- has a high degree of self-discipline, an ability to concentrate, and a belief in his or her ability to succeed;
- can be described as tenacious, spirited, uninhibited;
- is open to the irrational and has emotional sensitivity to others and his or her own external environment; and
- is nonconforming, accepts disorder, is not interested in details, is an individualist, does not fear being different, and is spontaneous.

The conditions necessary for the creative spirit to excel include an absence of a serious threat to self, a willingness to take risks, self-awareness, self-differentiation (seeing self as being different from others), being open to the ideas of others, and having confidence in one's own ideas. As these concepts indicate, the features and traits required for full creativity may well encouraged in some cultures and discouraged in others. As a result, creativity capabilities and levels will vary from culture to culture.

JAPANESE CREATIVITY

Five potential roles exist in the creative process: the explorer (searches for new information), the artist (turns the information into new ideas), the judge (evaluates the merits of an idea), the warrior (carries the idea into action), and the antique dealer (recycles old ideas for new applications). This cyclical form of creativity can be viewed as comprised of five related phases (see Figure 1.1):

1. Idea recycling (new uses for old and existing ideas)
2. Idea exploration (the search for new ideas when existing ideas are inadequate)
3. Idea cultivation (the seeding and incubation of new ideas)
4. Idea generation (new breakthrough ideas)
5. Idea refinement (improving and adapting new ideas to the changed environment)

Western creativity is clearly stronger in phases 2, 3, and 4. The Western scientists have traditionally excelled in pursuing basic research and exploring new scientific frontiers, activities that require maximum intellectual curiosity and a sense of adventure. In contrast, the Japanese (who have not been the explorers or inventors that Westerners have traditionally been) are strong in cultivation, refinement, and recycling (phases 1, 3, and 5).

Figure 1.1
Japanese Innovation Cycle

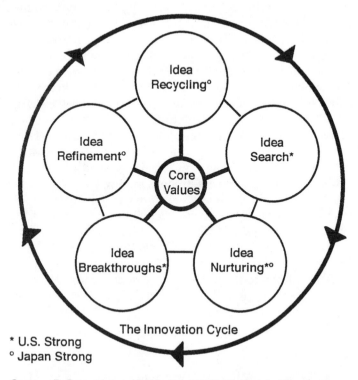

* U.S. Strong
° Japan Strong

Source: B. Bowonder and T. Miyake. (1992). "A Model of Corporate Innovation Management: Some Recent High Tech Innovations in Japan." *R&D Management* 2/4: 323. Reprinted by permission of Blackwell Publishers.

Two theories (Socrates and Protagoras), regarding the meaning and function of knowledge, dominate Western thought. Socrates held that the sole function of knowledge is self-knowledge: the intellectual, moral, and spiritual growth of the person. Protagoras, in contrast, held that the purpose of knowledge is to make the holder effective by enabling him or her to know what to say and how to say it (i.e., logic, grammar, and rhetoric). In the East (particularly Confucian thought), knowledge was similar to Protagoras' knowledge—that is, knowing what to say and how to say it is the route to advancement and earthly success. Knowledge for the Taoist and Zen follower meant self-knowledge and the road to enlightenment and wisdom. Knowledge to the Japanese traditionally has meant ability—not utility, not skill, nor the techne.

CREATIVITY—WESTERN STYLE

Western creativity reflects frontier thinking and is based on the concept of individual freedom, which favors the discovery of new ideas and product breakthroughs. Westerners (especially Americans) typically do better when targets are vague, which allows for more personal freedom and individual creativity. Western creativity is like growing wheat: It cannot be forced but must be allowed to develop spontaneously in its own way after the proper conditions have been provided. The land must be plowed, the soil fertilized, and the seeds planted. Thereafter, the process simply takes time and cannot be sped up. Western ideas are allowed to germinate quietly on their own. Western thought advocates allowing the strongest seeds to survive in an atmosphere of laissez faire (not predetermining winners and losers).

The Western view of creativity refers to generating new and novel ideas, whereas innovation involves applying the idea which will lead ultimately to increased profits or improved services. Creativity and innovation may be intimately related but are distinct concepts. Innovation is almost always a collaborative enterprise, requiring the cooperation of numerous individuals. In contrast, creativity is viewed as a flash of insight, an "ah ha" experience in which two bodies or matrices of thought, considered remote from each other, are suddenly joined. Within this definition, the Japanese are often not considered creative because they are group oriented and prefer to embellish existing ideas. Is this a true definition or a culturally biased standard?

The West values rational, scientific thought, the Socratic method of rationally framed questions and answers. This includes cross-examining, which (when combined with public debate) is the preferred tool for logical thinking or scientific exploration in the West. Americans tend to think there is always a scientific explanation for a problem. In Western creativity, individual brilliance has an opportunity to shine. American software programmers develop excellent software packages sold individually whereas Japanese programmers are believed to be better at developing integrated software for use in large-scale in-house systems. Western logic reflects its Cartesian heritage of a clear, linear path of reasoning. Westerners tend to be   straightforward and frank. The Western approach combines breakthrough, spontaneous creativity, creative fission, Cartesian logic, and unifunctional creativity. In contrast, the Japanese approach is one of adaptive and cultivated creativity, creative fusion, fuzzy logic, and multifunctional creativity. Whereupon in the West, the straightest path and quickest route to any destination, to solve any problem, is the straight line, in Japan, the circular way may be preferred.

CREATIVITY—JAPANESE STYLE

Japanese creativity is responsive, eclectic, focused, and practical. Japanese creativity is like growing rice. Japanese rice farming is an arduous, time-consuming process of cultivation. The field must be prepared and flooded with water; the seeds are raised in nursery beds and then transplanted to the main paddy field in orderly rows. The field must be constantly monitored, weeded, and controlled to obtain the maximum yield. Japanese creativity is more studied and deliberate and is maximized by cultivating minimal resources. Large Japanese companies cultivate their employees by training them, sending them abroad, rotating them, and providing long-term support for new product development teams.

The goal of Japanese creativity is not just to create new products and ideas but also to build teamwork and a sense of harmony. People who refuse to cooperate or continue to advocate unique ideas are distrusted, laughed at, or ignored by their peers in Japan. In the Japanese creative process, individuals are encouraged to contribute ideas for the benefit of the team, not to be overly spontaneous or different. The Japanese prefer to hide their ideas behind a facade of conformity to avoid being publicly embarrassed. Japanese creativity thrives on group interaction and brainstorming.

Japanese creativity is like fusion: Ideas from many people are gathered, assimilated, and squeezed into a new product. This fusion of an idea (*yugo-ha*), as in technology fusion, can trigger an intense explosion of new ideas and is extremely effective in creating new products. In technology fusion, hybrid technologies are interbred through interindustry technological fusion, combining different technologies and industries to form new ones. One such example is mechatronics, the deliberate fusion of mechanical engineers cross-fertilized with electronic engineers. Another such hybrid is the creation of fax machines which contain telephones, copiers, and printers.

Japanese logic, as influenced predominantly by Buddhism, is fuzzy, circuitous, and cyclical. The Japanese are much more comfortable with shades of gray—for them problems are rarely clear cut with few simple answers. Rather, everything is relative and open ended. Problems are viewed as complex, incoherent, and vague, requiring incremental, diffused solutions. The Japanese constantly seek multiple applications for new ideas as a consequence of their limited space and resources. Perhaps this is why they have taken such a fancy and interest in fuzzy logic, a new field of mathematics in which shades of gray exist and nothing is purely black or white (fuzzy logic was a Western creation!).

Zen meditation lies at the core of Japanese creativity because of the natural spontaneity and fresh insights it makes possible. Zen Buddhist philosophy does not place great value on rational thought alone but more on spiritual enlightenment and intuitive understanding. This emphasis on intuitive understanding explains in part Japan's traditional weakness in basic scientific research, in which logical reasoning plays a central role. Among the Japanese, there appears to be an absence of theoretical or systematic thinking and an emphasis on aesthetic and intuitive orientation. The Zen taste for refined simplicity and quiet with a predilection for visual design can be seen in many Japanese products. Japanese creativity is rooted in the design arts, which depend on synthesis and holistic right-brain thinking as opposed to rational left-brain analysis. Because of the nonintellectual nature of Zen, Japan's base of scientific knowledge and research methodologies has never developed as fully as that of the West. Western scientific discoveries may have involved intuitive leaps of imagination, but they were usually thoroughly grounded in scientific research. Relying on intuitive and spiritual enlightenment alone usually makes for bad science.

In Zen, no rational solution exists because the goal is enlightenment or intuitive understanding. Zen Buddhist philosophy does not place great value on rational thought alone. Intuition is self-knowledge of the whole in contrast to reason, which busies itself with parts. Intuition is the integrating principle, whereas reason always analyzes. Reason cannot work without intuition; parts are parts of a whole, never existing by themselves, and must be understood in their overall context or synthesis. Because of this nonrational or intuitive approach, discovery or enlightenment has had totally different meanings in Japan than in Western philosophy. *Eureka* (West) refers to the discovery of rational scientific principles, whereas *satori* (East) means personal enlightenment. This emphasis on intuition may explain Japan's traditional weakness in basic scientific research, in which logical reasoning plays a central role. On the other hand, the Zen heritage might also explain why the Japanese are strong in the design arts, which require synthesis and holistic (right-brain) thinking as opposed to rational (left-brain) analysis.

Muga—egolessness or self-effacement—is one of the principles taught by Zen Buddhism. Samurai training sessions combined physical with mental and spiritual training, giving precedence to the latter and a total lifestyle. To achieve mastery of any complex skill, mental training is as important (if not more so) than physical training. Tapping into ancient Zen Buddhism as a way of eliminating the ego can also release a measure of creative insight and energy. Most people are not truly creative because their thought processes are controlled by preconceived notions; they cannot think in new ways because unconventional thinking is blocked by psychological barriers. To remove this barrier is one of the goals of the mental stage of *muga*, a state in which the mind does not interfere with the actions of a trained body. If you have trained your body to perform the functions and have achieved a mental state of *muga*, the functions come as easy as thinking them.

Idea refinement is Japan's greatest strength. The Japanese are known for their ability to take seminal ideas (especially those overlooked or dismissed by skeptical Westerners) and transform them into something entirely different, novel, popular, and profitable. Two classic examples are the transistor and the VCR. Creative refinement is a disciplined method of transforming an idea into something new and valuable and it also engenders new marketing concepts and applications.

Another popular Japanese method of creating new products is to transfer an idea or technology from one industrial sector to another. Because Japanese workers tend to be generalists who move freely back and forth between divisions, they are easily able to transmit ideas rapidly between consumer and industrial product areas. Companies institutionalize crossover research by rotating their employees every two or three years through different divisions, thereby building multidisciplinary product development teams.

Truly creative research requires a considerable amount of curiosity, adventurousness, and risk taking, all traits endearing and comfortable to most Westerners but not to the average Japanese. Most Japanese still prefer the comfort of proven ideas and shy away from exploring risky technologies on their own; They prefer a more structured, team-oriented approach to avoid losing face or being left out. The Japanese envision a creative culture as one that leads the consumer, not follows him or her (Sony's Walkman and Data Discman are examples). To invent products properly, you don't ask people what they want, you ask them what problems they have when they get up in the morning.

Idea cultivation is difficult in Japan because of the tremendous competitive pressures which exist in Japan to bring products to the marketplace quickly. Commercializing ideas, not cultivating them, reaps the greatest rewards for companies in the hypercompetitive Japanese marketplace. As a result, pursuing unorthodox ideas is discouraged because it is risky and requires enormous patience and a willingness to swim against the tide. In Japan, it is not what is unique but what others are doing that commands the lion's share of corporate funding, attention, and support.

Another reason for the difference between the Japanese (who are good at miniaturizing, simplifying, and redesigning existing products) and Westerners (who excel at pioneering new ideas) is that Japan's culture works within its geographic resource limitations whereas the American frontier society explores beyond the horizon. Thus, for thousands of years, Japan's spirit of exploration and discovery was stifled. Its people became expert at taking their meager resources and maximizing their output. Production, not invention or discovery, was the means of daily survival. The Japanese have miniaturized many products, not because they are small or prefer small objects but because space is scarce and therefore the most precious thing in the world for them. For the Japanese, creativity meant shaping existing resources into usable items. Whereas Americans have traditionally sacrificed space for time, (they have lots of the former but were culturally short on the latter), the Japanese have sacrificed time for space (they had little of the latter and lots of the former).

For years, Japanese companies have boasted efficient spotless factories but their offices have resembled open bullpens overflowing with papers and files. For anyone trying to do any creative work, most Japanese offices are too noisy and chaotic, making it virtually impossible to concentrate or think. Little if any privacy exists in Japan. Telephone calls, visitors, and impromptu visits from customers are constant interruptions. (Japan's new breed of young people [*shinjinrui*] want better office layouts, carpeting, and wall partitions to reduce interruptions and allow for more individuality; as partial result of the pressure from this younger generation, Ricoh and Sanyo are building cubicles and offices for their researchers.) Meditation rooms, ergonomically designed offices, and "creation live" office furniture designed to produce the correct mood for promoting creativity and human interaction are becoming popular; however, the typical Japanese office still fits the traditional chaotic description.

In Japan, the group takes precedence over the individual (lifetime employment policies do not select brilliant mavericks). The *ringi* method of building consensus and harmony through *nemawashi* (which literally means root binding: a tree is prepared for moving by the protracted and gentle process of first freeing its roots and accustoming them to new soil. The same collective process shapes the major decisions of corporations and governments. Since all levels have taken part in the decision, it does not come as a surprise to anyone and policies are carried out with enthusiasm.). This cannot help but result in a stunting of individual creativity. As a result of these factors working against the individual, against individual achievement, the Japanese are better at adaption than independent invention.

The Japanese tend to make systematic small improvements in products. *Keihakutanshoka* is the Japanese term used to describe the process of making things lighter, slimmer, shorter, and smaller. Furthermore, corporate hierarchy and dependency relationships *(amae)* with superiors prevent researchers from contradicting their seniors. Being individualistic often means facing ostracism, ridicule, and bullying. Yet, most Japanese technological managers now believe that a working environment which encourages creativity is the key to their future.

Creativity *(soozoo)* is Japan's new battle cry. Creativity circles are the latest advance in Japan's attempt to propel creativity in a culture that is naturally adverse to it. These product development teams *(gonin-gumi)* generally consist of five people (the Japanese consider five an ideal number because it allows for both flexibility and a variety of opinions). Company groups of engineering, marketing, sales, and manufacturing employees are gathered to discuss not only problems with existing products but also ways to develop new hit products. Initially the team members are asked to suggest refinements to existing products. Over time, the teams turn to creative solutions by implementing some of the results of brainstorming sessions.

Part of this new effort also involves studying Western research methods and attempting to transfer them to the Japanese setting. More than 15,000 Japanese engineers and scientists are in the United States trying to learn as much about how their American colleagues *do* research as about *what* they are doing. Adapting, not creating has always been the strong point of the Japanese. However, Japanese companies are looking for different ways to overcome the psychological barriers to creativity. One method is to designate noted scientists as team leaders (with their own budgets) to bring together the leading researchers in the field. Each project bears the name of the team leader. Another method is the joint research projects sponsored by the government-funded Research Development Corporation of Japan. A third trend is joint work projects with foreign researchers (Berger, 1987).

The United States is considered an objective society, whereas Japan can be considered a polyocular society. That is, the Japanese believe that all phenomena can be seen from multiple points of view, and the more angles, the more whole and comprehensive the picture becomes; whereas the West tends to believe in a linear, one-correct-angle-point of view. The famous Japanese ambiguity is the result of this nothing-is-right-everything-is-right point of view. Prior to westernization, the Japanese had no word for objectivity; now the word is *kyakkanteki* (the guest's point of view), whereas *shukanteki* is the host's point of view (or subjective).

SUMMARY

Both American and Japanese experts agree that Americans tend to excel at breakthrough research and are stronger at independent creativity, whereas the Japanese are better at adaptive creativity (i.e., refining ideas and technologies to create new products and markets). This latter systematic approach is more suitable for process innovation and complex systems research, which require continuity of effort and team work. The Japanese excel when research targets are clearly defined and fixed and an incremental strategy can be employed. Japanese companies routinely recycle old customs and ideas and combine them with other ideas to develop new ones. Their emphasis is not on making breakthroughs but on humanizing and transforming these technologies for applications in everyday life. The Japanese are good at taking existing ideas and improving on them. Thus, in essence, they show creativity in process engineering and industrial design but are weak in thinking up entirely new ideas, especially in the basic sciences.

Although Japanese venture capital firms invested about $1.6 billion in 3,425 venture businesses in 1987, it is difficult for new venture businesses with creative ideas to secure financing, talented people, and customers. Japanese industry is still dominated by vertically integrated corporations with extensive ties to bankers, suppliers, distribution channels, and government ministries (*keiretsu*). The Japanese risk-adverse tendencies make new venture businesses difficult to start.

The Japanese have rarely made a spectacular discovery or product breakthrough that has lead to an entirely new industry. Most Japanese innovations are rooted in scientific theories and ideas developed in the West. When curiosity is lacking, creativity turns imitative. Coming up with new ideas is easy, but the hard part is to sort the grains of gold from the mountains of sand. In Japan, preference for benign neglect means that new ideas just lie on the table. So who sorts the winners from the losers? More often than not, it is the *gaiatu*, foreigners.

To an American, creativity involves a necessary break with traditional content and methods and implies the creation of a new idea or artifact (for at least an independent invention). Creation is a non-linear process, a break with the past, with the traditional, with the status quo. Not so, in Japan. In Japanese schools, originality comes after proficiency. An American conductor once remarked that the Japanese musicians he has encountered are technical professionals, experienced, perfectionists who knew their instruments thoroughly because they had practiced the music until perfect. However, they often lack soul and heart, the means to express the music creatively.

Most new industries have been created and defined in the United States, even though in several cases Japanese manufacturers have dominated them after a few, short years. New industry creations require market innovativeness as well as technological innovativeness and are the peculiar province of entrepreneurial high-tech companies in the United States. Product development to known specifications and process development to unknown specifications are the advantage of the Japanese when they either inspired or driven by the user (either the external customer or a firm's own manufacturing department) or by suggestions from throughout the company. The American high-tech companies are better able to capitalize on opportunities which are derived from or inspired by technology or by top-down management decisions. When the technological development primarily requires analysis, the Japanese have a significant advantage. When synthesis is involved (bringing together various technologies or matching new technologies with new market opportunities), American industry has had a substantial advantage over its Japanese competition. The fundamental technology for integrated circuits requires synthesis (a combination of multiple items) and the United States led in the early days of this technology. When the technology is pushed to provide greater density of circuits and higher yields, the emphasis is on analysis at which the Japanese excel.

Innovation is not a tradition in Japan, a country that before the nineteenth century invariably got its best new ideas (whether abstract or practical) from China, Korea, or Buddhism from India by way of China. For at least the last 100 years the source has been Europe and America. The benefits of a consensual approach to business planning do not apply as well to individualistic undertakings like invention. The Japanese value their similarities more than their differences. Making the intuitive breakthrough that opens an entirely new field is not the Japanese forte. Applying such a breakthrough to production and marketing is, however, their greatest strength.

In Japan, the struggle to be creative continues. The very same rigid hierarchical structure and consensus management system which served Japan well for so many years may be its undoing. Although Japanese companies have excelled at improving on existing products and methods, most are not pioneers. Future growth depends on if the Japanese can master the tasks of inventing new products, markets, and entire businesses. This will require more independent thinking and improvisation than has been tolerated in the past (Thornton, 1993a).

Chapter 2

Historical Evidence: The Japanese Perspective on Innovation

MEIJI—EASTERN MORALS, WESTERN TECHNOLOGY

The unprecedented nineteenth-century explosion of Japanese industry, with its concomitant relatively quick technical change, is due in no small part to the many new social, cultural, and economic attitudes developed from the Meiji Restoration. The Charter of the Five Oaths, the emperor's proclamation in 1868, was a key to opening up the rest of the world to Japan. A country which had condemned to death anyone traveling abroad was now determined to encourage its people to seek knowledge all over the world and thus to strengthen the foundations of Imperial policy. Japan went from a *sakoku* (closed country) to a *kaikoku* (open country) at a breathtaking pace.

Japan has consistently been underrated by the West. Japanese success has been based primarily on social innovation. Japan, after the Meiji Restoration of 1867, reluctantly opened itself to the world to avoid the fates of India and China, that is, to preserve its independence. Its basic aim, in true Judo fashion, was to use the weapons of the West to hold the West at bay and to remain Japanese. Modernization was seen as a weapon to free Japan from potential Western domination. "Eastern morals, Western technology" has been Japan's slogan and guiding principle for the past century. The social institutions had to be quintessentially Japanese and yet modern. The institutions had to be run by Japanese and yet serve an economy that was to become Westernized and highly technical at a fast pace. Technology that could be imported at low cost and with a minimum of cultural risk was perfect for the Japanese plan of modernizing without de-Japanizing. The Japanese accepted Western technology but took

Western institutions cautiously, assimilating them into their own culture. The Japanese understood that institutions, in contrast to technology, required cultural roots to grow and prosper. Imported institutions also tended to change or moderate existing institutions, rendering them impure. The Japanese, above all, wanted to remain pure, homogeneous, and Japanese. The Japanese made a deliberate decision 100 years ago to concentrate their resources on social innovations and to imitate, import, and adapt technical innovations (Drucker, 1985), to utilize Western technology but not at the expense of their own culture. They saw Westernization as a way of gaining strength and respectability in the eyes of the world's major powers, a way to be equal to and not subordinate to the West. For the next 100 years, their one driving ambition was not just to be equal to the West but to succeed and surpass the West, to prove to the entire world that Japanese culture was superior. Many would say that by the 1990s they had achieved this objective.

In Meiji Japan, the government actively pursued and aided growth and development. The earliest Japanese entrepreneurs insisted on the indigenous production of machinery. Although the machinery industry was not developed in the nineteenth century, it is easy to see how this attitude toward modernization and the active pursuit of its goals, aided by the Meiji government, led to a quick build-up of the infrastructure needed to initiate such an industry. Japan quickly began to set up training establishments and, before the turn of the century, had a substantial cadre of trained technicians and managers. The Japanese government considered creating an indigenous industry crucial to national security. At first, the emphasis was on the textile industry because it was a major source of trade imbalance and, consequently, foreign exchange and specie loss. The Meiji government considered trade imbalance a vulnerable point in the newly opened Japan (Sullivan, 1992).

The Japanese were not afraid of technology but rather embraced it. They searched the world over for technology, pursuing it with a passion and aggression second to none. Japanese firms accomplished this feat by absorbing and then extending foreign technologies, developing a skilled labor force and advanced manufacturing techniques, exploiting their robust domestic market, and adopting export-oriented strategies. Once imported, foreign technologies have been invariably adapted to specific industrial, commercial, and market requirements in Japan. Product development (including designs and packaging) has been tailored, wherever possible, to local needs and preferences, as have advertising, sales promotion, and customer services. Furthermore, imported technologies have frequently been improved and increasingly exported not only to third-world country markets but also back to their original exporting countries. The eager pupil became the instructor in many industries.

The supremacy of East Asia in manufacturing as opposed to engineering is not a recent development. In the eighteenth century, Europeans attempted to discover how to make porcelain, silk, cotton textiles, and paper that could match the quality of Chinese and Japanese products. The Japanese harmonious working atmosphere, on which workers are genuinely concerned with their company's welfare and in which there is a strong spirit of consensus, makes for efficient production and for effectiveness in some aspects of research and development. Innovation, however, tends to follow a linear rather than an interactive pattern in a society such as Japan's, in which individualism is not appreciated. Too ready an acceptance of consensus can inhibit vigorous discussion and dissent. Japanese innovation has been most successful when the Japanese had agreed-on objectives to work for. When development is linear, objectives can be readily agreed on and consensus works well.

Meiji Japan's desire to catch-up with the West led to a developmental strategy used by Japan which in many respects holds true today (Fruin, 1992):

1. A major role for the state in economic organization.
2. More centralized and coordinated investment strategies, with state planning.
3. A close cooperation between government and business in the establishment and management of national industries.
4. A greater stress on producers' rather than consumers' concerns, with more production going to the state.

Government policies, as well as the opening of Japan, helped to account for the explosive growth in the Japanese economy. Such growth never could have happened without the stimulus of foreign trade, the creation of political stability by the government, the economic unification of the country, the reform of the currency system, and the removal of feudal restrictions. The government's development of railways, ports, roads, and such urban services as water systems and street railways also contributed greatly to economic growth. In Japan, the government subsidized private industry by becoming its chief customer. Laws were also enacted which encouraged Japanese citizens to purchase Japanese products. These labyrinthian regulations discouraged foreigners from investing in Japan. Government subsidies for shipping and transportation abounded during those early days, cheap loans to industry were plentiful, and the continued build up of a vast support system for industrial development by the government all aided Japan in its effort to modernize. The warlike nature of Japan during the late nineteenth and early twentieth centuries also gave a boost to industry in the form of increased demand by the military and other sections of the Imperial government and new demand from their subjected vassals for goods.

One of the most important systems required and created by the Japanese was a viable central banking system, which was set up in the late 1880s. The financing of industries was given great importance. The nineteenth-century drive toward a strong country by imitating and assimilating Western thought and technology continued to be successful for the Japanese. During this period, they established themselves as a major world power and effectively ousted the foreigners with their own technology. Japan has a national industrial ideology oriented toward self-improvement (i.e., greater quality and efficiency), toward a world view in which exports are emphasized, and toward evaluation of performance on the basic of long-term rather than short-term results (Alston, 1986).

POST SECOND WORLD WAR INFLUENCES

The pattern set after 1868 and still prevalent to a large extent today was for Japan to import a product and copy it, making a product that might be inferior to the import in quality but sufficient for domestic use. Following a gradual improvement in production, the product could be exported. The domestic market became a controlled environment for nurturing export industries. The government promoted industries through subsidies and "buy Japan" policies and protected them from imports through high tariffs, import quotas, licensing requirements, foreign investment controls, and credit controls. Market access barriers included restrictive interpretation of customs regulations (ever-shifting standards), restrictive interpretation of product approval procedures, "buy Japan" biases in the procurement policies of public corporations or through administrative guidance, and the archaic Japanese distribution network. The Japanese generally have been unwilling to accept the results of tests conducted outside Japan, even when performed according to Japanese specifications; this adds to the costs of imported goods and can result in considerable time delays, which often give Japanese firms opportunities to develop competitive products. The Japanese government also lessened excessive competition among domestic firms through mergers and cartel arrangements. Often, when a foreign firm did become established in Japan, the Japanese government undertook action to limit that firm's market growth, particularly if the firm had the capability to dominate the industry (IBM in Japan is the classic example).

The principle of *ikusei* (cultivation) underlies the Japanese government's policies of protecting and promoting infant industries. The national government establishes national research projects, sets collaborative goals, and allocates research fields among participating companies, which are provided with financial assistance, special depreciation allowances, and tax incentives. Japanese business is regulated by strict, highly technical, and demanding laws and procedures. These regulation are not normally applied to everyday situations; they are consciously held in reserve as powerful social safeguards and are only applied when the situation seems to warrant it. The government thus acts as a powerful but benign parent. Discipline is managed by informal messages—administrative guidance.

During the 1950s and 1960s, while the United States held the edge in radio technology, American radios were banned from being sold in Japan, and firms such as Matsushita and Sony fought for control of the highly competitive Japanese market. Gradually, with application of technology licensed from the United States on a forced basis, the Japanese products rivaled those of overseas competitors. The Japanese manufacturers then took their products overseas based on price advantages created by economies of scale in the Japanese market. Cross-subsidization due to controlled high prices in Japan allowed market penetration pricing policies, which naturally led to market share domination and the exit from the industry by most American producers unable to compete against such forces. The government indemnified Japanese companies abroad against loss and condoned restriction on foreign construction bidding in Japan; neither at home nor abroad was there ruinous competition between Japanese companies.

Following the Second World War, the Japanese rebuilding effort focused on mass production industries, such as steel and automobiles. In Japan, the best personnel were poured into this endeavor. The large-scale mass producers in Japan embedded technological innovation in their production process, an example of which is the QC, quality circle. QCs organized team efforts in the production process. With lifetime employment, employees needed to rely less on professional associations and trade unions to counter their employer's power. Innovation, as a result, did not threaten worker jobs, but reinforced employees long-term prospects with the company. This produced happier, more productive workers. Besides enjoying stability of employment and good benefits, employees became members of a clan or tribe (Honda, Sony, Toyota) with the status emitted (Hull, Hage, and Azumi, 1984).

Japanese market development has undergone four distinct phases since the Second World War. First, immediately after the war, Japan focused on gaining a cost advantage through low wages. It began by concentrating on labor-intensive industries like textiles and garment manufacturing. The second phase was to move to a competitive advantage based on economies of scale (in shipbuilding and steel for example) by substituting capital for labor. Other industries, like textiles and garment manufacturing, that were not amenable to economies of scale were phased out. The third phase used competitive advantage based on low wages and scale economies. The industries that were attacked were automobiles, consumer electronics, and construction equipment. The segments selected were generally the least profitable portion of the product line or were in areas ignored by larger American producers. Using these segments as beachheads, the Japanese moved up and out to capture increasingly larger portions of the marketplace. The fourth phase is mass customization, the ability to produce customized units at economy of scale cost levels. Many Japanese companies have discovered that the increased flexibility and quick responsiveness developed during the third phase allowed them to increase greatly the levels of variety and customization in their product line (Abegglen and Stalk, 1985). Mass customization primarily focuses on total process efficiency.

The poor economic, social, and political conditions that existed directly after the Second World War during the U.S. military occupation provided the stimuli for the change phase; these conditions allowed the Japanese to become actors in implementing change. The occupation forces brought new technologies into Japan, creating a desire for the new technologies. The gains from the imported technologies spread to various sectors of Japan's economy. The importation of new technologies subsequently led to a dramatic increase in Japan's exports in several key industries, such as cameras, radios, textiles, and ships. The technology acquisition which resulted from the efforts from those first few industries subsequently stimulated Japan to place a greater emphasis on R&D than was done in the West. As a result of this newly determined emphasis in technology, Japan rapidly caught up with the West in many areas.

Even though the presence of foreign military helped implement change in Japan (and Germany), other channels of technological transfer were available: (1) direct foreign investment, (2) foreign collaboration, and (3) personnel transfer (Rodrigues, 1985). Japan adopted a bold liberalization policy and at the same time concentrated on upgrading scientific and technological capability through such complementary measures as expanding R&D investment, strengthening the cooperative research system, and securing of a sufficient number of qualified scientists, engineers, and technicians (Choi, 1989). Japan demonstrated the Japanese model of innovation technology transfer by emphasizing on the iron and steel, petrochemical, and electronics industries. They accomplished enormous economic development in a short period of time by carrying out the successive stages from importation and utilization of advanced technologies on a large scale, to demand creation, to investment for expansion of facilities, to reduction of manufacturing costs and reinforcement of international competitive power, to export increases and finally, to improve its balance of payments. The Japanese model of technological development represents a strategy of bold importation, digestion, and creative adaption of advanced technologies.

Japan has a long history of investing in new technology by buying it. Japan has imported a great deal of technology since the Second World War and as such is a good case study for newly developing countries. From 1950 to 1971, Japan introduced about 15,000 items of technology and has introduced more than 1,000 a year since 1963 (Choi, 1989). Japan's annual payments for licensing technology rose from around $50 million in the early 1950s to $2.7 billion in 1970 to $3 billion by 1985. The Japanese have begun selling technology as well (almost $900 million by 1985); most of this technology, however, is obsolete technology exported to the Third World.

Particularly important among the postwar factors in its economic success were: (1) a high rate of capital investment made possible by a high savings propensity, which provided ample, low-cost funds for producers; (2) a steady flow of innovation from the importation of advanced foreign technologies at reasonable prices, the availability of well-educated and well-trained technical and scientific labor and the favorable international economic climate in which Japanese industries were allowed to import capital, managerial know-how, and industrial technologies; (3) the effective policy planning and implementation by a small government supportive of the private sector, which was made possible by a well-trained and well-motivated bureaucracy and long period of competent political stability under the Liberal Democratic Party (LDP) regimes (Hirono, 1986); (4) national development efforts that provided an effective infrastructure and a domestic demand, which provided a fertile ground and economies of scale for world-class competitiveness while being protected from foreign suppliers; (5) an educated, disciplined labor force; (6) strategic security from and access to the United States and its markets; and (7) the postwar period of stable, low-cost supplies of raw materials and energy.

Little technical entrepreneurship has taken place since the Second World War, and the overall level of activity is low compared to the United States and Western Europe. The large number of small Japanese businesses are predominantly subcontractors with weak technology bases, modest ambitions for growth, and intimate ties to a larger company. Both banks and venture capital firms prefer to invest in lucrative, established firms, not start-ups (Riggs, 1984). An absence of employee equity participation implies the need for vast external financing at the start-up stage. The Japanese OTC (Over-The-Counter) market has traditionally been ineffective in providing financing to new firms and liquidity to investors and entrepreneurs due to restrictions (e.g., OTC entrants must be at least two years old, have paid dividends, and have had pretax earnings of at least 10 Yen per share). These requirements were revamped in late 1983. Yet the number of start-ups remains extremely low, nowhere near the numbers in the United States.

One reason for this is the scarcity of incubator organizations in Japan. The larger Japanese companies hire the better science and engineering graduates. The Japanese policy of lifetime employment, hiring only at entry-level positions, and typically avoiding mid-career transfer employees makes entrepreneurship extremely risky for the individual Japanese worker. Employees rarely change companies, let alone spin off on their own. General management experience is usually not gained until late in one's career, often well past the prime age for entrepreneuring. Little social and structural volatility also contributes to the low rate of Japanese entrepreneurship, and little foreign or domestic immigration exists in Japan. Japanese society can be readily described as stable and homogeneous. Companies prefer long-term, stable, close relationships with customers and suppliers. A relatively fixed industrial structure therefore exists. The emphasis on company loyalty inhibits the typical Japanese worker from leaving his or her company. Individuals striking out on their own know that acceptance will be minimal from important social groups and chances for future employment will be minimal if they fail. Risk is particularly great for the best graduates, who have the most to lose in the highly status bound Japanese society. To them, it is more important to be a small cog in a highly recognized company than a large cog in an unknown entity.

One of the important prerequisites for innovation is a substantial internal market. Japan is now able to produce new products in large quantities almost purely for export markets. However, Japan developed these export markets using incremental production from industries that had reached scale by supplying Japan's home-market demand (Gerstenfeld and Wortzel, 1977). This affluence and increased standard of living for the populace was essential to the Japanese success story.

The Japanese experience has been characterized by a paternalistic governmental protectionism to encourage decentralized innovation and manufacturing by large industrial houses. South Korea and Taiwan have followed the Japanese approach. Firms in countries that practice an export-driven economic philosophy enjoy a host of structural advantages, including low-cost capital, undervalued foreign exchange rates, favorable debt financing relationships, domestic procurement subsidies, protected home markets, superior tax systems, superior labor markets, supportive education systems, positive industry structures (including industry associations and cartels), and positive government relationships.

POSTWAR TECHNOLOGY AND ECONOMIC POLICY

The characteristic features of Japanese technology policy today were in place even before the First World War and required a strong impetus from the central government that would promote modernization of the Japanese economy (Freeman, 1987). The Japanese government permitted the importation of very few items aside from technology, food, and raw materials. Determined to maintain tight control of the home market, the government pursued rigorously protectionist policies designed to minimize the entry of manufactured goods from abroad. These policies included tariffs, quotas, inspections, certifications, administrative delays, and tight control over multinational operations in Japan (McCraw, 1986). Other major factors included the importance of education and training; intense efforts to import, and whenever possible, improve on the best available technology in the world; and close cooperation between the government and large industrial concerns.

The typical pattern of Japanese success has been rapid penetration of a narrow but carefully selected segment of a broad, expanding world market in which superiority of production efficiency, economies of scale, and exploitation of learning curve effects were particularly important. By expanding more aggressively than its competitors and anticipating learning curve improvements and economies of scale, Japan has been able to capture an important share of selected markets. The Japanese then broadened from this point and moved gradually toward more sophisticated and higher value-added products in the same or a closely allied market segment (Utterback, 1987). Japanese willingness to plunge in and adopt a new technology on the basis of its ultimate promise before it was proven to be cost-effective has been combined with careful and thorough scanning of related world technological developments for their possible competitive threat or promise.

Technological innovation in Japan was pursued as an integrated process from the outset, including education, technology transfer, indigenous research, development, commercialization, and diffusion of technology and products. The integrated approach was a natural consequence of the efforts of late-coming Japanese industry and government to catch up with already highly developed industries abroad. Another element was the introduction of foreign technology. Japanese industries looked all over the world for any new technology or invention they could take advantage of. This was combined with active R&D that would adapt the technology to Japanese conditions and develop it into entirely new products. Most of the resulting successful innovation was characteristically strongly oriented to the consumer market because the typical Japanese corporate strategy was to expand first in the domestic market and afterward to export abroad.

The success of innovation in Japan can be attributed to the development of high-tech production technology including quality control. The focus was not only on new products but also on how to make them of high quality and with high productivity. This may be due to strong competition of companies in the domestic marketplace, which continuously pushed each other to improve the quality and price of the products (Oshima,1984). Efficiency includes both productive and unproductive time (unproductive time is the time materials spend in inventory or in other nonoperational activities) (Pine, 1993). With the Japanese, the focus is on seeking optimum quality and eliminating all waste in the process. Continual process improvement flows from discovering defects and correcting them to yield higher quality and less waste for all subsequent production runs. Inventory is viewed as waste that adds costs and inefficiency. High utilization of and investment in worker skills reinforce the positive aspects of the entire system. A sense of community exists that begins with good labor-management relations and extends to suppliers, distributors, and others involved in the production process. The end result is less total costs and higher production flexibility. Flexible specialization is the strategy of pursuing permanent innovative efforts, accommodating and encouraging ceaseless change, and manufacturing a great variety of products to meet small market niches.

Japan, however, is hardly a fair and open market because it has systematically avoided rules of international free trade. Foreign goods that rivaled Japanese products were kept out of the home market either by discriminatory tariffs or a variety of non-tariff obstacles. Only after it had bought foreign expertise, given its manufacturers all manner of isolation from competition and thus time to catch up and build up economies of scale and experience, only then would Japan favor free trade. In the meantime, it often dumped goods abroad while keeping them highly priced in the home market. For example, a product certified as safe by Japanese testing authorities may be imported into the United States without a retest, but an American product certified by Underwriters Laboratories (UL) of the United States must still be retested in Japan. UL maintains facilities in the U.S. to conduct tests according to Japanese standards, but Japan will not go abroad to issue its JIS (Japan Industrial Standards) seal at the point of manufacture. Japanese product approval requirements are often based on design rather than performance characteristics which means that foreign goods with performance characteristics superior to approved Japanese products may not be approved because of differences in design. In addition, foreigners are excluded from Japanese standard-setting deliberations. The Japanese approval process often requires the submission of proprietary information about a product, which is not the case in most other countries. When a foreign firm does become established in Japan, particularly if it appears to threaten a Japanese industry's ability to compete, the Japanese government will take action to limit that firm's market growth through such items as procurement procedures, administrative guidance, or product approval procedures.

In Japan, most long-term investment capital is supplied to industry through banks, not open securities capital. In this way, Japanese authorities have been able to use control of the Bank of Japan as a way of funneling cheap credit to favored sectors and firms. Import controls were used to protect infant industries against foreign competition, to channel foreign technology to rationalizing sectors, and to prevent inflows of speculative capital. Export controls were used to prevent Japanese firms from expatriating capital except to invest in sources of raw materials. Tax subsidies were used to encourage exports, and accelerated depreciation allowances were used to promote investment in new equipment.

Internationalization to the Japanese means trade liberalization, expansion of Japanese investment abroad, and exportation of Japanese technology and managerial know-how, all directly relevant to Japan's economic interests. Internationalization means the acquisition of more information to facilitate the penetration of foreign economies. Japan has adroitly used the outside world as an adjustment mechanism for its internal economy: In times of recession, Japan exports to break recessions. A small country can protect its stakeholders from adjustments without causing a great deal of fuss internationally; but this same attitude is quite different for an important country like today's Japan, with its ever-present huge trade surpluses. This is especially true for a company wishing to be accepted as a major power.

In 1989, 265 cartels existed and were officially blessed by the Japanese government. Currently, over 350 industry associations exist in Japan. These associations set technical and other standards, manage joint R&D projects, manage capacity for the industry, occasionally set prices levels, and represent the industry in the political arena. Such groups can exist only in environments with limited or nonexistent antitrust policies. In the Japanese view, it would be foolish for the government not to intervene, because only results matter. They are not fettered by the dogmas of either free enterprise or socialism. The Japanese do not mind fostering cartels, as long as the cartels work to the national advantage. Although cartels among large companies are technically in violation of the Antitrust Act, the Japanese Fair Trade Commission (responsible for executing and enforcing the Antimonopoly Act of 1947) has chosen not to prosecute in cases in which agreements have been achieved in consultation with MITI. The basic Japanese attitude is that R&D activities are pro-competitive and should not be touched by the Antimonopoly Act, and thus the Japanese FTC exempts cooperative innovative efforts from the scope of the law. Thus, as one would expect in such an environment, competition is not that of a totally free market but of frequent collaboration for new products, new processes, and whole new sectors by enterprise groups (as much as one fourth of all new R&D). Often six to ten new firms, each backed by an enterprise group (*keiretsu*), emerges with each new sector. The new firms are often joint ventures among firms within each enterprise group.

Japan feels uneasy about the concept of consumer sovereignty. At the heart of the doctrine of consumer sovereignty is individual preferences, interests, goals, and legal rights. The elevation of the individual is foreign to Japanese society in which everyone is subsumed within a collective interest. Thus consumers have been accorded secondary priority in Japan's industrial policy and development. Producer interests have been uppermost in importance. What consumer benefits occurred were from spillover benefits; that is, what is good for Japanese business is good for Japan as a whole and therefore good for Japanese consumers. The Japanese favor established stakeholders over newcomers, both Japanese and foreigners. By initially favoring big producers, the Japanese government could channel resources more quickly into building an industrial base. This also allows for political efficiency; big producers are rich and concentrated, whereas consumers and small savers are disorganized and diffused (hence big producers tend to get their way). Purely domestic-oriented industries in Japan, such as services, retailing, agriculture, and construction, tend to be stagnant and inefficient in proportion to the extent they are protected from newcomers.

The typical government industry relationship in the United States is adversarial, whereas it is more cooperative and advisory in Japan. The American political culture views big business with suspicion. The regulatory environment is more litigious in the United States than in Japan. Japan's main policy objective has been to protect its economy—access to raw materials abroad, access to foreign markets, and the nurturing of powerful conglomerates in industry and finance that are big enough to perform stabilizing roles in society. In America, the purpose of economic policy is to provide individual choice and consumer satisfaction.

In essence, Japan is not a free market economy; it is a command economy controlled by a cartel of business and government interests. The government uses its revenue-generating and market-controlling influences to grow businesses and industries. This is done by providing support—ensuring a low cost of capital, providing advice, and limiting outside participants in the market through tariffs, patent restrictions, and outright blatant non-tariff barriers. Competition in the private sector may be stiff, but the combatants cooperate and carve up market opportunities. The notion of a free market—that is, a market free of or with minimal government intervention—has no deep roots in Japanese society. On the contrary, the Japanese believe that a free market sometimes leads to waste and inefficiency. Certainly the idea that the market will allocate resources to the appropriate economic sectors makes little sense to the Japanese. Rather, they assume that the government has a key role in directing economic development (Kash, 1989). Japan has a planned rationale system in which the government acts as the planner, whereas the United States has a market rationale system, in which individual buyers and sellers control events. This form of government-business relationship is not peculiarly or uniquely Japanese; the Japanese have merely worked harder at perfecting it and have employed it in more sectors than other capitalist nations. The United States had similar relationships during both world wars and the defense/aerospace industry after the Second World War most closely approximated the business-government relationships found in Japan. The differences between the two nations results from their differing orientations. The United States is oriented towards individual choice and naturally emphasizes consumer welfare and a bottoms-up type of consumer economic power in the marketplace. Japan, in contrast, is oriented towards the group, the collective body, and thus emphasizes top-down economic power conducive to the producers, not its consumers. These differences, emanating from cultural differences between the two societies, echo throughout each country.

MITI

The Japanese believe that the ideal functioning market is flawed by such things as imperfect information, narrow short-term pursuit of incremental gain, primacy of individual company pursuits over collective interests, and inattention to national goals. Japan compensates for these shortcomings in numerous ways. Japan's Council for Science and Technology promotes a comprehensive national policy and is composed of the Prime Minister, several cabinet ministers, and prominent experts. The Science and Technology Agency (STA)consumes about a quarter of government R&D, funds research, oversees a worldwide collection of science and engineering publications, and directs a technology transfer corporation. The Ministry of Education receives about half of the government R&D money (compared to 4 percent for the defense agency) and administers Japan's system of ninety-five national universities and their affiliated research institutes. Corporate subsidies take the form of direct aid, tax benefits, low-interest loans, assured purchases by governmental entities, and protected markets. Tokyo also allocates large sums (in 1992, nearly $30 billion worth of direct loans and twice as much in loan guarantees) to small and medium-sized enterprises.

MITI (The Ministry of International Trade and Industry), which receives about 13 percent of R&D funds, is the most active agency in industrial policy (Adam, 1990). MITI articulates a long-term vision for industries, sets sectoral priorities, allocates subsidies and facilitates financial flows, adjusts the industrial structure (by mergers or prohibiting expansion), protects infant industries, regulates excessive competition, develops ways to reduce risks and diffuse costs, promotes exports, and mediates trade conflicts. MITI often divides research work among companies and makes them share results. Often, MITI will also grant *hojokin*—low interest loans that need only be repaid when the project succeeds. MITI's legal powers are relatively unimportant. Its influence derives from its ability to obtain funds and channel them for research and development in areas deemed critical to national competitiveness, the respect it enjoys from both government and business, and its skill in securing the cooperation of industry rivals for joint projects. In 1980, to promote use of robots, MITI encouraged the establishment of the Japan Robot Leasing Company, Ltd. (JAROL), a joint venture between twenty-four robot manufacturers and ten insurance companies. The Japan Development Bank provided JAROL with low-interest loans for easy leasing terms. By 1982, Japan had 32,000 robots in place, four times as many as in the United States, and had taken over leadership for good in robotics.

Relations between industry and government can conform to any of three possible scenarios: adversary, interest representation, and rationality. The rationality view holds that the bureaucracy plays a complementary role to the market and that good and close relations with business ensures coherent macroeconomic and industrial policies: The efficiency of the market is enhanced. The Japanese Mercantilism model is an extreme expression of this position: Market efficiency is replaced with alternative objectives, which are pursued by the state in tandem with business. The adversary role argues that government intervention is, at best, irrelevant to the success of Japanese business and, at worse, positively harmful to it. The interest representation view holds that the specific value and institutional structure in which the Japanese bureaucracy is embedded places it in two inseparable roles: that of a semiautonomous rational regulator (policy maker) and that of a quasi-agent of specific interests in the economy (Aoki, 1988). Figure 2.1 shows a graphic representation of Japanese industrial policy. The Japanese industrial policy goal has been to enhance economic growth by anticipating dynamically efficient allocation of resources by the criterion of world as well as domestic prices; it has selected certain key industries as essential for preferential treatment and it has provided such treatment through a comprehensive, coordinated set of policy instruments. The linchpin in this model is MITI.

MITI coordinates Japan's industry, identifies and ranks national commercial pursuits and business opportunities, and guides the distribution of national resources to meet those goals (Morgan and Morgan, 1991). MITI encourages Japanese companies to pursue targeted opportunities. These goals are predicated on the long-term viability and strategic value of the technology or product area involved, the market share potential, and the competitive outlook worldwide. MITI gets the required cooperation by offering government-sponsored inducements, such as subsidies and market protection, to the complying firms. Cooperation between firms in technology development is coordinated by MITI. Four or five major firms are selected and funds provided for technology development. This reduces duplication of effort, promotes standardization of output, reduces overcall cost, and ensures success. These projects cover all stages of the technology development cycle—from idea generation, through design, prototype manufacturing, testing, and commercial production. For example, in the late 1980s, MITI targeted areas for Japanese industry were superconductivity and biotechnology: Forty-four Japanese companies took part in the MITI-sponsored International Superconductivity Technology Center, which opened in 1988. When MITI calls, few dare not answer its call.

Figure 2.1
Industrial and Competitive Policy in Japan

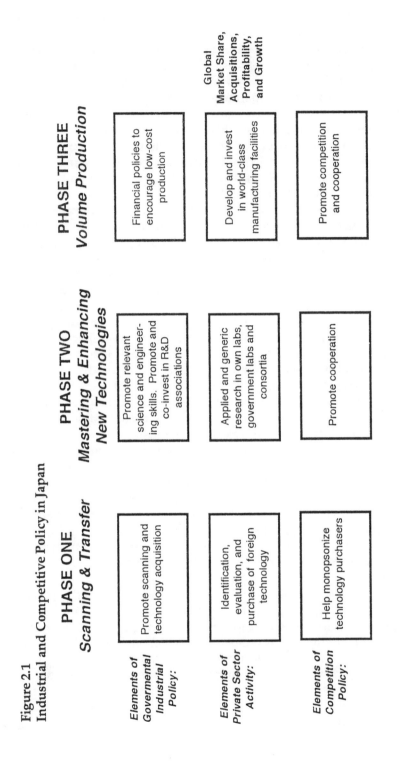

Once MITI selects an industry, a comprehensive package of support, including accelerated depreciation allowances, special R&D funding, tax benefits, and loans is created. By providing such incentives, MITI uses the marketplace to encourage business behavior. As a result, consumers pay relatively high prices especially in the early stages while non-Japanese firms are prohibited from operating in Japan. The result of such dynamic oligopoly encourages efficiency and productivity and reduces costs to allow such firms to become internationally competitive. MITI does not choose individual firms as national champions nor does it favor one company over another. High-tech markets have three major needs: assured markets, encouragement of R&D, and finance. Government-related procurement provides an immense market, possessing a wide range of "buy Japanese" regulations and incentives for Japanese corporations. However, such activities tend to benefit larger firms. This old model no longer works; MITI is no longer able to impose, without discretion, foreign exchange or import restrictions, tariffs, quotas, or non-tariff barriers to help new industries. The world has changed; no longer can Japan live in isolation and impose such protectionist policies with utter disregard to the impacts on its trading partners. With the advent of GATT and the World Trade Organization, further actions will get intense scrutiny and denials from the world trading body.

MITI officials believe they can anticipate the long-run strategic needs of the economy better than the marketplace, which inevitably has too short a time horizon and is unwilling to assume enough risk quickly enough. They believe they can anticipate where the market will go, thereby speeding up its operation. Their goal is to reach the same place as the market solution, but more rapidly and at less social cost. MITI chooses which projects to organize and subsidize carefully, in close consultation with industry. To quality for government assistance, a project must meet four criteria:

1. The proposed project must be of seminal importance to Japan's technological progress and future economic well-being.
2. The research must be of the pre-commercial variety so that the participating companies do not gain a decisive advantage over excluded firms.
3. Government assistance must be indispensable for the project to get underway and be completed.
4. The timeframe for the project's completion must be realistic. Government financing supplies the critical missing ingredient for launching projects of high capital costs and risks, relatively long gestation, fundamental technological importance, and broad commercial applicability (Kash, 1989).

Areas in which MITI has actively intervened include

- consensus building and articulation of a long-term vision
- setting of sectoral priorities
- allocation of subsidies to priority sectors
- adjustments of industrial structure
- infant industry protection
- investment guidance in certain industries
- regulation of excessive competition
- downside risk reduction and cost diffusion
- export promotion and mediation of trade conflicts.

A major reason MITI has been so successful in guiding corporate efforts stems from the closeness of its personnel to the business elite. MITI is considered a prime endpoint for top university graduates, and many graduates of top universities choose MITI. They thus have old school ties to the captains of industry. They develop long-term relationships with business leaders, often rising in rank with their counterparts in private industry. Often, retiring MITI managers will undergo *amakudari* ("descend from heaven," i.e., retire into a board or executive role in a Japanese corporation regulated by MITI). When MITI asks a business to risk precious resources in the development of a strategic area, trust must be present. Consultation and collaboration begin far before it is publicly announced that a technology is targeted for cooperative development. Protracted planning and exhaustive consultation take place at all levels among competitors, users, suppliers, and the government. Collaborative research is conducted by multiple parties and along several avenues. Cooperative R&D is diverse, though not overly duplicative. Participants work separately in their own facilities, and at least two firms will usually be assigned to a particular element of technology.

MITI does not manage projects directly but provides guidelines, priorities, and advice about financing, foreign exchange, and technology transfer. It sets targets for long-term growth and standards for modernization of plants, and it even promotes mergers of companies that lack the capital to meet those standards. MITI bureaucrats try to restructure industry, concentrating resources in areas where they think Japan will be competitive internationally in the future. In the 1960s, these industries were capital intensive; after the 1973 oil shock, MITI pushed Japan into knowledge-intensive industries (Feigenbaum and McCorduck, 1983).

MITI has policies for both declining and emerging industries. It is the power of persuasion rather than statute. Corporations cooperate with MITI because MITI provides superior information and analysis of worldwide industrial trends and meets with companies to exchange information. MITI works toward harmony and agreement. Company officials know that when the time comes for them to request licenses, permits, choice locations, and tax breaks, MITI will respond more favorably to cooperative than to uncooperative companies. MITI's displeasure can be costly to a firm; it can use delaying tactics, raise difficult questions, take a narrow view of tax treatments, and even influence banks that lend to the firms. It is important to understand the power of a MITI endorsement. The significance is usually less a matter of money (although this is central) than it is the assurance given to cooperating companies that the government will help out in every way it can until the projects are successful. This greatly reduces the risk and leads to a lower cost of capital since the financial institutions are assured of a long-term commitment. The risk is thus limited to the capability of the individual company. A Japanese company working on a strategic product or technology will know that it has deep-pocketed resources to draw on. For MITI, the purpose of cartels, tariffs, and other market controls is to promote production rationalization. MITI also administers a planned reduction in production capacity for depressed industries and a regional adjustment program for depressed areas.

In the early days and to a lesser extent today, MITI acted as a gatekeeper to the Japanese market, limiting access of foreign firms and targeting industries and firms for promotional policies. Capacity expansions and reductions in various industries were often planned firm by firm. Cartels and other informal mechanisms for market sharing and risk sharing were overlooked and actively encouraged by Japanese policy makers. Controlled levels of competition was preferable to market competition (Johnson, Tyson, and Zysman, 1989). Foreign direct investment (FDI) was precluded and the import of foreign technology was strictly controlled by MITI, which often acted as the intermediary between domestic firms and foreign suppliers of technology, benefiting the former and disadvantaging the latter. Interest rates were held below market, credit was allocated to targeted firms and activities at preferential rates, and non-priority borrowers were credit constrained. Exports were promoted by a variety of tax, credit, and protectionist policies that raised the returns to exports. Infant industries were protected against imports and foreign companies investing in Japan. Imports were controlled by tariffs and the foreign currency allocation system. MITI was permitted to decide who imported what.

MITI's interference with the computer marketplace as reflected in Japanese industrial policy is but one example of rough treatment forced on foreign firms (discriminatory treatment to foreign firms is the norm even today). IBM was compelled to license its key computer technology to its Japanese competitors in order to conduct business in the Japanese market. MITI told IBM it would take every measure possible to obstruct the success of its business unless IBM licensed its patents to Japanese firms and charged them no more than a 5 percent royalty. IBM capitulated, sold the patents, and accepted MITI administrative guidance on the number of computers it could market domestically in exchange for the right to manufacture and market in Japan. Approval for IBM to produce new models was held up in Japan if the products could compete with products being developed by Japanese firms. Despite being a Japanese company with an almost entirely Japanese staff, IBM Japan was (and basically still is) kept out of policy-making decisions that its competitors were allowed to be involved in. Likewise, Texas Instruments could not form a Japanese subsidiary unless it transferred technology to the Japanese. Its applications to establish a Japanese operation were ignored. Eventually it was permitted to form a joint venture with Sony in exchange for a general licensing of its critical semiconductor patents.

During the boom years, the Japanese government set the market rules while MITI controlled external access to the domestic economy No technology entered the country without MITI's approval, no joint venture was agreed to without MITI scrutiny, no patent rights were ever bought without MITI pressures, and no program for importation of foreign technology was ever approved by MITI until it was agreed that the time was right and the industry involved was scheduled for nurturing. Closed markets gave Japanese firms a protected base of demand that facilitated the rapid expansion of production and innovation in manufacturing and served to negate whatever product or production advantages foreign firms may have had.

MITI bureaucrats do not regard the market as sacrosanct. They have fewer inhibitions about trespassing on the private sector than exist in the United States. MITI believes that the market mechanism cannot be expected to generate economic outcomes that are always in the nation's best interests. To further the collective good, market forces need to be harnessed and guided by the state (Okimoto, 1989). Yet fallout from such efforts is not widely distributed or equal between companies in Japan. Key companies in the new technology are identified and become the haves. They will pioneer the commercialization of the technology and will receive special government status subsidies. Thus, companies are divided into haves and have-nots. Intermediates receive some direct government aid but basically rely on aid from quasi-governmental sources. The have-nots do not receive aid from any source. This industrial dualism is a mainstay of the Japanese economy and the source of many innovative disadvantages in Japan.

MITI is not infallible. In 1953, a small start-up asked MITI for permission to spend $25,000 to buy transistor manufacturing rights from Western Electric; permission was denied. Only the persistence of the founder, Akio Morita, who badgered the government into giving permission, saved his company, which later became known as Sony. In the mid-1960s, MITI wanted to create a world-class petrochemical industry. MITI facilitated the industry's rapid development by providing favorable incentives for heavy capital investments. Just about the time of completion, the energy crisis hit Japan. MITI set prices, allocated production quotas, and discouraged foreign competition. Japan's uncompetitive petrochemical industry, totally dependent on imported oil, was left with a large excess capacity. Gasoline and other refined petroleum products in Japan typically cost three or more times the price paid in the United States.

Although seven major auto makers exist in Japan, during the 1960s MITI tried to rationalize auto manufacturing into three major concerns; Honda successfully fought MITI's conclusion that Japan needed fewer rather than more automakers. Other disappointments included debacles to build up the aluminum and nonferrous metal industries (the aluminum smelting industry alone lost $2.5 billion). Efforts to develop Japan's aircraft and aerospace industries have produced only inferior products at absurd prices with little or no demand from outside Japan. Decades-long attempts to jump start the biotechnology industry have been just as disappointing. With the encouragement of MITI, several major Japanese electronics firms attacked the semiconductor memory industry with fierce determination. They ended up competing not only against themselves but against Korean and Taiwanese competitors, driving prices down well below costs and although securing market dominance, ended up with smaller revenues and little, if any, profits.

Other MITI or Japanese governmental industrial policy errors have been major catastrophes. Japan's landscape is littered with technological boondoggles. Industrial planning has often gone astray, saddling the nation with projects that go on for decades, consume billions of dollars, and end up with little of lasting value. Japan's fondness for consensus sometimes locks it into technological inferiority and rigid operational inertia. The strong consensus behind any given project tends to shield it from criticism, no matter how badly it falters or obsolete it may become. *Mutsu*, Japan's nuclear-powered merchant vessel, has sailed under nuclear power successfully only four times in twenty-five years and has had operational expenses exceeding $300 million during that timeframe. The government plans to spend in excess of $200 million to develop a high-speed magnetically levitated train, although even the Transportation Ministry doesn't know whether the system will ever be commercially feasible. Similar plans are being drawn up for a class of technological superliners, high-speed cargo ships 50 percent more expensive than ordinary ships. Japanese developers locked themselves into an HDTV (High Density Television) standard which uses analog signals (in typically Japanese fashion improving significantly an already existing technology), allowing American companies to leapfrog them with superior digital technology (in typical American fashion, pioneering a new technology by pushing back the state-of-the-art frontier). Even when a senior bureaucrat in the Ministry of Posts and Telecommunications suggested that Japan might have to abandon its home-grown HDTV standard, NHK and electronics makers reacted with outrage, forcing the bureaucrat to retract his comments (indicating that deviation from the hard-won Japanese consensus, even in clearly mistaken or obsolete decisions, is difficult in collective Japan). The emperor's clothes have been removed; MITI is certainly not infallible. Japanese governmental industrial policy has had more than its share of boondoggles. However in the media's eye, its successes have more than made up for any of its innumerable failures.

MITI directs the nation's capital to the larger companies at specific industries. MITI has also protected domestic companies from foreign capital. When industrial policies fail (as is often the case, as seen in the preceding examples), the consequences must often be offset by numerous countermeasures. These include sectoral targeting, industrial restructuring, government-sanctioned cartels, investment guidelines, or regulatory controls. Temporary cartels have had to be organized to control excessive competition (i.e., to correct for the aftereffects of excessive capital investment motivated by favorable incentives). The rationale is that is preempts warfare; it keeps the level of market concentration from increasing; and the bankruptcy of big corporations would have serious effects in Japan. As a result, not unsurprisingly, cartels increased tenfold between 1955 and 1973. Even today, blatantly public cartels are not unusual in Japan.

Japan's preventive approach suggests a more active posture based on a disposition to steer the market in desired directions. The "pure" market is flawed by several shortcomings: imperfect information; narrow, short-term pursuits of gain; scant spirit of cooperation; inattention to national goals; opportunistic behavior; structural changes and social dislocations; and potential subordination to foreign commercial interests. The market offers no guarantee that broader political, social, or economic security interests will be served. Thus, MITI must rely on industrial policy to compensate for the shortcomings in the marketplace.

COMPETITIVE STRATEGY

To the Japanese, technological self-sufficiency is the key to success. The Japanese tend to look at an emerging technology or market area from the perspective of vulnerability rather than risk. To them the question is how vulnerable a firm is if it does not enter a new technology rather than what the risks are of entering it. This system of decision making imposes a predisposition to entering a new technology and thus to keeping up with or gaining an advantage on competitors. The Japanese approach and undertake a research project not because it will solve a particular problem but because it may contribute to solving a number of seemingly unrelated problems. Americans tend to be more narrowly focused (Methe, 1991).

Industrial development typically follows a set of expected phases. The first phase finds Japanese firms at a disadvantage both in product development and production costs. Foreign firms could dominate the market and build up their own distribution and service systems if allowed to; if so, displacing them would be difficult. Tariffs or quotas encouraged foreign firms to start-up production in Japan. Outright discrimination often prevents foreign firms from distribution, service, and production in Japan, which can then preserve the domestic market for domestic producers. These bans force foreign firms to transfer technology and to distribute through Japanese channels. In the second phase Japanese firms, by borrowing technology, close much of their product and production disadvantage. Having built up distribution and service channels, they begin to dominate the Japanese market. Foreign firms lose competitiveness due to their mandated distance from the Japanese market. By the end of this phase, direct interventionist protectionist policies are no longer necessary because the Japanese market is dominated by Japanese firms. In the third phase, Japanese producers begin to build world markets. Cost advantages from economies of scale generated from oligopolistic, protected home markets give Japanese firms advantages. Cross-subsidization effects from excess profits gained in the home market allow the firms to battle for market share without regard for profits. Japanese firms tend to succeed in industries for which they dominate the final product market at home or are able to control access to the Japanese market.

The Japanese have turned manufacturing into a competitive advantage. They did not invent the host of consumer electronics products which now lead the world market. They did, however, develop designs and manufacturing systems that created a decisive competitive advantage. Equally important have been their changes in the organization of production, which permit them to introduce new products rapidly and constantly to improve and adapt the workings of that system. Small firms permitted large Japanese firms to establish economies of scale while retaining flexibility. These subcontracting links required small firms to adjust to market changes.

Market dynamics in Japan drive firms to pursue market share aggressively as a means of maximizing profits. As all firms seek to maximize market share, excess capacity and excessive competition results. This leads to efforts to regulate or bound competition. Because Japan was relatively closed to foreign firms, foreign technology could be readily borrowed and implemented and financial resources could be channeled to expanding channels. As long as the Japanese were aggressive and systematic technology borrowers in a rapidly expanding domestic market, a market share maximization strategy yielded a profit maximization result. Additional market share pushes a firm down the cost curve. As a firm increases volume, it takes additional market share, which lowers it costs, making it able to increase sales and starting the cycle over again. Firms are thus motivated to move down their costs curves faster than their competitors (i.e., to grab or steal market share) and to force a sharp reduction in their costs for each increment in production volume. The firm with the largest market share is in the best position to drive costs down and continue in a dominant position. Firms are induced to establish capacity to capture the market share they require in order to be successful. However, the flaw in this strategy is that if all firms build such capacity, excess capacity inevitably results.

Domestic competition in Japan has typically substituted for the pressures of the international market. Promotional incentives attracted many market entrants. The resulting battle for market share resulted in excessive or disruptive competition, which then had to be controlled. A variety of mechanisms existed to control competition: mutually agreed-on expansion plans by government and industry, exemptions from antitrust laws, debt financing of rapid expansion, and recession cartels. The Japanese government has encouraged the creation of cartels in designated industries to avoid the pitfalls of excess competition. In sunset industries, this is done to allow scrapping of excessive capacity. Nonetheless, after structural adjustment, shares of the export market and the domestic market of firms in Japan's declining industry are not likely to decrease appreciably. In sunrise industries, this is done to create advantage and to rationalize industries. Exports were encouraged as aggressive firms competing for domestic market share reached the international market together. This simultaneous arrival of many firms in the same industry gave the world "Japan, Inc."

The thrust of developmental policy has been to prevent foreign manufacturing firms from entrenching their position in the Japanese market as a means of assuring the development and international competitiveness of Japanese producers. Import substitution is feasible due to the size of the domestic market. Such a policy produced a reduction in manufactured imports and an expansion in manufactured exports. This has also produced an enduring marketplace advantage in global markets for Japanese firms. Then the challenge became how to manage this advantage? One mechanism used was to export the excess output. This excess meant that sales could be at marginal costs, leading to extremely low costs and accusations of dumping. A second mechanism was to use cartels or production controls negotiated among firms, often with the assistance of the government.

Japan's decision to build communication satellites with public money is an example of targeting and industrial policy, of Japan not buying advanced technology produced abroad until Japanese products are competitive. The Japanese government refused to discuss with the United States the possibility of buying better and cheaper satellites from abroad, claiming it was a matter of national security, even though Japan had already made it clear that Japan intended to start exporting satellites to North America and Western Europe by the late 1990s. Japan launched its H-II space vehicle in 1994, after investing nearly $2.2 billion and being delayed for two years past its original dates. Despite being the market's most expensive rocket and coming at a time when the commercial satellite market was expected to cool off (1997), the Japanese are determined to see it through. Japan's determination is to escape dependence on American space technology, to do it itself. This is another example of a government project to build up an industry which is not needed or economically justified, and it is part of the effort to build up the aerospace industry. The H-II vehicle can at best only be launched during two forty-five-day windows each year due to agreements with Japanese fisherman who must clear out of the fishing grounds near the space complex on the southern island of Tanegashima. More than enough space capacity already exists; the additional capacity planned by the Japanese is not needed.

Closed Japanese markets are not passé. Biotechnology and supercomputers appear to be two new industries in which government policy intends to reassert the age-old pattern. Japanese bureaucrats and scientists intend to use Japanese hardware for Japanese processes even if American machines are currently available and superior to those found in Japan. NTT procurement until just recently excluded foreign firms and even foreign firms with local subsidiaries, like IBM Japan. This is the prime area for American SII negotiations with Japan.

EDUCATION AND YOUTH

Education in Japan has been a great success story, if one goes by the numbers. Over 92 percent of eligible Japanese children attend kindergarten; 90 percent of all Japanese students graduate from high school. Japan's illiteracy rate is under 1 percent. Teachers are highly valued in Japan; deference and respect for them is strong. More highly qualified teacher applicants exist than places available for them in schools. The Japanese place great stress on learning as a group activity. Rather than encouraging individual excellence, the Japanese seek to ensure that all members of the class attain the required standard levels of literacy and numeracy. Japanese graduates are molded to possess high competency and conformance so as to fit in to the company which recruits them and become members of a disciplined and skilled work force dedicated to improving the firm's productivity. However, the entire Japanese school structure of 1.3 million teachers educating 27 million pupils in some 66,000 schools is tightly controlled and regulated by the powerful Ministry of Education. Course offerings, textbooks, salaries, and even a school's physical plant are under its supervision. This yields intense rigidity and conformity.

In the Japanese educational system, very little student participation exists and little or no student discussion occurs. The teacher lectures; the students listen and take notes. The average Japanese student, therefore, has a difficult time responding quickly to questions and finds it hard to express feelings verbally with anywhere near the amount of freedom and enthusiasm expected by Americans. The Japanese education system produces a steady supply of young people with good minds trainable by industry. In the Japanese view, engineers are produced by industry, business administrators by business, and neither can be properly trained by universities. Educators use three measures as evidence of high achievement: high attendance rates, order in the classroom, and high scores in international comparisons of knowledge (which actually is an indication of good test-taking skills).

Although Japanese society is far from egalitarian as Americans would define it, the Japanese do have every chance to succeed. Ability and effort allow the ordinary Japanese worker to climb the latter of success. It is true, however, that who you know is important in Japanese society. However, every Japanese student is exposed to the same material in school, takes the same exam, and has the same chance of passing it. Tokyo University may be the key to success in Japan, but every Japanese student has equal opportunity through his or her own talents, abilities, and efforts to study hard, to do exceptionally well on the exams during "exam hell week," to get accepted, and to attend the elite schools. Japanese businesses use the "learning by experience" principle to develop employees; even those with masters degrees start at the lower rungs to learn the company's business thoroughly (Tokuyama, 1987). Contrast this to India, in which the caste system is still firmly in place and birth, not abilities, determine, even today, many an Indian's future role and status.

Education in Japan is highly structured and has strict routines for classroom performance intended to mold each student into a homogenized product of the culture. The Japanese have a highly developed sense of balance, form, order, and style; an intuitive feel and need for precision, accuracy, and correctness; extraordinary manual dexterity and the ability to work well on small, detailed items; the predisposition to applying themselves with a single-minded dedication to the task at hand; and an overwhelming desire to excel in anything they do and to be as good as or better than anyone else. The primary function of the secondary school system is to prepare students for the college entrance exam, the exam which determines which students will attend which universities and eventually what jobs each gets. This restricts intellectual development and concentrates on following guidelines at the expense of originality, eliminating extracurricular activities, and neglecting social development.

Japan has a policy of public primary education that prohibits private schools in the primary grades. It also has a compulsory system of drawing students strictly from a single district. No choice exists for students and parents. Students are mechanically fed a bureaucratically designated curriculum and advance through the system month by month, lockstep with the rest of the country. Instructional outlines are provided that dedicate the system to eliminating defects and providing instruction in inverse proportion to ability—the less accomplished one is in a subject, the more one studies it. The last thing a teacher will do is to give additional instruction in a subject a student can do well. The education system does not work to strengthen the strong but to shore up the weak. School rules, which enforce norms of clothing, haircuts, posture, walk, etc., are strong. This is because some "bad" students still exhibit some signs of personal likes and dislikes (i.e., individuality). School rules are used to outlaw any expression of those last vestiges of student individuality. This system eliminates all pleasure from school life and destroys creativity. It is, however, effective in instilling a common level of knowledge and skills and in getting students used to enduring long hours. Japanese education emphasizes enduring long, distasteful hours and patiently doing unpleasant tasks for protracted periods of time. It also fosters a spirit of cooperation so that everyone achieves the same knowledge and skills. It is effective in training a labor force suitable for employment in the workplaces of standardized mass production, which allows new workers to be trained easily. Since the employees are highly patient and cooperative, the employer knows they will perform their assigned tasks diligently and accurately.

Young Japanese students find that their social status and life opportunities are fixed at an early age. High school does not represent an opening up of choice but a narrowing of focus. It is a tight regime that does not encourage personal dreams, experimentation, individual variety, or idealism. Individual choice has often been sacrificed in Japan for the sake of economic survival. With growing affluence, this necessity no longer exists. For Japan's technopolises and high-tech industries, this suppression of individuality is the nation's major weakness.

Thus, Japanese youth are robbed of the opportunity to dream, explore and choose—the very essence of creativity. Early in life, they must adapt to a demanding society that does not forgive failures. They are told to sacrifice their dreams for the common good. Examination hell week is the focus of their total high school days; their life is made or broken by its results. Everyone must study the same material at the same time, an approach that enforces uniformity. They must enter the university immediately after high school instead of taking time off, as some no doubt would like to do. Rather than being viewed as an asset, diversity of experience is viewed as anti-social or as slacking off. As a result, most Japanese youth hide within the safety net of convention.

Although Japanese schools are good at picking winners, they also create a nation of losers who are forever burdened with an inferiority complex because they failed one exam. In Japan, there is no such thing as a second chance, different options, or late bloomers. Everything is fixed at college entrance; students cannot change majors or take courses freely in other departments. Frustration and disruptive behavior are becoming serious. The sense of purpose that drove the postwar generation to workaholic excess is missing. Rebellion against regimentation is not considered natural and is frowned on. Today's Japanese youth are considered by their elders to be devoid of perseverance, dependent on others, and self-centered. All seem to agree that reform is a must; but the talk focuses on the revival of moral education and increased discipline—just the opposite of what is truly needed for more creative environment. Although many clearly see the need for change, the current mood in Japan is to instill even harsher, more strict discipline in the schools.

Japanese excessive public preoccupation with academic careers is a direct outcome of the recruiting and employment policies of leading Japanese companies. First-rate companies limit their recruitment to new graduates of a handful of prestigious universities. They have expounded, if not created, the exam hell which has stifled creativity. Because their recruitment and hiring policies emphasize good graces, attendance at the right school, and sociability, they eliminate the protruding nails, the creative people who rebel against conformity and convention. In Japan, brilliant but second-rate students are never allowed into the company. Japan's most creative ventures have been begun by graduates of Japan's second-rate universities and corporate dropouts. Thus, Japanese companies have been hypocritical in demanding creative students from the educational system when their hiring policies discourage experimentation and creativity in the schools. If they indeed want creative people, they must take risks in hiring and promotion.

In Japan, a person's entire life is decided and dominated by his or her ability to secure employment within a large enterprise. This competition to gain employment in large enterprises is fierce. The examinations for entrance into a large enterprise are open to an individual only once in his or her life, immediately after graduation from school or college. Since an individual has little chance of gaining entrance to a company if the school or college from which he or she has graduated is not a good one, fierce competition exists to get into the good universities, whose hierarchy is well known to both students and employers. To do so, there is fierce competition to get into the right high school, the right junior high, the right elementary school—it is so relentless that it even extends into getting a child into the right kindergarten.

Universities are predominantly subject to the needs of big business. Universities do no more than give instruction in learning in accordance with the priorities of business enterprises; most students only study to gain employment with one of the top large enterprises. In a Confucian society, a person's worth is estimated not on the basis of whether he or she possesses money but on the basis of whether he or she has been educated. Industry uses the university as a filtering device, acting on the assumption that the strict entrance exams will identify the brightest and most tenacious. The quality of education is almost irrelevant because the firms reserve to themselves the actual training of talent. In Japan, only business can teach business, only technological firms can produce engineers. The system makes no allowances for late bloomers or for those changing direction.

LABOR-MANAGEMENT RELATIONS

The prototype for Japanese labor relations can be found in Meiji working conditions and relations. Managers were active in their businesses and kept a close eye on input and output changes. They were also generally highly trained and had substantial knowledge of textile technology and management. The traditional family system continued to be the basis of the entire economy; A close, almost personal relationship existed between the management and the workers. Reinvestment was high and debt/equity ratios were low. Reactions to the changes in the economic environment were rapid. The idea of the joint profit-maximizing capitalist cartel was clearly embodied in many Japanese cartels, both in Meiji times and since then.

Unions that exist in Japan are typically company unions that act in conjunction with the company and are not hostile to its management (as can be seen even today by their walking out over lunch or during weekends so as not to cause their company to lose any production time). Team work in Japan is industrywide. This phenomenon can be seen today by the rotation of employees throughout an organization. The development efforts of Japanese firms emphasize rotation of personnel among departments in ways that lead to the exchange of useful information and the formation of common goals. In many cases, close communication among functionally separate specialists is strengthened by the awareness of a commonality of interest flowing from stable, long-term employment (and supplier) relationships.

At least three distinctive characteristics of the Japanese labor market differ from that found in the American labor marketplace: (1) low labor mobility (due to lifetime employment at many top-tier firms); (2) limited port of entry for new employees; and (3) the low profile of labor unions, which are mostly enterprise unions rather than industry or trade unions. Limited port of entry in Japan refers to the lack of mid-career entry, especially among college graduates, since most hiring is done at the time of graduation from school (any new hire traditionally must start at the bottom). Employment in Japan tends to be centralized with the central control of hiring handled by the firm's personnel department; whereas in the United States, each division or each manager possesses hiring authority. The first two aforementioned points imply that labor allocation and reallocation must be more active to cope with changing demand conditions and changing technology. As a business fluctuation buffer, many Japanese firms rely on subcontractors more than American firms do; when the recession comes, the firms can first cut back on subcontracted workers instead of laying off their own core workers (Imai and Itami, 1984).

The Japanese have developed internal labor markets whereas the Americans have developed internal capital markets and internal good markets. This is due to cultural, economic, and legal differences between the two societies. Japanese society is generally more homogeneous, close knit, and tolerant of ambiguity than American society. This makes consensus formation among members of an organization easier. Japanese society also monitors its members' behaviors. Agency costs are thereby less in Japan. In addition, in the high-growth market that Japan had for almost forty years after the Second World War, conflict was lessened. Without growth, the Japanese firm's heavy reliance on internal labor markets will be hard to maintain; layoffs may become inevitable (as was the case in Japan in the early 1990s), insufficient growth may mean reallocation and job rotation may not be possible. (Transfer or rotation of workers enhances the process of knowledge acquisition and diffusion. Rotation within teams allows workers to familiarize themselves with various aspects of the work process. Workers are also rotated frequently from task to task to reduce the rate of repetitive motion injury.)

In most Japanese companies, human assets are considered to be the firm's most important and profitable assets in the long run. These human assets are promoted throughout the company by emphasizing long-term and secure employment, a company philosophy that shows concern for employee needs and stresses cooperation and team work, and close attention to hiring people who will fit well with the particular company's values and to integrating employees into the company at all stages of their working life. These strategies are articulated through slow promotion (based on longevity and seniority, not on merit or performance), job rotation through all phases of the organization, a complex appraisal system, the emphasis on work groups, open communications throughout the organization in all work settings, consultative decision making, and concern for the employee (Hatvany and Pucik, 1981). These organizational value differences (between Japan and the West) are shown in Figure 2.2.

Employees in a Japanese firm are recruited into general work roles for whichthe focus is on people rather than skills. The idea is to pick people as they come out of a school or university and shape them to the firm's skills requirements in a particular area of operations. This will be done mostly through internal training, and the skills acquired will not be readily marketable as such. Such a recruitment strategy is made possible by the lifetime employment system, which encourages both employee and firm to invest in each other over the long term and, usually, throughout an employee's working life. Japanese employees often have very strong expectations that the upward mobility within

Figure 2.2
Differences in Organization Values

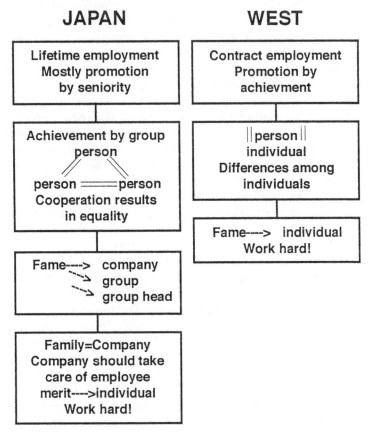

the firm will follow any training that they receive. Their gaze is upward toward their prospects within the hierarchy and not, as is typical in the West, sideway toward their opportunities in the labor market. In the West, it is the exceptional person who, after leaving school, has not been in the labor market at some time during his or her career; in Japan, it is the exceptional person who has. In the typical Western firm, both firm and employees share an interest in developing immediately useful, marketable skills; whereas in Japan both take a longer term view, preferring to invest in a thorough knowledge and experience of the organization's culture. The former aims at horizontal mobility because upward mobility offers inferior career prospects; but those who move to other firms find it difficult to get accepted in their new organizations unless they are very recent recruits. Indeed, in the typical Japanese firm, the greatest horizontal mobility is found at the lowest level of the hierarchy among semi-skilled or unskilled temporary workers in whom the firm has not invested. At the top of the firm, horizontal mobility is virtually nonexistent and none of the directors have been sought outside the firm: they are all confirmed and experienced corporate men (men, because Japanese business is still a sexist, masculine world) and their views on the world have been shaped in the same organizational mold.

Japanese workers do not regard their jobs simply as a means of earning an income; instead they attach a great deal of importance to the intrinsic compensation derived from the work itself—for example, based on opportunities to use aptitudes and abilities, belonging to a company can be interpreted as a sense of belonging to the whole company as a place of employment rather than to any specific job. The labor force identifies with the future of the company and is assumed to share its goals. This results in a high level of commitment and a willingness to accept managerial authority that would not be possible or acceptable in the West. Secure in their employment, people will allow themselves to be redeployed in jobs according to the needs of the firm. If this means a geographical relocation, they will subordinate the short-term interests of the family to those of the firm. The psychological contract between a company and its employees is long term. The acceptance of managerial authority shows up in a lower level of personal discretion in the performance of tasks than is usually found in the West. Jobs are set out in detailed written specifications, and their execution is subjected to tighter control procedures than would be possible in the West. Compliance is rewarded with upward mobility stimulated by that fact that rank and function are kept distinct. Seniority is an important determinant of rank. When vacancies appear, the expectation is that they will be filled from below, not from outside. This resulting hierarchical mobility ensures a high level of motivation, a low level of absenteeism, and a low separation rate. The *ringi* system provides for systematic consultation on a wide range of issues at different organizational levels, thereby achieving as broad as consensus as possible in planning and implementation.

In Japan, evaluations are usually based on daily observations by managers. Some companies have elaborate formal systems that specify evaluation criteria and formats, but in practice evaluations are informal and are carried out with minimal direct feedback to the employee. The annual face-to-face evaluation meetings that play so important a role in the United States are conspicuously absent in Japan. The opportunity that such interviews give employees to emphasize their accomplishments and for both parties to exchange information and receive feedback is replaced by an annual written self-assessment that employees are required to give to their managers. The employee, however, receives no formal feedback (Rosenberger, 1992).

This kind of evaluation system works well if there is a strong, trust-based relationship between researchers and managers. Without such a relationship, frustration levels can rise because there is no system that allows researchers to vent dissatisfaction. Despite the prevailing image of dedicated, company-oriented researchers in Japan, the levels of frustration are growing, especially among younger and more ambitious researchers. Frustration levels are growing with regard to the reward system in Japanese technical organizations. Even though most Japanese companies have adopted formally a more merit-based pay system, managers are reluctant to differentiate significantly among researchers in either base pay or bonuses.

The firm's investment in its human resources must be underwritten by the long-term commitment of its employees. The time-consuming efforts by these employees to acquire firm-specific and externally unmarketable expertise will only occur when advancement and employment are secure. This pairing is compounded by the lack of any effective and competitive labor market at the mid- and senior management levels. Lifelong employment necessitates continual wealth creation as the primary purpose of the enterprise; equity, security, and profits can grow only as much as the enterprise grows. A feverish pursuit of technology as an outgrowth of the culture at Japanese corporations exists primarily for the enrichment of employees not stockholders. Managers define their responsibilities first in terms of the people of the enterprise. Boards of directors are usually constituted by managers, not outside stockholders.

Employees tend to stay in the same firm for all their working life, no more thinking of deserting their firm than they would consider changing their name. The status system stresses seniority and regular promotion or increment based on length of service. Coupled with the consensus decision-making process, this means that the group, not individuals, is held responsible for mistakes. This, in turn, means that all pitch in to correct errors and little time is wasted searching for scapegoats. This keeps the organization focused on fixing the problem rather than fixing the blame. It also means that the lessons learned from a mistake remain within the corporation.

Japanese managers are much more willing to share firm-specific knowledge with union representatives than in the West. Although such knowledge might be used to formulate union demands and to develop negotiating positions, unions can be trusted not to abuse it or divulge it to outsiders when it is confidential. Union representatives remain company employees first and union members second. The bargaining process is typically subordinated to the imperatives of superordinate goals that favor the hierarchy and the company rather than the market, the union, or the employees. The relationship that binds firm and employee is insulated from fluctuations in the labor market by a buffer of subcontractors and temporary workers, who can be taken on or released by the company as conditions require. They absorb the environmental uncertainties that might otherwise threaten the company-worker relationship. The company's concern for the welfare and morale of its employees is repaid in loyalty and single-minded devotion of the employees.

The company union is granted a measure of legitimacy as a negotiating partner that does not typically exist in the West. It identifies with the company and its objectives, which makes possible a corporatist approach to industrial relations. This development of corporatism is further stimulated by the fact that all the employees are represented by a single union and that its concerns do not extend beyond the company and its activities. The union is organizational oriented, not market oriented, as it is in the West. In Japan, little sense of solidarity brings unions together in their disputes with their employers. The main role of unions is to reinforce the lifelong employment and seniority systems and to strengthen the company welfare programs. Union leaders must remain employees of their particular firm, to whom they continue to feel under obligation. After giving up active union duties, they can move into salaried staff status or junior management, as long as their conduct was satisfactory during their term of office.

Chapter 3

Japanese Innovative Strengths and Weaknesses

Patents, research and development spending in both aggregate and segmented forms, and technology transfer are examined in this chapter to reveal Japanese innovative strengths and weaknesses.

PATENTS

The custom of patents dates back to fifteenth century Europe when in 1460 the Republic of Venice granted two inventors a privilege stating that no one could reproduce their invention without their permission. By the middle of the sixteenth century, this idea had spread throughout much of Europe (Guile and Brooks, 1987). The importance of patents can be seen from the fact that British patent laws date from 1624, whereas those of France date from 1791 and those of other European countries date from the nineteenth century.

The original concept of patent protection was that by preventing others from imitating an inventor's invention or by putting the inventor in a position to license imitators only in exchange for compensation, patents would allow inventors to appropriate the economic benefits of their inventive contributions. The expectation of such rewards is what, theoretically, provides the incentive to invent. Absent patent protection, imitation might occur so swiftly that an inventor would not be able to make a return on the investment and hence would not have an incentive to invent.

Patents have been simultaneously praised for providing the economic incentives to innovate and condemned for creating monopolies that stifle competition and raise prices for consumers. Is it only coincidental that the periods of greatest innovation come during strong times of patent protection? The opposing viewpoint states that most companies need innovation for competition's sake, that patents represent "cream on the pie," and that patent protection in itself is not the primary incentive to innovate. Patents are far from perfect as a means of appropriating the benefits from the invention; rarely is a patent so strong that a determined effort to circumvent it does not succeed. Mansfield (1989) found that inventing around a patent requires substantially less cost and takes less time than the original invention. Although patents provide strong protection, they may also stimulate overinvestment in R&D as firms duplicate each others' inventive programs or when competitors attempt extensive R&D aimed at circumventing a patent.

Despite the imperfections of the patent system, any other form of protection or incentive has been found to work less well. Economists have determined that inventive activity responds elastically to the demand price of an invention, implying that it is influenced by the correct incentive policy. This should make the private rewards proportional to the potential social value of inventive output, which is precisely what the patent system achieves (Wyatt, 1986). More importantly, the patent system encourages ideas that represent departures from accepted practices, particularly radical innovations. In addition, patents are especially useful in assisting those who pursue unpopular or different ideas.

The number of innovations realized per patented invention varies considerably across industries. The relatively high ratios of patents per innovation in the chemical and petroleum sectors and the relatively low ratios in the computer, electrical machinery, lumber, and instruments sectors can be explained by the fact that the value and cost of individual patents vary enormously within and across industries. In some industries, like electronics, considerable speculation exists that the patent system is being bypassed to a greater extent than in the past.

Nonetheless, a society that wants to foster invention and innovation must make them worthwhile to the potential inventors and innovators. The patent process, by providing protection to inventors and giving them a monopoly on the rights to their inventions, spurs innovation. The importance given to patents is reflected in the Uruguay round of GATT (General Agreement on Tariffs and Trade). Intellectual property rights protection (of which patents are a part) were a key part of GATT discussions. In addition, the United States aggressively pursued patent protection for American inventors throughout the world during the late 1980s and early 1990s by using the threats implicit in its Super 301 trade clause. These two parallel efforts underscore the attention and importance accorded to patents in the United States.

Patents are often viewed as indicative of innovative skills. A review of patents issued by the United States during the 1980s has shown a strong trend upward in the numbers issued to the Japanese. In fact, in 1986 Hitachi ousted General Electric from its top position of receiving the most patents (Yoder and Lachia, 1988). However, numbers are not truly indicative of importance. Patents also vary widely in their significance. A patent in room-temperature superconductivity has greater potential than one that slightly modifies an electronic circuit; and yet both count equally as a statistic. The number of Japanese patents awarded to Japanese residents is greater than the number of U.S. patents awarded to U.S. residents. This is probably due more to the relatively lower costs of Japanese patenting than to any high productivity of Japanese R&D. The rapid increase in Japanese patenting efforts in the United States can be explained by the relatively small amount of technological advance incorporated into each Japanese patent (Pavitt, 1985). In fact, Japanese companies are being pressured by their backlogged government to curtail filings for minor patents.

CHI Research Inc. has developed more sophisticated measures that examine patents as indicative of innovation based on earlier patents cited as building blocks for new patents. The Current Impact Index (CII) measures how often a company's patents are cited relative to those of all other companies. The technological strength is derived by multiplying the impact index by the number of patents. Technology cycle time is the median age in years of patents cited in a company's new patents; the shorter the cycle time, the faster the company is developing new technology (*Business Week*, August 3, 1992, p. 68). A review of the data for 1991 shows that eleven of the top twenty-five American patents issued in 1991 were to Japanese companies. However, American companies tended to have higher current impact indices (interestingly, the two German firms in the survey had the lowest indices), thus making up considerable distance. Japanese firms by far have a lower technology cycle time, indicating their emphasis on speed for developing new technologies.

In the United States, patents are issued for significantly differentiated items and are secret until issued; in Japan, patents are regularly issued for what in the United States would be considered product line extensions and are public record when applied for. This provides more time to learn about the innovation, decide if it is worth developing, and then replicate, circumvent, or ignore the patent. Competitors can file to delay the patent and then proceed to explore the technology at will. In the United States, strong patent protection is provided to enhance R&D efforts and to provide incentives for a firm to innovate. In Japan, a family philosophy exists. An innovation does not exist merely for the inventing firm but for the benefit of the country as a whole. The entire system is aimed at avoiding conflict and promoting cooperation (cross-licensing) (Melloan, 1988).

Japanese patents tend to be narrowly focused on specific improvements to technology. For example, when IBM scientists in Zurich discovered warm temperature superconductors in 1986, Japanese companies duplicated the results and within the year had flooded their patent offices with hundreds of related but minor applications. Another example is the dispute between Mitsubishi Electric and Fusion Systems Corporation. In 1985, Fusion discovered that Mitsubishi had filed more than 160 patents in Japan for products similar to its linear microwave-actuated ultraviolet lamp, which Fusion had been selling in Japan since 1975. Mitsubishi argued in its defense that it did not infringe on Fusion's patent because the devices were significantly different in design; Fusion countered that Mitsubishi had made only trivial changes to its design. This underscores the real difference between the Japanese and U.S. patent systems.

The wide diversity between what a patent is, what it protects, and its primary national objective makes the number of patents issued a questionable usable variable for determining a nation's innovative capabilities. The Japan honors "first to apply," whereas the United States honors "first to invent." American applications must disclose all "prior art" and thus prove that they have something distinctly new and different; in Japan, it is possible to patent a relatively minor change. American patent applications are secret until the patent is issued; whereas in Japan, patent applications are made available to potential challengers at the time of application. Whereas the American system protects individuals, the Japanese system balances individual rights with broader social and industrial interests. As long as it is easier to copy under Japanese law, Japanese companies will continue to do so. Japan has been reluctant to tighten intellectual property laws, especially those concerning patents, believing that the country still needs easy access to the creative ideas of the West, particularly in the computer and entertainment software areas.

One of the main problems with the Japanese system from a foreign company's perspective is the extremely long patent application approval periods (an average of four to six years versus two in the United States); such applications are open to public scrutiny after only eighteen months. Japanese patents offer narrower protection and must be filed in Japanese, and there is a dire shortage of patent attorneys to pursue the interests of foreign companies. If a foreign company has a strategic technology, it should expect to wait a long time in Japan for a patent. Another concern is that domestic companies using patents pending rarely have to pay royalties for periods of use prior to patent award. In rapidly changing markets, the value of the patent protection may have evaporated by the time the patent is issued. In 1960, John Kilby of Texas Instruments applied for a patent on the integrated circuit. The patent was not awarded by the Japanese government until 1989. In the meantime, of course, the technology had far transcended Kilby's early design. American companies have seen their prime patents stalled on Japanese bureaucrats' desks as Japanese competitors used the technology to gain new markets. Corning Glass applied for a patent on its optical fiber in the United States in 1974; the patent was granted two years later in the United States. Corning applied in 1975 for a Japanese patent, which was granted in 1985 (Yoder and Lachia, 1988). The Japanese patent process, in comparison with most other industrialized nations, limits the issuance of patents to foreigners. In Japan, only 10 percent of all patents are foreign, versus 48 percent in the United States, 56 percent in Germany, 71 percent in Britain, and 78 percent in France.

The enormous rise in Japan's patent productivity can also be partly attributed to the sustained and steep increases in R&D investment. Real growth rates in Japanese R&D expenditures rose faster than those of any other major industrial state. Other factors may be superior company incentives; greater research continuity made possible by lifetime employment; closer contact and better communications among divisions engaged in research, production, and marketing; fiercer competition among firms; and greater company prestige derived from patenting. International comparisons of patent data tend to overstate Japanese technological accomplishments significantly. Quantitative indicators provide little information about the quality of patents. The Japanese have applied for and registered more patents than others because the knowledge they seek to protect tends to be less significant technologically and of lower quality, and the Japanese have a greater propensity to seek patents for know-how that others would consider too mundane or short lived to bother about. Nearly half the applications made by the Japanese to their own patent office are turned down, compared with less than 20 percent of foreign applicants. Patents provide a skewed and misleading picture of the present Japanese position. Experts indicate that one American patent is worth seven Japanese patents (Heiduk and Yamamura, 1990). Japanese researchers tend to apply for patents for everything as proof of research activity, and as a consequence the majority of Japanese patent applications in Japan are rejected. The turn-down rate of Japanese patent applications is also significantly higher in the United States than for any other nationality. In the United States, the pace of technological change may be so rapid that it makes a lengthy patent approval process an ineffective device for protecting property rights; with public access as patents require, many companies believe that patents will disclose vital information that will help competitors and hence they do not file. Despite the Japanese lead in pure numbers, considerable doubt exists regarding the quality of each patent issued. Patents are sufficiently vague that any inferences regarding innovative strengths and weaknesses are impossible.

R&D EXPENDITURES

Japan's R&D expenditures as a percentage of GNP have continued to rise to their current level, which approaches 3 percent and leads the industrialized countries (see Figure 3.1). R&D as a percentage can be misleading: Belgium spends 1.5 percent of its GNP in R&D, a percentage comparable to the United States; however, this factors out to $168 million, roughly 1 to 2 percent of total American non-military R&D spending. Figure 3.2 shows trends in R&D intensity between government and industry in Japan, Germany, and the United States. In Japan, the salaries of all university and college science teaching personnel are counted as if they were full-time researchers. This leads to a substantial overstatement of Japan's overall R&D expenditures, a substantial overstatement of the academic sector's role in Japanese R&D, and a substantial overstatement of the role of basic research. This overstatement can be as much as thirteen times (Okimoto and Saxonhouse, 1987).

If percentage of GNP were the only indicator, the former Soviet Union (with R&D spending equivalent to 3.75 percent of its GNP) should have led all nations; but one would hardly qualify Russia, now or then, as a technological leader. R&D expenditures represents inputs, not output. It is important to consider not only the level of R&D spending but also its effectiveness. Capital is a necessary component for innovations but is not in itself sufficient. Not only is the quantity of dollars important but the efficient use of that money. The United States' level of productivity is as high or higher than that achieved overseas in most industries. The United States puts as much resources in R&D as Japan, Germany, and France combined; twice as much as does

Figure 3.1
Japanese R&D Expenses and Economic Growth

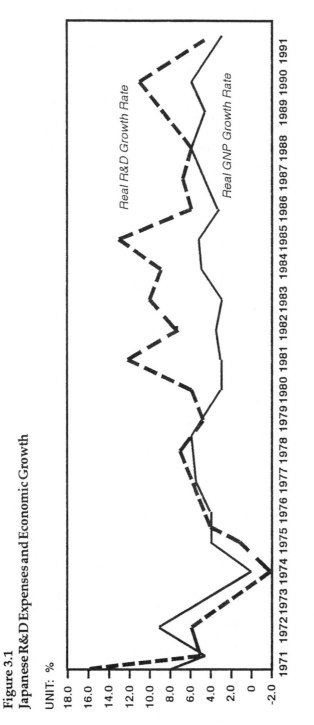

UNIT: %

Source: MITI

Figure 3.2
Trends in R&D Intensity

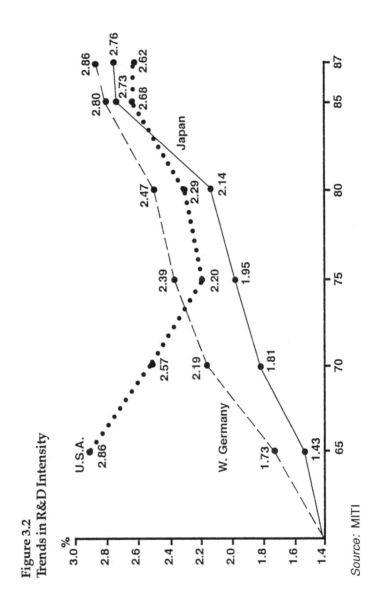

Source: MITI

Japan. The much feared and publicized Japanese effort to build a fifth-generation supercomputer aided by a government grant of $500 million over ten years (which has little to show for the effort) must be compared to the $3 billion IBM alone spent on R&D in 1984 (Baily and Chakrabarti, 1985). Percentage of GNP also is too elusive and inexact to be used to measure innovation.

When it comes to research scientists and engineers relative to the size of the labor force, the United States still has more than any other country. In 1981, only about 4 percent of Japanese R&D dollars were paid to universities or independent institutes for contract work or in support grants (Clark, 1984). In 1981, more than 75,000 engineers graduated from Japanese universities but only 7,000 masters and 1,200 doctorates were awarded in engineering. The United States produced about the same number of engineering graduates but three to four times as many masters and doctorates. American receipts for sales of technological licenses to the rest of the world far exceed those of any other country. Americans write 35 percent of all of the scientific and technical articles published in the world (Thurow, 1987). If one were to compile a list of the most important innovations of the last twenty years—for example, the transistor (Bell Labs), the semiconductors chip (Texas Instruments), the small computer (Apple), and the video recorder (Ampex)—one would see that they were all American ideas. The United States still leads in research efforts, but the lead is smaller than it used to be.

Differences in gross spending, numbers of scientists, and GNP percentages tell little. However, dramatic differences between Japanese and American firms in their allocation of R&D resources between process and basic research do exist. American firms devote about two thirds of their R&D expenditure to improved product technology (new products and product changes) and about one third to improved process technology (new processes and process changes). Among the Japanese firms, the proportions are reversed: two thirds are spent for improved process technology and one third goes for improved product technology. In fact during 1987, 54 percent of current Japanese R&D expenditures focused on development, 43.7 percent on applied research, and the remaining minimal expenditures—2.3 percent—were in basic research (Mansfield, 1988a). The Japanese devote a much larger percentage of their R&D dollar to tooling, manufacturing facilities and capital equipment—applied R&D—almost double proportionally than is spent in the United States. The largest proportion of Japanese R&D activity has continuously gone to development research.

A study by MITI indicated that from 1960 to 1980 the Japanese came up with only twenty-six technological innovations whereas the United States had 237; however, only two of the Japanese innovations were classified as radical whereas the number of U.S. radical innovations were sixty-five (Harper, 1988). In Chakrabarti, Feinman, and Fuentevilla's (1978, 1982) studies of 500 industrial innovations introduced in major industrialized countries from 1953 to 1973, the United States was given credit for 257 innovations, of which over half were considered radical; whereas twenty-five of the twenty-seven credited innovations from Japan were of the improvement variety. Their studies noted that over a quarter of the Japanese innovations (a proportion twice as much as found in other countries) were for the innovating firm's internal use and meant for productivity or quality improvements. Of the U.S. innovations, greater than half of the total of sixty-eight were deemed radical or major technological shifts. Of the Japanese innovations, only 7 percent were radical and the majority were of the improvement variety. Figure 3.3 shows the distribution of innovations between improvement, major technological advances, and radical innovation for each of five major industrial powers. Figure 3.4 shows the distribution of radical innovations between 1940 and 1980 between the industrial powers in the world. According to a 1968 OECD study, Japan has contributed only five major innovations from a list of 139 major innovations which have been invented since the Second World War: the bullet train, the transistor radio, the compact videotape recorder, the electron microscope, and the synthetic fiber Vinylon. Few examples exist to date of Japanese originality in technological development.

Nobel prizes are awarded for creative breakthroughs; what do these statistics say? Pure science is a field in which geniuses reign; but geniuses often do not fit standard molds, and nonconformists do not fit well into Japan (Taylor, 1983). Only five Japanese scientists have ever won Nobel prizes (the same number as have been won by Denmark, a country considerably smaller than Japan), and most of the winners did their prize-winning work elsewhere. The 1988 winner in medicine had not lived in Japan since 1963. Leo Ezaki won the Nobel prize in 1973; he left Japan in 1960 to work for IBM in the United States. He bluntly said that Japanese society is not conducive to originality. Tadatsugu Taniguchi who discovered the structure of beta interferon, says that "geniuses get kicked out (of Japan)." He escaped the fate of others by getting his Ph.D. at the University of Zurich and studying in Italy and the United States (Yoder, 1988). The few Japanese Nobel Prize Winners have few kind words to say about Japan.

Figure 3.3
Distribution of Innovations

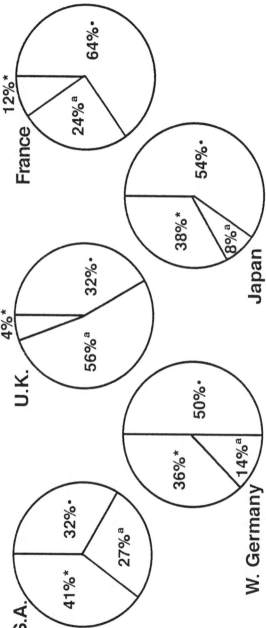

France
64%•
24%ᵃ
12%*

U.K.
32%•
4%*
56%ᵃ

Japan
54%•
38%*
8%ᵃ

U.S.A.
32%•
41%*
27%ᵃ

W. Germany
50%•
36%*
14%ᵃ

* Improvement of Existing Technology
ᵃ Major Technological Advance
* Radical Breakthrough
Source: Hudson Research Europe S.A.

Figure 3.4
Distribution of Radical Innovations, 1940s–1970s

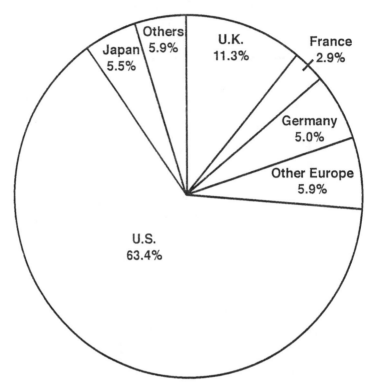

"What should Japanese researchers do if they want to develop into first class scientists? Go overseas. If they're really interested in science, then that's what they should do. In Japan, there are no opportunities for young researchers to do independent research. Japan's science is definitely inferior to America's in terms of real creativity. It is very clear that Japan is making money by taking and applying the fruits of science that the West creates at great expense." So spoke SusumuTonegawa, Japanese Nobel laureate in medicine and physiology (1987). He critiqued the profit-oriented nature of Japanese government research programs, which tend not to pursue fundamental research but only applied research. They are stifled by a rigid hierarchy, archaic rules, inadequate funding, and enormous pressures to conform. That nearly all the Nobel Japanese winners went to the West is an unpleasant reminder of Japan's continuing failure to produce world-class scientists.

Very few mathematicians or scientists who have done significant original work are Japanese. Visiting physicists are typically unimpressed by Japanese research, which is mainly derivative in nature. Western scientists complain that Japanese labs tend to offer too little space, poor equipment, inadequate maintenance, and too few technicians. Japanese scientists rank third behind American and British researchers in contributions to scientific literature each year. Few of their research papers are cited by scientists abroad, and even fewer research papers are co-authored by Japanese and foreign scientists. It appears that the United States excels at basic science whereas the Japanese lag far behind. The vast majority of Japanese effort is not only commercial in orientation but is directed at improving on or advancing existing technology. In contrast, the West, particularly the United States, France, and the United Kingdom are extraordinarily fertile in giving birth to radical breakthrough innovations. Japanese output in this most creative related part of Research and Development is trivial by comparison.

Only a small proportion of all Japanese innovation has had the primary end result of using less labor in production. Labor saving and the substitution of capital for labor in production via automation are American traits. Although robots have been utilized in great numbers, the vast bulk of the Japanese economy is made up of small Japanese firms, which account for 70 percent of the total Japanese employment and which employ inexpensive but disciplined Japanese workers. Only the top-tier Japanese companies have been diligent and consistent in automating their factories. A large proportion of Japanese innovation (more than one third) has been oriented toward raw material and energy conservation. This has had a tremendous impact in that these cost savings have been applied to commercial products. A large proportion of Japanese innovations have been oriented to a particularly Japanese problem: space saving and miniaturization. These specific Japanese orientations begin in the Japanese home market in an attempt to meet the special needs of the Japanese people (Franko, 1983).

Twenty percent of Japanese R&D is paid for by the Japanese government compared with 54 percent in France, 47 percent in America and 39 percent in Britain. Japanese governmental R&D is almost nonexistent compared to the industrial sector. The Japanese government's share of R&D expenditures have consistently been near 20 percent, of which expenditures on industrial technology are 13 percent. Thus, the proportion of industrial R&D financed by the Japanese government is less than 3 percent, which is one tenth of that found in most other industrialized countries. The other nations show a balance between the sectors which does not exist in Japan. Figure 3.5 shows the breakdown of Japanese Research and Development expenditures among government, industry, and universities; whereas universities and government R&D expenditures have remained relatively consistent between 1977 and 1991, industrial R&D has multiplied fivefold. This shift and preoccupation is unique to Japan. Figure 3.6 shows those shares of R&D financed by the industrial and governmental sectors for five major industrial powers. Excluding defense-related research, the breakdown in research expenditures among research establishments are similar among all the major industrialized countries (*The Economist,* September 28, 1991, p. 96).

The strength of Japan's system lies in its capacity to convert breakthroughs swiftly into tangible products on store shelves. Continuous innovation in production technology is pursued at all times by most Japanese companies, almost to the extent of fanaticism, a religious zealotry. Incremental improvements to the innovation drive competition for market attention and more competitive costs. The system is based on consensus building, government industry cooperation, an emphasis on advancing the not glamorous but commercially decisive area of process technology, cost-effective resource allocation, and commercial applications. Japanese firms follow strategies which may be suboptimal to the members of the group in the short run but optimize the group's performance in the long run. Due to the unique aspects of the Japanese labor-management system (lifetime employment and practically no mid-term employment hiring or firing), information is quick to pass among members (divisions of the same company, sister companies within the same *keiretsu*) but slow to leak outside, to non-associated entities. Innovations are driven by identified commercial markets. Since the Japanese domestic market is highly competitive and demanding, competitive pressures in the private sector drive high R&D investments throughout all the firms in the industry.

Japanese managers prefer incremental improvement over radical breakthroughs as a mechanism for growth, dividing risk into smaller elements through short product cycles and quick market response. This is both culturally induced as well as operationally by the Japanese corporate and political environment. This preference for small but constant improvement is matched by a continuing search for emergent technologies outside the firm and industry. If nothing else, the Japanese are extremely vigilant about monitoring and absorbing external technologies. If it is interesting, if it may be usable at some later date, it is picked up, no matter the source. The Japanese have this fascination with technologies, the newer the better. If a competitor has it or is thinking about it, the more adamant it is to get.

Figure 3.5
Japanese R&D Spending

UNIT: 1 Billion

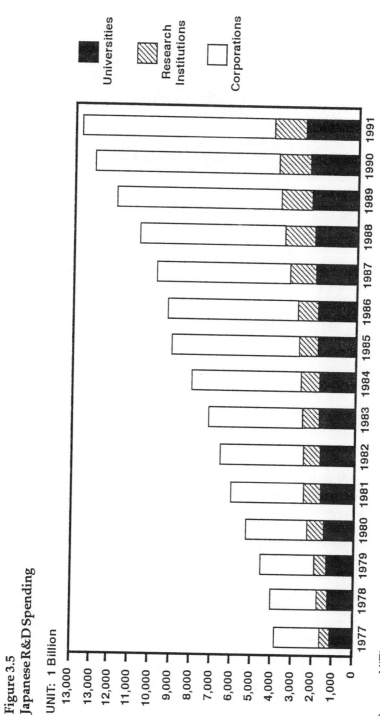

Source: MITI

Figure 3.6
Industrial R&D Expenditures by Industry and Government

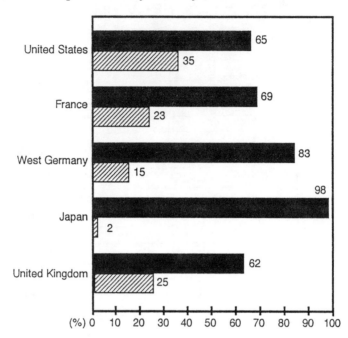

Source: International Science & Technology Data Update
(NSF USA, 1988, Vol. 21.)

The primary Japanese vision has been civilian application of technology, which involves improving the methods of production with process innovations usually acquired from abroad. This preoccupation with non-military applications is derived from the American Military Occupation and MacArthur's insistence that the Japanese energy be diverted into non-military endeavors. That this has become so inbred in Japanese politics and economics has come back to haunt the U.S.

Companies have been encouraged by the government to emphasize finding ways to adopt and add to imported technological knowledge and thus to improve efficiency and produce quality. The Japanese view product and process innovation as equally important and originating from the factory engineering staff. Figure 3.7 shows Japanese R&D/sales ratios by industry; the huge increases seen between 1975 and 1991 are indicative of the importance accorded to research and its primary placement in traditional industries.

Figure 3.7
Japanese R&D/Sales Ratios by Industry

UNIT: %

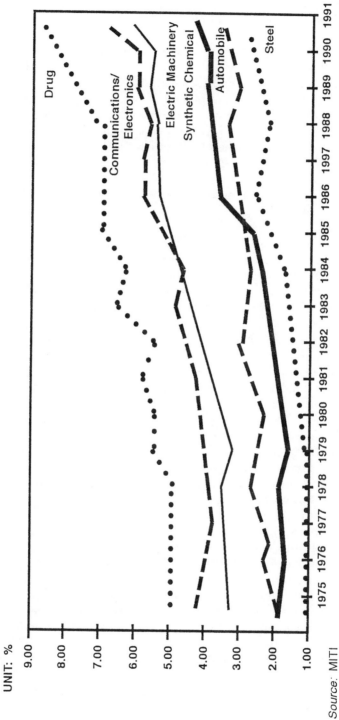

Source: MITI

TECHNOLOGY TRANSFER

For the last forty years, the Japanese have been accumulating technologies and patents at an incredible rate. Between 1950 and 1968, Japan entered into some 10,000 contracts with foreign countries and made transfer payments of more than $1.4 billion. This inflow of foreign technology stimulated the modernization of old industries and helped create new ones. This inflow of technology not only matched but exceeded that seen when Meiji Japan decided to modernize after the Meiji Revolution in 1867. Such technical know-how was made available on a relatively inexpensive basis. Technology was purchased in the form of royalties and license fees; seldom was there any direct investment by foreigners. These royalties and license fees were obtained at the best rates obtainable; often times foreign firms were prohibited from doing business in Japan unless they provided to selected Japanese corporations those intellectual property rights deemed most important and vital to Japanese national economic interests. Although not necessarily done at the point of a gun, the technology transfer was conducted on terms and timing most favorable to Japanese interests. This has allowed the Japanese to maintain control over most economic enterprises, an objective deemed particularly important by the Japanese government and policy-makers.

Japan is calculated to have spent only about $11 billion dollars between 1950 and 1980, perhaps $25 to $30 billion (in 1980 dollars), for the whole stock of Western technology (Dore, 1989) obtained during the proceeding thirty to thirty-five years. The main pattern in Japanese technological development since the Second World War has been to absorb European and American technology (at bargain store prices) and then to improve and upgrade it. Japanese manufacturers have been finding it increasingly difficult in recent years to import advanced foreign technologies when they have had no technologies in return to offer. This situation can only increase in the coming decade. Nonetheless, Japan's situation to date has not created a demand or an overwhelming need for creativity.

Between 1950 and 1980, a total of 26,804 separate technologies were imported from abroad by Japanese industry. General machinery, electrical machinery, and chemical products manufacturing industries were the major importers (Hirono, 1986) (However, the Japanese were rarely discriminatory, if the technology was usable or easily foreseen to be usable in the future, it was obtained.) Between 1950 and 1967, Japanese industry purchased 4,135 licenses (mainly from the United States), over half in the field of machinery construction and about 20 percent in the field of chemical industries. During the same time, exports of licenses amounted to only about 1 percent of the money spent on imports of patents and licenses. Once imported, foreign technologies have been adapted to specific industrial, commercial, and market requirements in Japan. Product development, including design and packaging, has been tailored to local needs and preferences, as have advertising, sales promotion, and customer services. Imported technologies have frequently been improved on and exported not only to Third World markets but also often back to their own originally exported countries. Japan remains a net importer of technology through license agreements and other purchases of technology. Its basic shortcoming in research stems from its weakness in creativity. Japan's deficit in technology trade (payment and receipt of money for patents or technical know-how) underlines its weakness in this stage of research. In 1985, Japan's technology imports surpassed its total exports, as they have every year.

The United States has been both giving and receiving technology, whereas Japan is primarily a recipient (Chakrabarti, Feinman, and Fuentevilla, 1978). Five times more Japanese researchers work in the United States than Americans in Japan. Japan exports less technology than most other industrialized countries. At the same time, it is the largest importer of technology in the world. Technology transfer from America to Japan is on the order of three to four times greater than the reverse flow, whereas technology transfer from Europe to Japan is twice as great. The ratio between imports and exports of technology in Japan was .10 in 1965 and rising but was only .26 by 1980. The amount of British technology exports in 1980 amounted to over twice that of Japan. In every category except steel and synthetic fibers, Japan buys more technology than it sells. Japan has also run a sizable deficit in its technological balance of trade, relying heavily on imports of foreign know-how to upgrade its manufacturing capabilities. The majority of Japan's technological exports are being sold to developing countries (unlike that of the United States in which 85 percent go to advanced countries). Much of the Japanese technological exports are in the category of incremental improvements in production technology for heavy manufacturing sectors (Okimoto and Saxonhouse, 1987). It is clear that Japan is selling off its technology in declining industries while continuing to be a net importer of technology in such key future areas as communications equipment, pharmaceuticals and computer manufacturing. This suggests that for mature technologies, the Japanese export technological advances while importing key portions of new, frontier, state-of-the-art technology from the West (particularly the United States).

Contrasting Japanese strengths and weaknesses in different market segments within industry sectors, some patterns become obvious.

- •Japan exports middle-of-the-line ready-to-wear clothes and textile fabrics. It imports high-fashion items (from the West) and inexpensive garments from the LDCs.
- •Japan exports massive quantities of inexpensive watches; it remains one of Switzerland's largest markets for fashion and jewelry timepieces.
- •Despite having the world's second largest pharmaceutical market, Japanese firms have made a negligible impact on international markets. Japan imports several times as many pharmaceutical products as it exports.
- •Japan exports massive quantities of basic number-crunching hand-held calculators; it imports advanced complex HP programmable machines.
- •Japan produces and exports large quantities of standard integrated circuits and RAM memory chips. Yet it imports virtually all its microprocessors and microcomputers. The difference is that the former are hardware, whereas the latter have a majority of their value added in the software (the programs).

Most innovations based on external technology are imitative in nature and can be adapted and improved at a relatively low cost. Japan's greatest technological strength is the speed at which it develops products and processes, improves and cost reduces them. In no other country can production engineers take the very latest technological breakthroughs and quickly build them into inexpensive consumer products which they then mass produce. However, these advantages of time and cost seem to be confined to innovations based on external technology (25 percent less time and 50 percent less money). Many innovations based on external technology are new products that imitate others in important respects. Among innovations based on internal technology, no significant difference in average cost or time between Japan and the United States exists (Mansfield, 1988c). The Japanese have great advantages based on external technology but very little comparative advantage in carrying out innovations based on internal technologies (Mansfield, 1988a). Their ability to absorb and adopt Western technology is well documented, but their ability to create knowledge in return is questionable. Thus, Japan continues to lag behind the West in basic research and number of radical innovations produced (Boisot, 1983). Japan seems to have been more likely than the United States to make significant technical adaptions of the imitated product and to reduce its costs substantially. This reflects, of course, Japan's emphasis on process engineering and efficient manufacturing facilities. As Mansfield (1988b) concluded, no solid evidence exists that basic research has been fruitful in Japan. Any product advantages are largely confined to applied R&D—particularly R&D concerned with adaption and improvement of existing technology.

Japanese firms absorb and then extend foreign technologies; develop a skilled labor force and advanced manufacturing techniques; exploit their own robust domestic market; and then adopt export-oriented strategies (Rosenbloom and Abernathy, 1982). The Japanese have been making the most progress in fields in which incremental improvements on imported technology are possible. The high-technology industries chosen by the Japanese government as key to Japan's future show two key characteristics: extremely high market growth potential and the ability to link synergistically with technological advances in other industries.

The Japanese have developed techniques for cooperative analysis of process quality well beyond anything given them by Deming and Juran, including many techniques for cooperative analysis in quality control. These, however, are largely group process innovations. It appears that Japan excels at evolutionary and (especially at) process innovations but not at radical innovations or basic science. The United States appears to excel at radical innovations and inventions but does poorly (comparatively) at evolutionary and process innovations. Optical computing is a technology of tomorrow. Although Japanese firms are investigating the technology, it will be the Americans who perfect its usage. Most Japanese experts cite their wish to continue the traditional pattern wherein they do better at perfecting a technology than inventing it. Japanese companies develop many systems, but the fundamental motive is commercial. In the United States, the most important thing is the frontier spirit (Hooper and Schlesinger, 1990).

Common knowledge supposedly has it that Japanese quality management is superior to that in the United States. Data show this to be a myth. Vendor relationships are often thought to be of longer term duration in Japan than in the United States. The median duration of supply relationships in the air conditioning industry was found to be ten years for Japan and eleven years in the United States (1984). Myth has it that single sourcing is more prevalent in Japan; in reality 80 percent of purchased parts and materials in Japan are derived from, on average, three firms. Another myth is that incoming parts and materials in Japan come directly to fabrication or the assembly line without receiving inspection. In reality, nearly 70 percent of incoming parts and materials were used without inspection. The median number of assembly line inspectors in the air conditioning industry was thirteen for Japan and only nine for the United States.

SUMMARY

Japan's manufacturing processes have an overwhelming advantage over those of the rest of the world; if the index for Japan is 100, the comparative American index is 93, Germany 75, United Kingdom 45. The Japanese are very quick to introduce new machinery. They do not hesitate to dispose of facilities even if they were installed only five or six years ago; if they are obsolete, they are considered out of date no matter how old or young. The time lag between Japanese manufacturing industry R&D and commercialization is estimated at 3.3 years, and the lifetime of the technology is estimated at 10.2 years, superior to any other major industrialized power (Watanbe, 1991). The rapidity of introduction can be seen in the fact that the stock of technological knowledge in the Japanese manufacturing industry in 1987 was seven times as great as that in 1970, equivalent to 9.3 percent of GNP.

Even the more rapid exploitation of robotics in Japan appears to be due to the alacrity with which Japanese firms modified and simplified product design to accommodate new robotics technology. It has probably been more sensible to simplify the design of products so that robots could readily assemble them—thus reducing the number of component parts and simplifying the method by which part are attached to one another—than to design robots of more general, and therefore more sophisticated, assembling capabilities. Sendai, the Japanese radio cassette recorder manufacturer, massively automated its factory in 1985. It installed 850 industrial robots; the new assembly line required only sixteen workers compared with 340 before. The chief reason for Japan's commitment to automation has been a serious labor shortage. Robots were initially deployed in repetitive or dangerous jobs, which relieved workers of unpleasant tasks and promised enhanced productivity that would be reflected in annual bonuses. The use of robots also aided in preserving Japan's commitment to racial homogeneity instead of importing thousands of guest workers.

Several important differences appear in the nature of the innovation policy process, in the policies adopted, and in the types of policy tools employed. In the United States, the policy process is highly political, decentralized and involves a great deal of inter-group negotiation and bargaining; partisanship (strong lobbies) and high visibility appear to be important to policy stability. At the opposite end of the spectrum, policy making in Japan is based on public and private consensus with strong central direction. Throughout Europe, the policy process varies between nations but lies between the two extremes indicated by the United States and Japan (Rothwell and Wissema, 1986).

Americans often leave their competitors with a host of opportunities for imitation and modification for improving performance or reducing costs. The Japanese are skilled at rapid adaptation of a new invention for mass production. Many companies give birth to new inventions only to abandon them; and the foster parent Japan picks them up and develops them. The Japanese realize this. In a 1988 survey by the *Japan Economic Journal*, 80 percent of the technology executives at 100 Japanese manufacturing companies felt that Japan must strengthen its basic research facilities.

Japanese success in each of these areas can be traced to the cumulative impact of its great development capabilities. Japanese success in development has often been able to overcome America's much-heralded innovative capabilities. The more specialized an activity becomes, the greater the importance of efficient information exchanges if inappropriate tradeoffs or inappropriate optimization criteria are to be avoided. For specialists to work well in a large organization, there must be an intimate familiarity with one another's goals and priorities. A set of shared understandings and concerns must exist. The development efforts of Japanese firms strongly emphasize rotation of personnel among departments in ways that lead to the exchange of useful information and the formation of common goals. In many cases, close communication among functionally separate specialists is strengthened by the awareness of a commonality of interest flowing from stable, long-term employment (and supplier) relationships. Japanese firms appear to make more systematic use of engineering skills.

Once the Japanese decide to adopt a product, they tend to do so faster and more thoroughly in an industry than occurs within the United States (especially process innovations). The maximum diffusion rate is higher in Japan than it is typically within the United States. However, the evidence suggests that the hesitation rate (time until first trial) is longer for Japan than for the United States. This patterns generally holds for all three types of innovations (process, evolutionary, and radical). However, diffusion tends to be quicker for the more familiar, less risky type of innovation (i.e., evolutionary or process innovations) and less so for radical innovations.

The success of Sony, Matsushita, and JVC as innovators can be ascribed primarily to their strategies and organizational methods, but they also benefited from their location in a mercantile economy such as Japan. In all of their consumer electronics businesses, they served a large protected domestic market that provided the basic bread and butter for cash flow and dramatic market growth. Furthermore, that market was not fragmented; and the leading companies tended to have large shares, giving them a significant scale of operations. American manufacturers had a large and concentrated domestic market also, but they lacked two things the Japanese had from the start—access to an even larger foreign market (the United States used the same technical standards) and protection against import competition.

The Japanese approach to the R&D workforce is to have a clearly defined objective, analogous to the dive bomber. The American approach to R&D is akin to carpet bombing: Researchers investigate every possibility, checking out all related technology from every angle: this requires vast amounts of money, a huge research support effort, long periods of R&D, and a certain amount of waste. R&D organizations in the United States are independent of production centers. In Japan, they are incorporated and interwoven into the production center. Japanese R&D workers are not necessarily in R&D because of their speciality or abilities, but often just because of job rotations. They must either cram and acquire enough specialist knowledge or find someone with expert knowledge to work with, gradually learning by watching the expert. *Shugyo* is the Japanese concept that people who are experts in one speciality can demonstrate the same degree of ability in another. Japanese R&D workers must have this kind of transferred knowledge.

One major advantage of the Japanese in their pursuit of process innovation is that Japanese workers welcome technological change. Few try to sabotage productivity improvements. This is not so in America. To the average American factory worker, automation can only result in the exchange of people for machines: Introduce labor-saving machinery into a plant and someone becomes unemployed. Make one worker more productive and someone else loses his or her job. Or install a robot which can work twenty-four hours a day on the assembly line and three workers are no longer needed. In contrast to this fear of unemployment in the United States, many Japanese corporate workers are lifelong employees. They will not be fired except for criminal behavior, insanity, or the company's bankruptcy. The Japanese worker with lifelong employment does not fear being replaced by machines. If a worker's duties become automated, the worker will be moved elsewhere. Their company would look after them until they retired, after lifelong service with the same company.

Many Japanese companies have also almost completely automated their own blue-collar work, and no one has been dismissed after being replaced by tooling machines. The blue-collar workers whose duties became automated were retrained and transferred to sales, testing, and computer programming; many now program the very machines which automated their work. This is why Japanese employees submit tens of thousands of suggestions per year without any significant monetary reward. Group unity and loyalty help stimulate suggestions and a spirit of participation (Alston, 1986). Increased productivity results in higher pay and other benefits. Higher profitability is translated into higher pay in the form of semi-annual bonuses, often worth four to six months' wages. In Japan, increased profits go to the workers in the form of bonuses, not to the managers in terms of executive bonuses or to the stockholders in the form of dividends, as is often the case in the United States.

The Japanese system appears to promote imitation and process innovation, and to work best in established industries in which their perpetual fine tuning can give the Japanese a competitive edge when complacent competitors fail to respond. The Japanese ability to absorb and adopt Western technology is well documented, but their ability to create knowledge in return has not been as strong. Japan's computer leadership hopes have encountered a major weakness in the production of software. Software is more of an art than an effort; the best programs are written by talented individuals and not by teams, which is why the United States still leads. Meanwhile, Japan spends millions trying to find hidden patterns to reduce software design from an art to a process (Boisot, 1983; Taylor, 1983).

IMITATION VERSUS INNOVATION

American attitudes toward imitation reflect a cultural bias that copying is less reputable than inventing and imitation is less honorable than innovation. The terms that Americans use for imitators—such as clones, borrowers, pirates, copycats—all reflect this bias (Bolton, 1993). Innovation as implemented by many American firms is a learning-by-doing strategy involving primarily experiential learning within the firm; a firm's competitive advantage stems from an internal source of competency. In contrast, Japanese companies emphasize the external development of new knowledge, importing ideas and technology across boundaries and "learning by watching." Japan has no problem with the concept of making exact copies because it studies only the technology, ignoring the philosophical systems of the culture behind it (as a conscious decision to maintain cultural purity). Japan does this by selectively adopting only the desirable features of foreign cultures. It has a national industrial ideology that is oriented toward self-improvement (i.e., greater quality and efficiency), toward a world view in which exports are emphasized, and toward evaluation of performance on the basis of long-term rather than short-term results.

Japanese firms achieved unbelievable growth in the 1960s by absorbing and then extending foreign technologies, developing a skilled labor force and advanced manufacturing techniques, exploiting their robust domestic market, and adopting export-oriented strategies. Table 3.1 compares the United States learning-by-doing preference to the Japanese learning-by-watching approach.

Imitation consists of two essential components: strategic followership and learning-by-watching. Strategic followership occurs when a company purposely delays in adopting a new product or practice—judging when consumer acceptance of a rival's new product will create an even larger market for a lower priced, less expensive, higher quality product Matsushita's low-cost strategy is predicated on being a second mover; it deliberately arrives late in the marketplace, competing successfully through an outstanding global distribution system and low-cost, high quality production. Matsushita waits and watches, judging when consumer acceptance of a rival's new product will create an even larger market for a lower priced, less expensively produced product of equal or better quality (Bolton, 1993). Matsushita's name in Japanese, *maneshita denki*, translates as "electronics that have been copied."

Learning-by-watching refers to activities directed toward external knowledge sharing and acquisition, through observation and assimilation of external knowledge. An example of this is benchmarking, wherein a company searches for existing best industry practices to improve performance. This may also take the form of partnerships or strategic alliances. Both types help firms benefit from the experience of pioneers and reduce the uncertainties accompanying innovation. The Japanese perspective focuses on the learning component; the Japanese word *manabu* ("to learn") is extremely close to *manebu* ("to imitate"). Successful imitation rarely occurs in a vacuum; it requires considerable expertise to transfer a borrowed technology to a different environment. The recipients of borrowed technology must also invest in substantial research and development and related competencies to transfer technology successfully and integrate external knowledge into existing systems and product lines.

Expertise acquired during the knowledge-transfer process typically results inmodification or improvement. A pure imitation strategy is seldom effective; it is the rare follower who copies a technology exactly without trying to modify or improve on it. An imitating country must be highly selective and adopt only those practices that fit comfortably into its unique circumstances and culture, a strategy which Japan has mastered for over a century.   Japanese businesses fanatically

Table 3.1
Comparison of U.S. and Japanese Mechanisms to Develop New Technology

UNITED STATES: INNOVATION: LEARNING BY DOING
Competitive Environment

- Two-tiered industrial structure: large, vertically integrated producers and smaller, independent, specialized products
- Spinoffs (employee mobility, diffuse new technology)
- Limited government role in diffusing new technology
- Government encourages diffusion of basic research through military expenditures and university research
- Centralized, hierarchical coordination of innovation
- Emphasis on quantitative decision making and vertical information flow
- Short-term, two-party, arm's length, cost-focused strategic alliances
- Internal corporate ventures to foster innovation
- Development of new technology through centralized corporate research and development
- Scattered information collection strategies (staff function)

JAPAN: INNOVATION: LEARNING BY WATCHING
Competitive Environment

- Horizontal coordination of innovation through stable networks
- Diffusion of new technology through external trading alliances
- Government agencies actively guide diffusion of new technology
- Limited industry-university research relationships
- Decentralized, horizontal coordination of innovation
- Emphasis on qualitative and quantitative decision making and horizontal information flow
- Development of new technology through shopfloor modifications
- Learning-focused joint ventures and strategic alliances
- Emphasis upon "redundant" data collection
- Specialized investment in date collection (line function)

pursue competitive information, conduct widespread technology surveillance, consult foreign specialists, call frequently on suppliers, cull operating manuals, send students to foreign universities, send managers on Western tours, translate technical journals, and attend large numbers of professional meetings. Few firms successfully combine both imitation and innovation strategies; it is difficult to stretch resources across different approaches. American attitudes towards imitation reflect a definite pronounced cultural bias: copying is less reputable than inventing, less honorable than innovation.

Imitators typically will outperform innovators in those industries with weak intellectual property rights protections, in technologically interdependent industries, in industries with high market and technical uncertainty, in industries with rapid technological change, and in industries with rapid information flow. Imitators in industries with extensive information flow can outperform innovators. Innovation in these circumstances has many risks, and companies find it increasingly difficult to realize economic benefits from innovation. State-of-the-art research is different. When Japan was a follower, the research direction was clear: Observe the successes and false starts of the pioneer. Now at the frontier, the paths are not so clear. Setting such technological targets involves greater uncertainties and risks.

Although the United States does fairly well in process and evolutionary innovations, that it does not excel is evidenced by the tremendous deficit to Japan and the large number of once American products no longer made in America by American-based companies. But if the United States excels anywhere, it is in radical innovations, inventions, and basic science. The Japanese excel at evolutionary and process innovations but traditionally have failed to contend in radical innovations or major inventions and basic science.

Chapter 4

Innovation—Japanese Style

ORGANIZATIONAL INFLUENCES

Organizational influences on the Japanese innovative process can be derived from four sets of dichotomies: the use of generalists rather than specialists, the predominance of large firms over small firms, the preference for established firms rather than new firms, and the predominance of commercial applications over military expenditures. Figure 4.1 portrays the elements of information strategy and new business development and shows the central role innovation has in the conduct of the typical Japanese business.

Generalists versus Specialists

The Japanese approach to innovation relies on generalists taking ownership of the problems at hand. The technological function is embedded throughout the organization. The advantage of the Japanese approach is that it is good for company-related, incremental innovations. The innovation management process, such as QCs, builds teamwork into problem identification and solution. This collective effort makes technology implementation more easily accomplished. The potential disadvantage of the Japanese approach to innovation is that one company does not always have enough specialized expertise. A dependence on in-company generalists may reduce the opportunities in highly specialized fields of high technology, such as genetic engineering. To the extent that high technology needs to generate new knowledge in scientific specialties, the Japanese formula may be somewhat restrictive.

Figure 4.1
Elements of Information Strategy and New Business Development

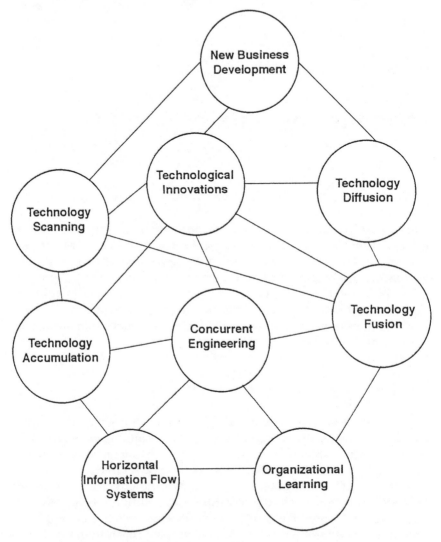

Source: B. Bowonder and T. Miyake. (1992). "A Model of Corporate
Innovation Management: Some Recent High Tech Innovations
in Japan." *R&D Management* 2/4: 328. Reprinted by permission of Blackwell Publishers.

The advantage of predominantly using specialists, the American approach to innovation, is that it often can generate technological breakthroughs. However, breakthroughs are idiosyncratic and may have little relevance to the company product lines. The very specialization on which American industry is based necessarily makes communications more difficult between R&D and different functions, such as marketing, production, and finance. Thus the disadvantage of the American approach to innovation includes its irrelevance for a company employing an R&D staff. Increasingly today, R&D labs are being directed by financial and marketing executives to produce to company needs. This is due to the requirement that R&D cost-justify its activities and demonstrate how it benefits the bottom line. To the extent that R&D needs to be managed differently from factory production to operate efficiently, over-direction stifles innovation in American industry. The development efforts of Japanese firms strongly emphasize rotation of personnel among departments in ways that lead to the exchange of useful information and the formation of common goals. In many cases, close communication among functionally separate specialists is strengthened by the awareness of a commonality of interest flowing from stable, long-term employment (and supplier) relationships. New industry creations require market innovativeness as well as technical innovativeness and are the peculiar province of entrepreneurial high-technology companies in the United States, the classic example being Silicon Valley.

Innovation and venture business differences between Japan and the United States revolve around differences in cooperative R&D efforts among otherwise competing producers or between the buyer and seller (more in Japan). The well-developed internal market and low mobility of researchers in Japan make the benefit of cooperative R&D greater and more easily recognizable by each member firm and spreading the results of the R&D throughout the firm. American expertise in radical innovation and Japanese expertise in incremental innovation can also flow from labor allocations. In the United States, mobility means that a manager can assemble an R&D team from outside members with ease, which is the generation of radical innovation. On the other hand, incremental innovation comes from knowing the details of the existing technology, its relationship with other related technologies, and the strengths and capabilities of the firm. Low labor mobility, labor reallocation, and job rotation in Japan encourage this activity. However, the generalists bred in Japan are often not sufficiently narrow in their expertise to generate necessary radical innovations, as the specialists which exist in the United States appear to do more easily and often (Imai and Itami, 1984).

Aoki (1990) indicates that horizontal coordination among operating units based on knowledge-sharing (generalists), rather than skill specialization, is an important internal characteristic of Japanese firms. Japanese firms depend on employee competition to achieve higher status within their hierarchies of rank as a primary incentive device. The hierarchical nature of the incentive scheme, therefore, complements the non-hierarchical tendency of operational coordination and helps maintain organizational effectiveness and integrity.

Aoki speculates that the key to understanding Japan's industrial performance can be found in the ability of firms to coordinate their operating activities flexibly and quickly in response to changes in the industrial environment as well as emergent technical and technological exigencies. The most well-known example of this is the *kanban* system of just-in-time deliveries to the assembly line. Other examples include quality control and product development. In the Japanese system, engineering and manufacturing are not mutually exclusive but are integrated, even to the point of constant rotation of personnel between the two groups. This integration, overlapping of sections, and flexibility can also be seen in the typical Japanese product development effort and accounts, to a large degree, for the observed Japanese success in commercialization of products.

In the Japanese firm, work-related communications between people with different specialities and from different departments are extremely trouble free, resulting in a high level of interdepartmental cooperation. Most new employees are graduates fresh out of school and enter the company as one large group in April. Each year's new hires are put through an extensive in-house introductory training program, which provides them with an intense, shared experience and develops a strong group spirit that establishes the basis for the horizontal communications they will utilize and depend on for the rest of their career. Horizontal linkages between departments or divisions are kept extremely close through the personal relationships enjoyed by these cadres of employees, who have all entered the company at the same time and thus have a shared set of experiences and a common lifestyle. For example, of Hitachi's thousands of R&D staff, the majority are distributed among the various factories and operational divisions. As many as 90 percent of NEC's R&D workers work in the factories. Most Japanese companies give high priority to the production process, so much so that most employees undergo rotation in the factories as a matter of fact. Most Japanese CEOs come from the production side, in contrast to the United States. Production, not sales, is often the path to success in a Japanese company. This emphasis is also a partial explanation to the predominance of process innovations seen in Japan.

Preference for Large Firms over Small Firms

Japan excels in what is called industrial dualism or industrial gradation. This has caused a polarization of Japanese industry into very large and very small businesses. Over 90 percent of all firms are small scale, employing less than twenty workers; over 50 percent have three or fewer employees (over twice the proportion as found in the United States). The wage disparity between large and small companies has been estimated to be as much as 50 percent. The larger firms obtain preferential financial treatment from banks and government. Smaller firms have serious disadvantages in capital and labor markets; in status-conscious Japan, the top graduates tend to choose larger, more prestigious firms over small ones. Other factors providing an edge to larger companies over smaller firms include the price of land, overall competitiveness, and the herd instinct of *keiretsus*.

The largest Japanese corporations may be considered modern *hans* (contemporary fiefs). The parent company is the *daimyo*, the supreme power, the apex of a pyramid in which production flows from the bottom-up and rewards from the top-down—a vertical hierarchy. In the pyramids are layers of subcontractors whose only function is to produce a small quantity of goods for the company just above them in the pyramid (Sasaki, 1990). No matter how bad times may get, companies can never leave their industrial group to seek employment elsewhere. If they tried, no one else would hire them.

In Japan, carmakers deal directly with only 200 to 300 fairly large suppliers (compared to over 1,000 in the United States), who in turn subcontract part of their work to other lower tier suppliers. Over 50,000 suppliers serve Japan's major automotive makers. Wages at firms with fewer than thirty workers (with no employment guarantees) are typically 40 percent lower than at large firms, which usually offer such guarantees. The system depends on a large labor force willing to work long hours for low pay and no job security; today's young Japanese do not want these jobs and have other options, thus subcontractors must often employ foreign workers to keep the line going.

Japan has over 800,000 small and medium-size manufacturing companies (*chu-sho kigyo*), which increasingly find themselves captive of larger companies. By 1980, two of every three companies were classified as subcontractors of larger firms (Kotkin and Kishimoto, 1988). Subcontractors and suppliers, those in the second and third tiers, do not have the protection of lifetime employment. The parent firm helps the subcontractor with supplies, technical assistance, and investments in machinery. The firm will not usually turn to cheaper subcontractors. The lower-tier firm, however, must accept its role as a shock absorber in periods of economic downturn—meaning that it must be willing to accept lower prices (usually mandated by the parent), larger inventories, and hand-me-down personnel from the parent company. The subcontractor is expected to be loyal to its parent company at all costs and is often forbidden to accept orders from any other company, even when times are slow and equipment remains idle. Parent companies expect *keiretsu* suppliers to help them design their components and constantly improve them; price is subject to frequent negotiations. These smaller companies conduct most of the research and pass the results up the line to the larger companies. Many smaller companies have gone bankrupt due to the constant price squeeze from their parent companies. They are the ones that must cut their profits in times of lower revenues for the larger companies and lay off workers in times of depressed sales. They are told what to produce, when to produce it, when to deliver, and how much they will be paid for their product or service. If the superior company requests the smaller company to buy a new and expensive piece of equipment, it is purchased. The parent companies, however, remain healthy, which is the purpose of the system. The system is regulated to preserve the status quo and protect the big banks and members of the *keiretsu* from competition, which makes it difficult for entrepreneurs but easy for big companies to launch new businesses.

Large Japanese firms have two major areas of competitive advantage in technology over United States firms. First, they have developed ways of embodying technology in products and moving from development through manufacturing to the marketplace quickly, with high quality and with a relatively low purchase price. Second, the larger Japanese firms have extremely effective systems of global technology scanning, developed over decades of playing catch-up in science and technology. These include systems of global patent scanning, in-house international scientific and technical information systems, and high-level technology scanning systems in their foreign affiliates (Westney and Sakakibara, 1985).

The intensity of competition in Japanese industry is another reason for innovation. Japanese markets are typically more competitive than elsewhere throughout the world, producing dozens of similar products seeking to attract the customers' favor. Hence, technical innovation assumes enormous importance for both manufacturers and consumers in differentiating their products. In their annual reports, most Japanese firms discuss their R&D efforts in great detail, providing information not only about research in general but also about individual patent and royalty agreements. This excessive competition makes research more important as a predictor of success in the marketplace. This fierce competition on a wide front forces companies to put more effort into development than basic research in order to bring out new models and improve old ones. By the very nature of the competitive playing field, Japanese companies tend to be risk adverse. They put their effort mainly into development along highly predictable lines with quick returns. This naturally, to a certain extent, precludes creativity.

Kaisha (Japanese corporations) belief purposes (goals) are often formally written and displayed in their offices and factories. These goals often include creating wealth through growth, employee welfare, customer value through improvement, and survival. Most *kaisha* beliefs include that failure to add customer value is a waste and must be eliminated, being competitive depends on continuous improvement via employment involvement, and people are the major asset—trained to identify problems freely, they will find solutions.

Dominance of Established Firms versus New Firms

Venture business activity is not as likely in Japan as in the West due to low labor mobility and the Japanese capital market. The supply of capital for potential entrepreneurs is limited in Japan due to an underdeveloped equity market; the bank loan market tends to lend primarily to large sister *keiretsu* firms. The cost of failure for an entrepreneur has traditionally been much higher in Japan due to a lack of mid-career entry opportunities. The cost of breaking into a market is also much higher in Japan due to *keiretsu* structures and interconnecting relationships; hence the higher likelihood of failure in Japan for entrepreneurs.

Entrepreneurial activity is much more numerous in the United States than in Japan. In the United States risk takers are encouraged; the entrepreneur is often the society-changing catalyst for radical innovations. One reason for this high level of activity in the United States is the wide availability of venture capital. In the United States, people cheer those persons who take risks. Venture capital is still not freely available in Japan, probably because large Japanese companies are horizontal in structure and typically have the huge resources necessary inhouse to fund their new projects. This puts the small entrepreneur at a disadvantage. Since banks are reluctant to lend money to unknowns, and extremely limited amounts of private venture capital are available, Japanese entrepreneurs have a difficult time.

Japan's R&D system differs markedly from that of the United States in three ways: the role of small companies in technological innovation, the government's role in R&D funding, and the character of advanced training for technical personnel (Okimoto and Saxonhouse, 1987). Small American firms play a more pivotal role in stimulating major technological innovations than do their Japanese counterparts. Japan has not fostered governmental policies aimed at allowing small research-oriented firms to play a critical role in the development of new technology, as the United States has. R&D tax credits, when offered, could offset all income tax liability in the United States but only 10 percent of total tax liabilities in Japan. Venture capital partnerships are unknown in Japan, in contrast to the United States. The United States R&D system fosters the constant formation of small venture firms through favorable labor and capital markets, strict antitrust enforcement, and generous tax provisions on capital gains. In contrast, the financial system in Japan is not nearly as supportive.

The only firms which have entered the biotechnology industry in Japan are from established firms. In the United States, hundreds of firms have been formed. Venture capitalists in the United States have invested billions alone in biotechnology, a number ten times greater than the entire amount of venture capital available in Japan for all industries. Newly established firms in the United States account for about half the participants in biotechnology in the United States and typically spend a much greater percentage of their revenues in R&D activities than do larger firms. Japan's thirty or so venture capital companies' combined assets of less than quarter of a billion U.S. dollars pale in comparison to the United States' hundreds of similar companies with tens of billions in assets. Japan's over-the-counter (OTC) equities market is at most 1 percent the size of its United States counterpart. Only 16 percent of what MITI defines as venture businesses have ever received venture capital financing. Thus, the Japanese entrepreneur is severely handicapped no matter where he or she turns, approaches, or seeks advice from. In retrospect, what is surprising is not the small number of entrepreneurs seen in Japan, but the fact that, considering the obstacles they must overcome, *any* exist at all.

Japan has an advantage over the United States when advances are inspired or driven by the user (the user being either an external customer or the firm's own manufacturing department) or by incremental suggestions emanating from within the company's organization. The American high-tech companies are better able to capitalize on opportunities (than are Japanese companies) which are derived from or inspired by technology (the research lab) or imposed by a top-down management decision.

Commercial Applications Preferred to Military Usage

Japan's low level of defense-related procurements has had important implications for Japan's R&D system: Macroeconomic policies aimed at expanding aggregate demand have played a greater role than targeted industrial policy in promoting the growth of high-technology products. MITI has had to rely predominantly on supply-related incentives, using no demand-pull measures. Thus, inefficient resource allocation, waste, and politicization have been kept under relative control; this has prompted Japanese management to stress applied R&D instead of basic or prototype development research. With no assurance of government demand for new products, Japanese companies have followed a fairly conservative approach to R&D, emphasizing reasonably high prospects of commercial feasibility; this may be one reason why the Japanese have not been noted for creating whole new industries or major new product designs.

Japanese engineers and scientists have not been diverted from commercially oriented R&D to carry on highly specialized research for military and space applications. The differing locus and character of training in Japan (in-house training of Japanese R&D) has led to much lower interfirm mobility than in the West as well as much less of a professional and occupational orientation. The transfer of know-how is a positive byproduct of the highly mobile U.S. labor force. Such an R&D system is apt to be more accommodating of diverse research approaches than Japan's. Less structural leeway for research pluralism exists in Japan because of rigidities in labor and capital markets: more technological knowledge than scientific knowledge, and learning-by-doing and experimentation more than theories and interpretation.

RESEARCHERS

Japanese R&D capability is primarily located in three organizational settings: universities, government laboratories and industry. Japanese universities do not play the powerful research role that American universities do. Their research faculties are not tightly tied, through common substantive interests and funding, to mission-oriented government agencies and industry in the way that many American university faculties are. The vast majority of funding for research in Japanese universities is provided by the Ministry of Education, Science, and Culture. This Ministry controls half of all government R&D funds, and two thirds of its total R&D monies go to universities. The general purpose of the Ministry's support for universities is to ensure an adequate supply of research and technical personnel rather than to fund specific substantive research. The Japanese have often substituted in-house research and training within the corporation for what in the United States is a university function (Kash, 1989).

Over half the respondents of a 1988 survey agreed with the statement that "the Japanese environment is not adequate to foster unique and creative research" (Cross, 1990). The weaknesses found in universities and university research is widely admitted: In a 1988 *Japan Industrial Journal* survey of 1,000 businessmen, respondents ranked the following reasons for Japan's poor showing in basic research: inadequate national funding (53 percent), educational system (45 percent), corporate environment (44 percent), low status of researchers (41 percent), hyper-competition (33 percent), weak industry-university ties (29 percent), weak university research (22 percent), and lack of international exchanges (16 percent). In the United States, about half the research funds come from the government, of which 70 percent is given to private research institutions. In Japan, private businesses bear 70 percent of R&D costs, with government contributing the remaining 30 percent. Japanese industries invest more money in foreign universities (nearly twice as much) as in domestic ones. The meager monies received by Japanese universities are typically directed toward applied research and specific projects. The government's share is mostly spread among government-affiliated research departments and universities, notorious for their lack of motivation in Japan. The recovery rate of government R&D investment totals under one twentieth that of private R&D. This could be one reason behind for the severe lack of basic research found in Japan.

The institutional history of Japanese universities makes them less likely to carry out the same role as U.S. universities. Their mission is primarily knowledge dissemination rather than knowledge generation. The Japanese university's primary focus is on developing student potential and developing strong personal links between professors and students. Students are not expected to acquire directly skills needed by industry—that is the job of industry. A decreasing pool of qualified university graduates to do research is one of the most serious problems confronting Japanese companies. The more talented graduates have increasingly been entering the more favored occupations: banks, trading companies, and other service-oriented firms.

Although Japanese companies have been generous donors to foreign universities, often funding full professorships to buy goodwill and access to top researchers, they are still miserly with the Japanese universities. Corporate donations to Japanese universities are not tax deductible, as in the United States. Money making is viewed with a great deal of disdain in Japanese academic circles; it is considered beneath one's professional dignity to work with people more interested in profits than in theoretical research. In Japan, the humble educator is the exemplar of academia. Consequently, few Japanese professors work as consultants or serve on corporate boards.

Severe budgetary constraints exist at many prestigious Japanese universities. The typical university infrastructure is poor. Industry hiring practices have discouraged serious study since employers do not place a high value on academic excellence. Applicants in engineering peaked in 1987 and have since declined (Ishii, 1993). Why are Japanese research institutions so weak in basic research? The predominant reason is lack of funds. Japan's best and brightest are recruited to private industry to develop new products. In addition, three major obstacles were identified by Masanori Moritani (Ishii, 1993), senior researcher at Normura Research Institute:

1. College "examination hell," which rewards students adept at rote memorization and taking tests but penalizes students with inquisitive minds. High schools are so oriented toward college entrance examinations that almost all independent thinking and personal discovery comes to a complete halt in high school.
2. Japan's single-minded "herd" or "festival" mentality, in which companies and governments establish joint research projects to focus on narrowly defined goals.
3. Japanese lack of a spirit of play and a gambler's spirit, which means that researchers rarely risk the possibility of failure.

Many of Japan's best and brightest young scientists continue to find their creative urges stifled by a social fabric that seems to idolize seniority, loathe individualism, and muffle debate. The big culprits are the same ones that made Japan an industrial powerhouse: acquiescence to authority, strict seniority, a stable but immobile work force, and little debate (Yoder, 1988). These customs often inspire loyalty among factory hands and teamwork among the engineers who whisk product ideas to market. The presence of these traits stunt free thought and creativity in Scientists. In Japan, if you're different, you're a minus, not a team player; this attitude nips originality in the bud.

In addition, universities are not conducive to research. Resources are scarce, and bright students have little incentive to do postgraduate research. The strict hierarchy which prevails in universities is to blame. Young researchers spend their most creative years acting as personal assistants to older professors. Research is controlled by rigid hierarchies of elite professors and government bureaucrats. Equipment is often poor and obsolete. Few postdoctoral programs exist, and research positions for aspiring young scientists are few and far between. Inadequate funding has created "overdoctoring," a growing class of highly qualified Ph.D.s with scientific or engineering degrees who cannot find full-time work; less than 10 percent of Japan's Ph.D. candidates in the biological sciences are employed in either industry or academia upon graduation.   Industry is typically reluctant to take on employees of advanced ages (usually 27 or 28). Japanese universities are creative backwaters in the scientific world, severely and perpetually underfunded. Thousands of Japanese researchers have studied and worked abroad but are returning home to an uninspiring work environment. Those few who find spots in academia must wait until they are nearly forty (become a professor) before they can pursue their own research agenda.

A major obstacle blocking scientific creativity in Japanese universities is the *koza* (chair) system, in which professors and lab managers in their forties and fifties maintain absolute control over research topics and budgets. The 800 *koza* managers are the pillars of Japan's scientific establishment. They advise the Ministry of Education about the direction of scientific policies and the awarding of research grants. They influence the hiring of young graduates into university and government research positions. They direct teams of young scientists whose work appears only under the names of the *kozas* and whose only hope for doing independent research is to wait patiently until they too become a *koza*. This discourages risk taking and encourages younger people to defer to their *koza*. Young researchers may strike out on their own, but by leaving the system, they find it impossible to return.

Western universities contain a wealth of new ideas because they are relatively unrestricted institutions, open to a constant flow of outside professors, students, researchers, and visitors. Scientific creativity often results from this clash of opposing ideas. Japan's government-run universities, in contrast, are relatively closed institutions with the resulting absence of creative ideas. In Japan, *discipline* means that one must defer to seniors and agree with the thoughts of elders. Foreign researchers are a rare breed. Foreign students are a tiny often neglected minority. They are often not welcomed by school administrators and local neighborhoods and as a result often leave with bitter memories of their experiences.

Engineering students at Japanese universities are said to be firmly grounded in general theory and well trained in problem solving in mathematics and statistics, but they are offered fewer specialized courses in subfields of engineering. After they enter the Japanese firm, they spend considerable time becoming familiar with specific design processes during on-the-job training. Some selected researchers and engineers may be sent to graduate school abroad for more specialized training.

Recruitment of technical personnel is a corporate personnel department function in Japanese firms. Key professors in major Japanese universities routinely allocate their students to the major companies. The professor in charge of placement will write only one letter of recommendation for each student, and that will be to a major company that will accept without question that recommendation. For a company to disregard that recommendation would be to forfeit the opportunity to obtain future graduates from that professor. For the student to refuse to go to the company for which the professor has written the letter would mean that the student would forfeit all chance of working for a major Japanese firm, since the companies do not recruit students for which such letters are not written (Westney and Sakakibara, 1985). As a result, companies make ongoing efforts to establish and maintain close relationships with leading universities through the supply of equipment, research grants to faculty, and personal contacts.

Japanese Researchers

More than a quarter of the developed world's scientists are Japanese, more than those from any Western country except the United States. Nonetheless, basic research accounts for only 14 percent of Japan's research budget. Japanese government institutes also play a much smaller role. Any breakthroughs tend to occur in private corporate labs. Therefore, disseminations of findings tend to be more difficult in Japan than in United States, since in the United States research by universities or Department of Defense is considered public and open. In addition, language barriers exist. Estimates place the amount of Japanese scientific and technical literature that is translated into English at about 25 percent of the total. However, this does not mean that 25 percent of the total body of knowledge is available or is available in a timely fashion. As Japan's own research establishment grows, less is being written in English.

Researchers in Japan face serious obstacles in their efforts to produce creative research. Japanese national government researchers, like their university counterparts, live in a closed, isolated, highly stratified society that pays more deference to seniority and rank than to original research. Cloistered in their separate laboratories, they lead a highly compartmentalized existence with nothing like the rich cross-fertilization of ideas that occurs more freely in most open Western laboratories. They are also far removed from international activities. They rarely sponsor foreign researchers in their laboratories and do not mingle freely with colleagues from other ministries. A strict hierarchy of positions exists, which inhibits most scientists from questioning the decisions of their superiors as well as making any kind of decision on their own without the explicit approval of their superiors.

Japanese researchers tend to be reluctant to explore the unknown alone and to challenge their peers, especially Westerners, at international conferences. The Japanese tend to be much more self-effacing in their technical presentations and hesitant about putting forth criticisms and offering new thoughts which have not been thoroughly considered. Avoidance of conflict is seen as a measure of sincerity which should be admired. The Japanese are more likely to identify self with the idea and consider that direct criticism is a form of personal rejection. They prefer to follow the leaders into new fields. For decades, perfecting a device, not inventing it, was the surest way to professional security and economic prosperity. Japanese scientists view themselves as cultivators, not as pioneers exploring new frontiers. Japan's scientific community has reinforced this conservatism by belittling the work of unorthodox researchers who stray from the mainstream. Universities and government ministries ostracize outspoken, independent-minded people who challenge the accepted wisdom. The protruding nail is still being hammered down in Japan.

Japanese researchers labor under tighter governmental restrictions than most other researchers around the world. Grant proposals are often delayed or ignored if they fall outside the mainstream of research or cannot promise immediately useful applications. Laboratory officials are forbidden to dispose of obsolete equipment and replace it with state-of-the-art equipment. Until 1984, corporations were prevented from donating equipment because of concern over undue influence in the setting of research priorities. Scientists in Japan's corporate research labs are encouraged to care as much about the practical applications of technology as about pure research. In graduate schools in the United States, most every student wants to be in basic research. In Japan, the reverse is true. Most of the important work occurs within companies. Scientists and engineers who join Japanese companies are not expected to pursue their own scientific curiosity but rather work toward breakthroughs that will help the company; Japanese corporations exist not just for the enrichment of stockholders but for the benefit of all their employees.

In Japan, journal publications do not necessarily contain new work, whereas most U.S. journal editorial policies insist on original work only. The Japanese technical journals often consist of progress reports as well as reports on setting up and testing methods of experimentation which may have been published elsewhere. The traditional Japanese attitude about originality is one which prefers to follow a pattern rather than to break new ground. Most Japanese researchers attend international meetings and two thirds have spent a year or more in the United States or Europe. Most Japanese scientists are usually encouraged to spend some time (usually two years) abroad at some laboratory doing similar research. This provides the administrators with first-hand information of the goings-on in an actual research environment and provides the scientists with an understanding of the management framework.

Fundamental engineering science is emphasized rather than basic scientific research and is typically done in groups rather than by individuals, largely consisting of experimental verification work. The principal sources of basic research information for Japanese researchers are journal articles published by leading university researchers in the United States and Europe. The typical Japanese researchers spend enormous amounts of time (two thirds of their available time) exchanging new ideas by participating in talks, meetings, and working with leading colleagues; the most efficient technology transfer mechanism most is people intensive, which the Japanese do well. Personal commitment, trust, and desire for cooperation among researchers serve as the glue which keeps the Japanese R&D organization together. The Japanese concept of project management starts with the fundamental belief in the coequal importance of all players needed to fulfill a task and continues with the continuous process of linking these players together horizontally, of creating a flawless, contiguous team.

Job security encourages and allows time for scientists and engineers to exercise mobility within the institute, thus giving them a better baseline understanding of the breadth of the research. On the other hand, the hiring quota is low due to the extra long-term expense of each new individual; thus, rarely is anyone hired at the technician level, and an alarming shortage of skilled technicians exists in Japan. Fewer Ph.D.s are hired in Japan; typically, scientists are hired at the B.S. level and are trained at the lab for their assigned role. Scientists are thus extremely overworked. In addition to research, they must either do all their own routine maintenance or call on outside help. Japanese institutions tend to be equipment intensive but labor short.

In Japan, a close relationship exists between researcher and technician, scientist and laborer. Practically no difference in salary exists between the classes because salary is usually decided by age and working period, not job definition or merit. The joint work of researcher and technician is often carried out together from the planning phase through to the experiment. Technicians frequently join planning discussions and understand the essential experimental purpose. This is not considered efficient in the West. However, the Japanese prefer this since there are many possibilities for finding new phenomena in the course of experiments. In Western countries, a large gap exists between researchers and technicians, who typically work separately. The researcher makes a plan and the technician or laborer does the work according to the researcher's direction. The researcher learns of a result after the experiment. In this Western organization, fewer possibilities exist to find unexpected new phenomena. Figure 4.2 shows the different R&D practices in the West and Japan; the egalitarian position of the Japanese and the emphasis on joint work is clearly seen.

Cooperative research is the norm in Japan. The Japanese tend to hold many more technical meetings on an industrywide basis than their American counterparts do. Major research labs become familiar with work at other labs, leading to rapid dissemination of new results and less duplication of effort. The Japanese government actively promotes the formation of research associations among the leading companies in particular fields for the purpose of developing and transferring new technologies. Patents from these arrangements are pooled for participating companies to use. The system also works well because of the strong leadership of the university professors, who serve as committee chairpersons and the strong ties between these professors and their former students. In Japan, Ph.D.s are not nearly as widely respected or utilized in the R&D function as they are in the United States.

The Japanese R&D decision-making process in such institutions tends to be slow and deliberate, never without consideration of every option in detail. It is performed in a highly systematic fashion, with everyone involved at all stages. Meticulous attention is paid to the details of the research project. A supervisor will never go ahead with something until everyone is fully informed. These scientists have a much better view of the scope of the research project and where it fits into the big picture. Once a decision has been made, it is difficult to reverse.

Generally in Japan, researchers consider that the experimental result is the most important part of the scientific process, although they also investigate theory and previous data. Previous theories may

Figure 4.2
Different R&D Practices

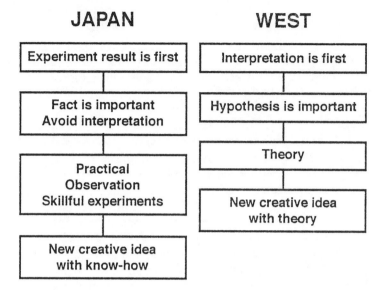

change and new ideas appear through experiment. Experimental facts are the most important, and most learning theory is done through experimentation. Interpretation comes after the experiment. For this approach, researchers need practical and precise observations and skillful experiments. Scientists and technicians tend to work together as one body. New phenomena are often discovered by precise observation, and new creative ideas with know-how come as a result of this way of thinking. Contrast this approach to approach taken by the typical Western researcher, who typically believes that the more important steps are the interpretation and hypothesis aspects of research. If the hypothesis is proved, the researcher is proven right. In the West, this theoretical approach is considered the most effective way to develop,test, and define new ideas. New creative ideas come with theory, theory which must be proven or disproven. Figure 4.3 shows the different ways of thinking about the scientific process in the West and in Japan. The Japanese emphasis is on empirical rather than theoretical knowledge. The Japanese believe that the experimental result is primary and the theory and data are secondary. Japanese believe that achievement is effected by group effort, and success by any one person is only achieved with the help of his or her associates—a cooperative result. Honor is usually only given to a company or group, not to an individual.

Figure 4.3
Different Scientific Systems

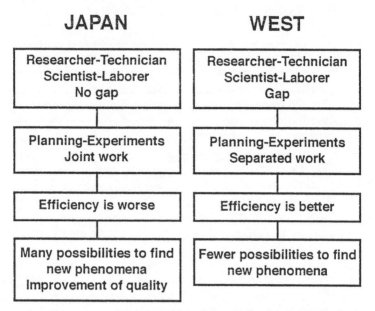

Japanese technology policy is both mission-oriented and diffusion-oriented and emphasizes rapid upgrading of the nation's technological skills. It is mission-oriented by being extremely focused on the end goal of securing the technology by whatever means from whatever source, constantly improving upon it by forever minute process imporvements, and expanding upon the technology. The mission of such a policy is to dominate the world in the chosen technology and to continue to remain at the frontier of the technology to provide the comparative advantage necessary to maintain dominance. The diffusion-orientation of the policy can be seen in the collectivist orientation of the Japanese, the Japanese corporations, and the Japanese government. Cross-licensing is not only encouraged but many times required. Diffusion of technology between sister divisions and sister *keiretsu* companies is rapid and thorough. Once the technology has been selected to be transferred, the engineers and scientists are absorbed in learning everything there is to know about the technology. The technology policy emphasis can be seen by the promotion of leading-edge industries through tax policy more than direct financial assistance, facilitating technology transfer, and upgrading the human capital base on a more general, less industry-specific basis. That it has succeeded can be seen by the level of technological capabilities seen in Japanese companies.

THE JAPANESE PROCESS OF INNOVATION

In the internal organization of their firms, the Japanese commonly provide for much closer interaction between product designer and production engineers; they devote considerable attention to the refinement of the appropriate process technologies, and they assign a prominent role to the engineering department. In considerable measure, then, their skill in imitation can be attributed to their skill in and concern with developmental activities.

Japanese companies prefer to do it themselves rather than contract it. They favor trial and error over the systematic stepwise techniques more widely used by United States companies. This means that many of their development phases overlap, with planning and action taking place simultaneously. The end result is a high adaptability to making mid-course adjustments that compensate for new information (i.e., a drive for continuous improvement). The cultural and business environment within which the *kaisha* operates includes a long-term perspective on growth, a customer focus, cooperation at all levels and, above all, the survival of the firm (Kennard, 1991).

The technological behavior of Japanese firms is oriented toward shorter development times, an effective identification and acquisition of external technology, a higher propensity to patent, design toward manufacturability, incremental product and process improvement, competitive matching, an innovation system dominated by large firms, a tendency to combine technologies, interfirm technical cooperation, and a much stronger role of technology strategy in the corporate strategy.

When technological development requires primarily analysis, the Japanese have a significant advantage over the United States. Japanese manufacturing organizations are dominated by engineers and technical workers. The distinction between research and development and manufacturing and marketing is much less pronounced than in the United States. Engineers dominate in Japanese companies, but their goal is not technological elegance, it is competitive advantage in the international commercial marketplace. It is assumed in Japanese companies that engineers involved in product development will frequently lead marketing specialists in the identification of sales potential, it is development first and find the potential applications and segments after the product has been defined. Japanese engineers are much more likely to have been assigned courses of study by the company to broaden their work skills and improve their productivity within the company; American engineers are much more likely to take educational development for their own career improvement opportunities.

The Japanese approach to product and process design is to have R&D integrated with engineering design, procurement, production, and marketing. The aim is to acquaint all those affected by technical change with the problems that are likely to arise and to give them some understanding of the relationship between various operations in the firm. Japanese firms often seem to take a relatively long time making the first decisions about design and development because doing so involves a great deal of internal debate, discussion, experiment, and training. Nonetheless, as this consensus evolves, the whole organization becomes firmly committed to the new product and processes, and the resulting lead time is brief. In Japan, it is long to develop and short to produce. When synthesis (bringing together various technologies or matching new technologies with market opportunities) is involved, U.S. industry has had (and most experts agree will continue to have) a substantial advantage over its Japanese competition. American development and design groups have been much less closely linked to manufacturing than their Japanese counterparts (and much more closely linked with marketing and sales than is usually found in Japanese companies). In Japan, the locus of responsibility for the engineer's career lies unquestionably with the firm, whereas it lies with the individual in American firms.

A track record of participation in successful projects is important for technology managers in both countries but for different reasons; in Japan it indicates the ability to manage a team successfully; in the United States, it is an indicator of technical mastery and individual ability. In Japan, the project leader is principally powered by seniority and the leader's role is more of an effective chair, encouraging and guiding the research firm; in American firms, the project leader is expected to be a technical leader who has won his or her position by individual successes and commands respect by virtue of mastery of engineering and his or her ability to find solutions to problems.

In Japan, the typical engineer for a firm's central labs is recruited directly from universities with a master's degree. Very few mid-career engineers are ever recruited from other companies. Neither salary nor rapid promotion are used to reward exceptional performance. All engineers proceed up the salary ladder at the same pace. The principal rewards for outstanding performance are intrinsic (the respect of superiors and peers) and long term (the opportunity to go abroad for advanced study and the prospect of staying in the central labs rather than transferring to a manufacturing division). The organizational structure of R&D groups is the same as that of manufacturing or sales with section chiefs and department heads carrying the same status and same salary across functions.

Researchers and engineers in their twenties in the typical Japanese company are rotated among various projects, but they are not given administrative tasks such as drafting research proposals, which are assigned to more senior researchers. Although they normally progress through a special promotional hierarchy that is distinct from those for blue-collar and white-collar job categories, salaries differ very little at the lower ranks of all these promotional hierarchies. Salaries are dependent upon seniority and age, not ability or title. By the time they reach thirty, researchers and engineers are promoted at virtually the same speed, and outstanding contributors are not immediately rewarded, except that their reputation is enhanced (and some may be sent to a foreign graduate school as a reward noting their potential). However, contributions at a young age may still have important implications for one's long-term career within the firm. By building a good reputation, divisional engineers may be promoted in their mid or late thirties to line managers in the manufacturing division and may be screened for further advancements in the managerial ranking hierarchy within the division. Many of the members of top management in leading Japanese manufacturing firms have been selected from the divisional background of the selected president, from which the strategic orientation of the firm may be discerned. In short, politics, while somewhat downplayed at the typical Japanese company, still exists, as it does everywhere else in the world.

The researcher first assigned to the central research laboratory may move to a divisional engineering department after the age of about thirty-five and may act as a carrier of a development project in which the researcher had been previously actively involved. This means that the researcher will be responsible for moving a new design to a more detailed stage of design and testing. In view of the strategic position of the engineering department with respect to career advancement, this transfer is normally considered a major promotion. Further promotion at about the age of about forty leads to entry into the managerial ranking hierarchy. Although entry to the managerial ranking hierarchy may entail better prospects for lifetime income and prestige, some researchers want to stay in the central research laboratory, where they can pursue careers as project leaders and managers of corporate research and development. Under the ranking hierarchy of the Japanese firm, researchers and engineers are rewarded for their performance by salary increases and rapid promotion at an early stage of their career. This is unusual in Japan where typically promotion is tied to one's age and seniority at the company; that it is so indicates the importance in Japan of the technologist and the recognition that even in collectivist Japan, individual paths may be necessary.

Japanese governmental programs contribute to commercial innovation by stimulating ideas and allowing companies to learn from each other in cooperative rivalry. Cross-licensing is actively encouraged and sometimes required in Japan. The immobility of research workers discourages the rapid diffusion of technology between firms (but increases it between divisions and sister companies). In industrial labs, the proportion of fully qualified researchers is higher and the number of technicians and ancillary workers is lower than in other countries. In Japan, the researchers have little technical help, and as a result research tends to take longer than in the West.

The Japanese have been successful in applied, not basic, technologies in part because of an educational system that is excellent through the secondary level but is weak at the graduate and postdoctoral levels. Applied technologies demand a distinct set of skills which the Japanese culture fosters and encourages among its citizenry and scientists. Nevertheless, at the same time, these traits and skills which allow superior execution at the applied level also often inhibit development at the basic innovation level. For the Japanese too be more successful in the basic technologies, a significantly improved postgraduate educational system would have to emerge. The education system does not produce either innovative thinkers or people who are supportive of individualistic behavior and ideas. Management style would have to move from strictly rewarding seniority to rewarding individual creativity.

The Japanese improve the methods of production by allowing process innovation to dominate. The government encourages companies to emphasize finding ways to absorb rapidly and add to imported technology and thus improve efficiency and produce quality goods (Methe, 1991). The method of assimilating and improving on imported technology was typically some form of "reverse engineering" (Pavitt, 1985). This involved trying to manufacture a product similar to one already available on the world market but without direct foreign investment. Japanese management, engineers, and workers typically think of the entire process as a system and begin to think in an integrated way about product design and process design. In factories, workers are more flexible, and more engineers are typically present. In Japan, operators themselves rather than engineers take the initiative in studying the task, work, and tools by using computer simulation. Japanese engineers and managers use the factory as a laboratory. The R&D department is closely related to the work of production engineers and process control. Reverse engineering involves not only the firm but all contractors and subcontractors associated with the final product, as well as an emphasis on high-quality results.

Japanese firms allocate half their research budget directly to the central R&D labs and half to the business divisions, which can use their funding either to carry out development activities within their own facilities or to commission specific research projects from the central labs. These divisions have their own development labs. Hence, their engineers play an important role in the R&D process and ease of manufacture is a major consideration in the design process. The research handoff is usually accomplished by dispatching one of the engineers from the central lab's project team to the division lab, a permanent transfer. In Japan, seniority and management skills are more important in encouraging and guiding one's research team.

Japan has an advantage in technological projects in which the target specifications can be well defined and are reasonably firm. That is, when the engineers know what they are looking for, Japanese industry is extraordinarily capable and highly innovative. On the other hand, when target specifications are vague (as they necessarily are when basic research is involved or when entirely new products for new applications are the objective), American industry seem to be particularly capable and creative. Thus comparative advantages occur in different levels of technological development. As products, processes, and markets mature, process technology becomes more dominant as competition and development efforts geared to known or firm-improved specifications take precedence over research efforts. It is   in   these areas   that   the   Japanese   excel.

The following factors indicate why the Japanese are good at analysis: consensus decision making, on-the-job training, job rotation and training, suggestion systems, technology monitoring, closeness to customers, the organization of research and engineering, and the intense competition. These factors yield intense communication, shared knowledge, and uniform and strong technological expertise. Technology thus transferred becomes widely disseminated within the company and serves as the basis for incremental improvements. Lifetime employment encourages user-inspired developments but sharply reduces the opportunities for synthesis of dissimilar technologies that arise from the mobility of scientists and engineers, as in the United States. In Japan, companies get very close to their customers (this is not necessarily equated with strong marketing) as relationships between vendor and customer usually is long-term and deep. This closeness explains the importance of customers as sources of ideas for product improvement and variety in Japan. Excessive dependence on customers, however,   also tends to inhibit the development of radically new products to fulfill needs of which customers are unaware or only vaguely aware.

Successful product innovation, development, and adaptation are the three pillars of Japanese innovation. The Japanese excel by drastically reducing the cycle time between design, engineering, production, marketing, and product redesign. In the Japanese innovation system, idea search, idea nurturing, and idea breakthroughs are given more prominence whereas in the American system, idea refinement, idea recycling, and idea nurturing are stressed. Japanese companies are particularly effective at creating system benefits for customers in mature industries such as automobiles and consumer electronics. American firms excel at technology-driven innovation that creates whole new industries. The Japanese excel at incremental advances in existing products and processes. The Japanese tend to make more use of companywide teams assembled to improve critical performance parameters.

The Japanese model of innovation starts with a market-finding phase followed by design, production, marketing, and distribution and use phases. Multiple paths exist from which innovation may arise, and there exist many forms of feedback: Research is not normally considered to be the initiating step (research occurs in and contributes to all phases in the innovation process) and the primary source of innovations is believed to be stored knowledge and technology. At the heart of the innovation generation process of Japanese organizations is the kind of cooperative utilization and learning through problem generation called learning-by-intrusion, in which overlapping information between members of the team is the norm, not the exception. Every member involved has the potential to create and suggest a solution to the problems at hand regardless of the member's status within the corporate hierarchy. When this form of information redundancy is present, loyalty and trust forming increases considerably within the team. However, this can also nurture group think. A hesitancy exists to submit creative ideas. Such a policy also incurs a high cost of human exhaustion in the process.

A major concern today in Japan is the all-too-often situation where upon a worker has literally work himself to death. This is called *karoshi*, salaryman sudden death syndrome. It is not uncommon for salaryman (as Japanese white collar employees in the top tier companies are called) to work eighty to one-hundred hour weeks for months on end or to commute across the ocean on a weekly basis. The cumulative effect of this human strain takes its toll. Many thirty-something and forty-something Japanese executives drop over dead, of plain exhaustion. Like footsoldiers for the Japanese military during The Second World War, they have given their all, made the ultimate sacrifice, for their company.

The Japanese tend to emphasize incremental process and product improvements based on existing technology and knowledge. They also tend to allot more of their resources to the middle part of the innovation process (process engineering and manufacturing facilities) than in United States (about twice as much). They treat the innovation process as a continuing, cyclical, iterative process. Each individual works as part of a team with a common goal. Outstanding coordination exists between product design and engineering groups. Research is ultimately performed with manufacturing in mind. Japanese firms and industries are characterized by rapid and efficient flow of information along vertical ties, providing ease in technology transfer. Japanese firms also place a greater emphasis on human resources and human relations, which are held to be more important relative to research or manufacturing results than in the United States. Customers tend to have greater input in the innovation process, and the resulting innovations are inherently geared toward meeting customer needs and desires.

Foreign scientific and technological knowledge is brought into Japan via extensive scanning and monitoring of publications, attendance of foreign conferences and trade fairs, sending of researchers and students abroad, joint ventures, acquisition of foreign companies and the relocation of R&D labs overseas. Japan has greater access to U.S. scientific and technological databases than the United States has to those in Japan. In addition, a strong relationship exists between companies, industries, and MITI. Employees from industry are commonly sent to MITI laboratories to participate in the development of new technologies. Japan's industry's strategy toward creativity is to stimulate it through the cross-fertilization of ideas within a project team.

New, state-of-the-art technology tends to be like a ladder: Climb it and you acquire new knowledge that confers a competitive advantage, but only until your competitors learn the new technology then you have to climb the ladder again. It is the proverbial Alice In Wonderland scenario of having to run ever faster to stay in the same place. On the other hand, process-oriented innovation has no beginning and no end. Each turn of the wheel improves an existing product and its production methods. The company unveils not entirely new products that keep getting better, more reliable, and cheaper, and cumulatively the advantage adds up. This is the Japanese philosophy: little by little. This is combined with a fast cycle of development, whipping out new product and reacting quickly to shifts in consumer preference. This is the Japanese preference for innovation, a preference which has suited Japan well over the last century.

PROCESS INNOVATIONS

American firms are often good at innovation, since individual ingenuity and sharply focused specialization can overcome many obstacles. Although scientists are admired in the United States, production engineering ranks much lower and important industrial disciplines like welding are hardly respected   at all. Until recently, American firms tended to put their best engineers into R&D and their second best into production. Pay and promotions for those in production tended to lag behind those in the R&D group (Thurow, 1987). The United States has many fewer production engineers than its foreign competitors. Many of America's most innovative firms often find it difficult to make the small steps that are crucial to the ongoing development process. Weakness in production innovation is central to America's competitiveness and trade problems. A firm cannot control what it cannot produce competitively; a production disadvantage can quickly erode a firm's technological advantage. As products, processes, and markets mature, process technology becomes more dominant as the basis for competition, and the process improvement effort takes over from the radical innovation research effort.

Japanese success can be traced to the cumulative impact of its great development capabilities. Japanese success in development has often been able to overcome America's much-heralded innovative capabilities. Twelve centuries ago, Japanese swordsmiths made the world's finest blades, patiently folding and hammering the metal into 10,000 microlayers of steel. To control impurities, craftsmen painstakingly selected the best woods to burn for charcoal. This same dedicated effort exists in Japan today. The more specialized an activity becomes, the greater the importance of efficient information exchanges if inappropriate tradeoffs or inappropriate optimization criteria are to be avoided. For specialists to work well in a large organization, there must be an intimate familiarity with one another's goals and priorities and a set of shared understandings and concerns. NASA's zero-defects program was a great influence on Japan's QC efforts. The Japanese learned about American high-quality standards during the Korean War, when United Nations' military procurement in Japan gave an enormous boost to Japanese industry and introduced military standards that required higher quality than was common for ordinary civilian products. The patron saint of Japanese quality control is an American named W. Edwards Deming, who is credited with bringing quality control to Japan in the early 1950s; today he is regarded as a national hero in Japan and the world famous Deming Prize for Quality is named for him.

The integration of innovation and production, called innovation-mediated production by Kennedy and Florida (1993), has five basic dimensions: (1) a transition from physical skill and manual labor to intellectual capabilities or mental labor; (2) the increasing importance of social or collective intelligence as opposed to individual knowledge and skill; (3) an acceleration of the pace of technological innovation; (4) the increasing importance of continuous process improvement on the factory floor; and (5) the blurring of the line between the R&D lab and the factory. This model is not uniquely Japanese, although the Japanese no doubt perfected it. What matters most in this model is not just radical new breakthrough technology but the ability to upgrade and improve those products constantly and manufacture them as efficiently as possible once they leave the lab.

Kaizen

Masaaki Imai (1992) described issues which are essential in achieving quality management and continuous improvements: setting standards, maintenance and improvement, *gemba* (the place where the action takes place), and the tools for problem solving. in Japan, everyone's job includes finding a better way of doing the job and improving the existing standard.

The essence of Japanese style management, or *kaizen*, is that there should be a willingness and recognition for gradual, constant, and incremental improvement. *Kaizen* is different from the idea of innovation because it includes those actions that make the best use of the resources at hand without using money. The Japanese feeling that the customer comes first is structured into the *kaizen* concept as is the need for long term satisfaction. The *kaizen* style of operations, according to the Japanese mode of thought, has three key pillars: (1) concepts which involve the way of thinking, (2) systems to implement the work, and (3) tools, the concrete means to effect the process. This philosophy is universal; All companies, regardless of nationality, regardless of background or education, have the inherent potential to implement the *kaizen* approach. The *Kaizen* approach, when applied to the workplace, means continuous improvement involving everyone—managers and workers alike (Imai, 1990). (This is remarkably like the American total quality management fad now in progress. This similarity is evidence of its universality and applicability to all workers throughout the world.) Figure 4.4 shows Japan's *kaizen* concept and its central position in Japanese business organizations.

Figure 4.4
Kaizen

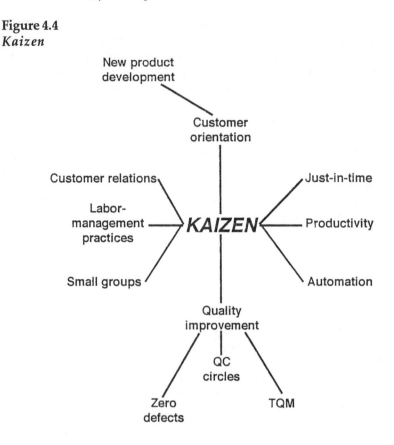

Understanding the concept of *kaizen*—constant improvement—is central to understanding Japan's approach to creative refinement. Improvement in Japan is a mind-set inextricably linked to maintaining and improving standards through delegating responsibility to the lowest unit—the worker on the line in most cases. Japanese companies prefer a series of small, incremental improvements in their daily operations, hitting for singles and doubles not home runs. (Small change is acceptable, large changes are not desired.) Japanese workers are constantly encouraged through the use of quality circles, suggestion boxes, meetings, and consensus decision making to offer new ideas for reducing costs, increasing quality, simplifying procedures, and developing new products. Small improvements, no matter how minor or seemingly insignificant, are crucial for the ultimate success of the company. This concept has also been adapted to the development of basic research and new technologies.

One example of this is the suggestion system. Every year, tens of thousands of suggestions are submitted by the employees of Japanese plants. Many are actually put into practice. Usually no significant monetary reward is given to the suggester. Rather, recognition takes the form of a certificate of appreciation and possibly a token gift. The cumulative results of these suggestions amount to important advances in efficiency, quality, and new technology. Group unity and loyalty help to stimulate suggestions, and a spirit of participation is what makes the worker submit. There is no comparison between the numbers of suggestions proposed by Japanese employees and the number of suggestions proposed by their American counterparts on a percapita annual basis; the Japanese win hands down.

The following are required to make the *kaizen* process work:

1. Worker cooperation. A long-term relationship between the worker and the company, job security, and the commitment that suggestions for productivity improvements will not cost workers their jobs.
2. Management commitment. Top management needs to back the *kaizen* team with the resources and authority to make sweeping changes, if need be, in search of radical efficiency gains.
3. Measurable goals and results. Besides validating the team's successes, measuring enforces a reality check.
4. Diverse teams. *Kaizen* teams should draw from disparate backgrounds—not just manufacturing—to elicit a variety of ideas.
5. A bias for action. The teams should favor immediate action on many fronts, opting for small improvements over costly, technological big fixes.
6. Follow-up. Not everything can be done quickly, so follow-up work is needed to implement medium-term suggestions.

Kaizen has been described as an umbrella embodying a considerable number of techniques, including customer orientation, TQC (total quality control), robotics, QC circles, suggestion systems, automation, discipline in the workplace, TPM (total productive maintenance), *kanban* (just-in-time), quality improvement, small group activities, cooperative labor management relations, productivity improvement and new product development (Imai, 1988). The TQC system produces a structure in which close communication is maintained between members of an organization. A strong and appropriate leadership is required to activate the structure and attain the highest productivity. Management targets must be understood by each member of the firm to reach the desired goals. The *Kaizen* system, to be fully understood and truly implemented by a firm, Japanese or foreign, must be viewed from the lens of the Japanese culture and understood in terms of the cultural scenario from which it arose.

The starting point for improvement is to recognize the need for it. This comes from recognition of a problem. *Kaizen* emphasizes problem awareness and provides clues for identifying problems. Once identified, problems must be solved. Improvement reaches new heights with every problem that is solved. To consolidate the new level, however, the improvement must be standardized. Thus *kaizen* also requires standardization. A precise standard of measurement must exist for every worker, every machine, and every process as well as every manager. In *kaizen*, standards exist only to be superseded by better standards as a result of constant revision and upgrading. Each standard carries with it the following characteristics: individual authorization and responsibility; transmittal of individual experience to the next generation of workers; transmittal of individual experience and know-how to the organization; accumulation of experience (particularly with failures) within the organization; deployment of know-how from one workshop to another; and discipline. Standardization in *kaizen* spreads the benefits of improvement throughout the organization.

Imai (1988), in his book *Kaizen: The Key to Japan's Competitive Success,* suggests that the reason for the extensive use and success of *kaizen* in Japan is that Japan is a process-oriented society, whereas the United States is a results-oriented society. People, machines, materials, methods, and environment are the inputs of a common process. A Japanese employee is typically concerned with the means, whereas the American is only concerned with the ends. Japanese management tends to emphasize attitudinal factors (i.e., many of the process-oriented criteria as well as the end result); the process is considered just as important as the obviously intended result. A Japanese process-oriented manager will be interested in discipline, time management, skill development, participation and involvement, morale, and communications—people-oriented management.

Once the process has been identified, with its outputs, inputs, customers, and suppliers, a need usually exists to obtain feedback on process performance and the effects of any changes that were made. Imai (1988) argues that it is the Japanese management system, *kaizen*, that is the key to Japanese success. *Kaizen* generates process-oriented thinking, since processes must be improved before improved results are achieved. The continual process can be thought of as the PDCA cycle Plan, Do, Check, and Action.

The Japanese institutional framework, in which competition is built-in, can be argued to be an advanced form of offensive management, in which product-cum-process innovation has resulted in the coupling of continuous innovation and industrial evolution. Japanese scale-intensive industries, such as automotive manufacturing and consumer electronics, have been shown to be two such industries in which the generation and utilization of new technologies in a continuous process produce well-known successes (Baba, 1989).

Baba discusses in detail the Japanese industrial policy, which includes a system of intrafirm promotion (or rotation), the lifetime employment system, age-based salaries, firm-based unions, bottom-up decision making, and horizontal information structures, in which knowledge and skills are shared among neighboring subunits. He also indicates the influence of other Japanese-specific factors, such as Japanese universities (which tend to restrict themselves to generalized knowledge with the firm providing specific job-related knowledge), less interfirm mobility between researchers and engineers, problem solving by learning-by-doing, and, in general, what Baba calls "strategic identity." All these items are in contrast to the typical American firm and American industry modus operandi.

Table 4.1 compares innovation to *kaizen*. *Kaizen* nurtures small and ongoing changes, whereas innovation is random and erratic. *Kaizen* calls for continuous effort and commitment. This is nearly the opposite of what is required by classical innovation. Imai (1988) has likened innovation to a stairstep and *kaizen* to a slope, gradual and incremental. Even the Japanese admit that they are stronger on the *kaizen* side whereas the West excels in innovation, a preference easily explained in terms of culture. Whereas the Americans stress innovation and sophistication, Japanese production managers and engineers often enjoy as much prestige as researchers. Whereas the Americans stress the short-term but dramatic effects of innovation, the Japanese stress the long-term, mundane effects of *kaizen*.

In summary, the dominant elements of the Japanese innovation system are as follows (Bowonder and Miyake, 1992):

- overlapping phases of development
- a wide range of suppliers capable of supplying sophisticated components
- firm-specific and factory-specific incremental innovation
- long-term transactions involved in such relationships, including social trust and loyalty
- extensive information sharing of technology and product through relationships
- applied R&D, not pure science
- commercial, not military, focus
- process and production technology
- quality control
- miniaturization
- standardization and mass volume production
- core competencies in technologies which have spillover effects

Table 4.1
Kaizen versus Innovation

	KAIZEN	INNOVATION
1. Effect	Long-term and long-lasting but undramatic	Short-term but dramatic
2. Pace	Small steps	Big steps
3. Timeframe	Continuous and incremental	Intermittent and non-incremental
4. Change	Gradual and constant	Abrupt and volatile
5. Involvement	Everybody	Select few "champions"
6. Approach	Collectivism, group efforts, systems approach	Rugged individualism, individual ideas and efforts
7. Mode	Maintenance and improvement	Scrap and rebuild
8. Spark	Conventional know-how and state of the art	Technological breaktrhoughs, new inventions, new theories
9. Practical requirements	Requires little investment but great effort to maintain	Requires large investment but little effort to maintain
10. Effort orientation	People	Technology
11. Evaluation criteria	Process and efforts for better results	Results for profits
12. Advantage	Works well in slow-growth economy	Better suited to fast-growth economy

The technological behavior of Japanese firms can be summarized by the following:

- shorter development time
- acquisition of external technology
- higher propensity for patenting
- design for manufacturability
- incremental product and process improvement
- technology strategy more important than corporate strategy
- competitive matching
- innovation dominated by large firms
- weakness in science-based industries
- combination of technologies and interfirm cooperation

Chapter 5

Japanese Product Development Strategies

HISTORICAL PERSPECTIVES

The postwar Japanese competitive strategy evolved from one of low wages (1945–1950s; labor-intensive industries such as textiles), to capital-intensive scale economies as rising wage rates eroded the advantage of low labor rates (1960s–early 1970s; market penetration and automation—steel, shipbuilding, autos, consumer electronics), to focused production (late 1970s and 1980s; high-volume segments and establishing a production facility that minimized complexity), to flexible production (producing a range of products on the same production line using just-in-time inventory techniques to provide both lower cost and greater variety in a shorter time and with a shorter life cycle) (Musselwhite, 1990). This was done by absorbing foreign technologies and making continuous improvements while maintaining quality consciousness (Best, 1990).

Taiichi Ohno, chief engineer at Toyota during the 1950s, learned many valuable lessons from Detroit which would later be instrumental in the way the Japanese economy prospered. He found a way to reduce the time required to change dies from a day to three minutes. He discovered that it cost less to make small batches, since making small batches eliminated the carrying costs of huge inventories required by mass production techniques. Making only a few parts before assembling them caused mistakes to show up almost immediately. This caused Ohno to concentrate on quality to eliminate the waste of large numbers of defective parts. To make this system work, Ohno needed both an extremely skilled and a highly motivated work force. As a result of a postwar strike, an agreement was worked out between the company and the union: Employees were guaranteed lifetime employment and their pay would be steeply graded by seniority rather than by specific job function and was to be tied to company profitability through bonus payments. This essentially made the employees members of the Toyota family, with rights of access to Toyota facilities (housing, recreation, clubs, etc.). The employees also agreed to be flexible in work assignments and to initiate improvements rather than merely respond to problems. Hence, the Japanese labor policy was born (Womack, Jones, and Roos, 1990).

Japanese companies tend to market technology-intensive products. First, R&D focuses on continual incremental improvement, which naturally extends product technology. This can push the most mundane products (automobiles, watches), over time, into the arena of high technology. Second, new technologies provide the best possibilities for serving market niches and fragmenting larger, more homogeneous markets (Pine, 1993). Japanese firms emphasize meeting consumers' needs with good quality and reliable products at competitive prices. Japanese companies appear more adept at exploiting strategic windows—opportunities created by new market segments, changes in technology, or new distribution channels.

FACTORS IN THE PRODUCT DEVELOPMENT STRATEGY

The eight factors discussed in this section contributed to Japan's speedy and flexible postwar development process.

Top Management as a Catalyst

Top management plays a key strategic role in new product development in the typical Japanese company. Management provides the initial kickoff to the development process by signaling a broad strategic direction or goal for the company. This is done by constantly monitoring the external environment (competitive threats and market opportunities) and evaluating company strengths and weaknesses. The Japanese firm continuously scans the globe for new ideas and is able to assess with more foresight the technologies that have a large future growth and diffusion potential. Top management rarely hands down a clearcut new product concept of a specific work plan. Rather it intentionally leaves considerable room for discretion and local autonomy to those in charge of the development project. A certain degree of built-in ambiguity is considered healthy, especially in the early stages of development of the product or technology. Management also implants a certain degree of tension within the project team. This tension, if managed properly, helps cultivate a must-do attitude and a sense of cohesion among members of the crisis-solving team. A Japanese company comes in contact with an appropriate series of generic technologies through in-house research and a considerable capacity to integrate the latest scientific developments. Such contact becomes possible through high-level collaboration with university laboratories, public and private research and information organizations, and other companies (Giget, 1988). Outside research is analyzed to provide material for directing in-house applied research programs. All this is guided subtly by top management.

Self-Organizing Project Teams

A new product development team, consisting of members with diverse backgrounds and temperaments, is hand picked by top management and is given a free hand to create something new. Members of this team often risk their reputation and sometimes their career to carry out their role as change agents for the organization at large. To become self-organizing, a group needs to be completely autonomous, it must come up with its own challenging goals and then try to keep elevating those goals, it can not be content with incremental improvements alone being in constant pursuit of a quantum leap, and it is usually composed of members of diverse functional specialization so that the whole becomes much more than the sum of its parts. Cross-fertilization then occurs. Ambiguity is tolerated. Sharing of information is encouraged. Decision making is intentionally delayed to extract as much up-to-date information as possible from the marketplace and technical communities. Sharing of responsibilities is accepted by all group members. For all of the advantages that this group consensus provides, it also has some potential drawbacks. For example, collective thought often leads to isolation and elitism (as is the case for Japan and the Japanese people themselves). However, in the Japanese view of the team and teamwork, workers are encouraged to have multiple skills and are valued and paid for their versatility (the number of different roles they can play within the team). This allows teams to assume major responsibilities and to solve problems spontaneously as they arise rather than asking the engineers for a new blueprint and the staff for new work procedures. The work is more varied, flexible, and challenging and may make levels of supervision superfluous. The Japanese search for goal congruence is continuous and never ends until consensus is reached.

Overlapping Development Phases

The concept of division of labor is not well adopted in Japan; rather, redundancy (excess information sharing), and shared division of labor are the norms with every phase of innovation generation loosely connected and overlapping, expanding and contracting as necessary. The unique characteristic of Japanese enterprise is that, rather than dividing each phase and operating remotely, every phase is made to overlap in a process that moves through the joint efforts of the participants. As a result, the time required to develop an idea is halved in many projects. However, information redundancy can nurture group think as well a hesitancy to submit creative ideas. The Japanese innovation generation process has an unusually high cost associated with it in terms of the generation of problems and solutions, high degree of social interaction (work is the reason for existence and family often gets shortchanged), human exhaustion and overwork (*karoshi*), mental exhaustion, and burnout (Nonaka, 1990).

Considerable overlap exists in the phases of the new product development process in Japan. This overlap between R&D and marketing enhances shared responsibility and cooperation, stimulates involvement and commitment, sharpens a problem-solving focus, encourages initiative taking, develops diversified skills, and heightens sensitivity to market conditions. Phase management is holistic and overlapping rather than analytical and sequential. The search for information and experimenting at all points delays until the last moment the narrowing of options. In an overlapping program, many groups are working on a project at the same time. The overlapping approach has both merits and faults. The obvious merits include (1) faster development, (2) increased flexibility, and (3) information sharing. This approach also helps foster the more strategic view of a generalist, enhances shared responsibility and cooperation, stimulates involvement and commitment, sharpens a problem-solving orientation, encourages initiative taking, develops diversified skills, creates grounds for peer recognition, and increases the sensitivity of everyone involved to changes in market conditions. On the other hand, the burden of managing the process increases exponentially. By its nature, the overlapping approach amplifies ambiguity, tension, and conflict within the group. The burden to coordinate the intake and dissemination of information also increases, as does management's responsibility to carry out ad hoc and intensive on-the-job training (Rosenberg, 1986). As a result, the division of labor often becomes ineffective.

Multilearning

An almost fanatical devotion to learning occurs in a Japanese institution, both within organizational membership and among outside members of the network. Learning, for the typical Japanese person, is something that takes place continuously in a highly adaptive and interactive manner. These continuous interactions with outside information sources allow workers to respond rapidly to changing market preferences. The constant encouragement to acquire diversified knowledge and skills helps create a versatile team capable of solving a wide array of problems in a relatively short period of time.   Learning is institutionalized by the Japanese practice of job rotation.

Subtle Control

Subtle control is exercised by management to prevent looseness, ambiguity, tension, or conflict from getting out of control. The emphasis is on self-control and on peer pressure. Management selects the right people for the team, constantly monitoring the balance and adding or deleting specific members if deemed necessary. An open and visible working environment requires one to think about what is best for the group at large. Management also encourages team members to extract as much information from the field and to share the information with other team members. The Japanese evaluation system, which is based on group rather than individual performance, encourages the formation of a self-organizing team, fosters multilearning among team members, and builds trust and cohesion, and peer pressure. Management establishes overriding values shared by everyone in the organization.

Organizational Transfer of Learning

Technology and knowledge are transferred to other divisions or subsequent projects and become institutionalized over time. Personnel are rotated as well. Successful, highly visible projects will be studied and copied by others in the company. Due to the Japanese emphasis on lifelong learning and the job rotation which exists in most every large Japanese corporation, the organizational transfer of learning to other individuals or to entire other groups can be accomplished easily, quickly, and cooperatively.

Japanese Teamwork

According to Peter Drucker (1993), three potential types of teams exist. One is the baseball or cricket team, in which all players play on the team but they do not play together as a team. Each team member has a fixed position. This version of a team has great strengths, specific tasks, measurable performance, and players that are well trained for the specific position the player has. This is excellent for repetitive tasks and for work in which the rules are well known. It is also the model on which modern mass production was organized. As team members get information from the situation, each receives information appropriate to his or her task. Traditionally, most work in large American companies was organized in this way.

The second type of team is analogous to a soccer team or the symphony orchestra, all with fixed positions which work as a team. This requires a conductor or coach and a score as well as endless rehearsals. This type of team has great flexibility if the score is clear and the team is well lead. Information comes largely from the coach or conductor. This is the typical Japanese model of work.

The third type of team is the doubles tennis team, or executive committee. This type of team is small and flexible with the players rapidly adjusting to each other. This team only functions well when the members adjust to the strengths and weaknesses of other player(s). This is the strongest team of all three types. The performance of the team is greater than the sum of the individual team members. This version of the team, however, requires enormous self-discipline and time together to work well. Information comes largely from each player or team member. This is the team most suitable for the information age of the twenty-first century.

Lean Production

Lean production is a comprehensive information system that makes it possible for everyone in the plant to respond quickly to problems and to understand the plant's overall situation. The *shusa* system pioneered by Toyota (or LPL—large project leader—as it is called at Honda) is one such example. *Shusa* is the boss, the leader of the team, whose job it is to design and engineer a new product and to get it fully into production. The *shusa* assembles a small team, which is assigned to the development project for life. Techniques of lean design include leadership, the *shusa*, teamwork, communication (resolving critical design tradeoffs at the beginning), and simultaneous development.

MARKET DEVELOPMENT

The Japanese establish themselves in a market and then begin to focus their attention on market and product development. This strategy allows them to achieve competitive leadership within the market. They continuously search for ways to upgrade and improve their product's performance, style, quality, and features. This allows the Japanese company to offer its customers newer and better products than the competition is typically able to offer. Even though the Japanese are aware that product innovation is their key for long-term survival and profitability within their market segment, they initially use aggressive pricing strategies to help secure their market share. When their product is not clearly superior to the existing product in the market, they "buy time" by the use of a lower pricing strategy to gain market share as they develop and begin to market a product that is superior to those of their competitors.

Market research for Japanese product development frequently begins in the home market. Japanese experience within this market provides insight into customer preferences, product deficiencies, and effective marketing strategies. Japanese firms collect extensive market data on consumers' quality preferences, expectations of product life, changing attitudes toward breakdowns and reliability rates, and perceptions of product performance and rely heavily on this information when redesigning old models and creating new products. However, the Japanese routinely export their highest quality products to other markets and keep many of their lower quality products for their own home market. The Japanese also export many of their lower quality products to developing nations.

Pre-competitive research is typically achieved through research associations, in which the goal is to create an engineering infrastructure as the basis for competition. Cooperation among rival firms requires that the subject for research is fundamental and of common interest to all participants. The resulting cooperative research effort emphasizes development of a prototype. The task of determining what to make and how to make it (i.e., articulating the needs of the marketplace) is shared by association members. Afterward, each competing company is on its own to produce its own version.

In any industrial or retail sector in Japan, ten to twelve competitors typically battle for market share. Displayed in many stores are rows upon roles of different products from different manufacturers, each priced closely to each other but each offering a slightly different feature that vendors hope will attract customers. The Japanese do not test market. They rush to market with the final product and let the market decide on winners and losers. This unique Japanese technique of being simultaneously competitive yet protected against foreign (non-Japanese) producers provides interesting results. Japanese firms are adept at what is called product covering—rushing out instant imitations. The rival manufacturers rush to produce their own versions just in case the pioneer's should prove to be a best seller. Japanese companies also use product churning extensively. Whereas Western firms use the rifle approach in market studies, testing the market constantly and revising the product each time until it exactly meets the customer's needs before launching it, Japanese companies tend to use the shotgun approach to market development. New product ideas are not tested through market research but by selling the first production batch and letting the market decide directly the winners and losers. Massive amounts of products are thrown at the market, and what sticks becomes the winner.

Thus, flooding the market with new products is important in Japan because firms are determined not to lose access to scarce and often rigid dealer and distribution networks. This is not as important overseas. Tarnishing one's corporate reputation with a poor product is also of less concern in Japan because many new versions are aimed at a core of sophisticated consumers who will try anything new. Abroad, outside of Japan, new products must be chosen and developed more carefully since a single dud can damage a carefully nurtured image. Isolated from their markets, Japanese manufacturers find its safest to offer as wide a range of products as possible. The presumption exists that being in a particular industry means doing what other companies in that industry do. This is cultural baggage left over from the rice culture mentality: In rice villages, a farmer is wise to copy the neighbors, but hunters and herders are only successful if they find their own particular niches.

Market penetration is a more important pricing objective than quick price skimming profit-taking. Entry into a market was viewed as a long-term investment. Individual markets were not seen as profit centers but as pieces in one large global puzzle. By generating sufficient funds at home and in some selected markets where the share positions were strong, the lower returns from a low price penetration strategy in newer markets could be sustained over a relatively long period of time. This is the niche approach or *sukima* strategy (a *sukima* is a small opening that remains when a sliding door does not quite fit its frame). The idea is that by entering through a chink in the armor, an unprotected niche or attacking a weak product, existing competitors would not take notice and not defend their product line strongly. From this "foot in the door," further inroads come naturally.

One major source of Japanese innovations and their commercial excess is the nature of user-producer interaction, which includes a sequential and dense communication between a demanding user and a producer. This is especially true between a user and a capital goods supplier. Designers list every market expectation they can identify, based on feedback from salespeople, market research, and customer interviews. Each general feature is broken down into more specific requirements and then into even more exact specifications. Each requirement is ranked in order of importance, and the completed list adds up to a product's true quality because it represents what consumers really want. On the other dimension of the matrix, designers list every conceivable product characteristic and then the developers assign a degree of correlation between market need and the product characteristic. This allows the designers to develop foolproof guidelines for the most appropriate product.

PRODUCT DEVELOPMENT—JAPANESE STYLE

Product development Japanese style is the dynamic and continuous process of adaption to changes in the environment. The key elements of this effort are self-organizing development teams (autonomy given to the groups to define their own activities, which entails members from diverse functional backgrounds), facing challenges collectively, overlapping development phases, and a commitment to continuous learning. Project teams are assigned to pursue a broad strategic product development goal instead of a specific new product concept.

The Japanese are known for their commitment to "gaining, maintaining, and expanding market share around the world through the use of product innovation strategies" that challenge their resources and technology (Coe, 1990, p. 22). They invest heavily in research and development, spending 3 percent of their GNP to create and develop non-defense related products. Since 1983, Japan has gained shares in total patents issued in thirty-eight out of forty-eight product categories (Dumaine, 1991, p. 57). The Japanese product research is market driven. Japanese organizations must pay for 98 percent of their research from their own revenues (Moffat, 1991, p. 88). The Ministry for International Trade and Industry (MITI) coordinates the *keiretsu* members to help on the research and development of products for global markets. However, it is the individual Japanese companies and their cooperative efforts which, for the most part, must end up doing the actual research and paying for its development. Direct government funding is extremely limited.

Japanese companies spend more time than Americans do in planning (40 percent versus 25 percent), suffer development setbacks in a smaller proportion of products (28 percent versus 49 percent), and waste less of their time debugging finished products (5 percent versus 15 percent) than does the average American company (Dumaine, 1991, p. 59). Japanese companies also invest more of their managerial time in new products (50 percent versus 40 percent) and receive more revenues from them (44 percent versus 28 percent) than the typical American company (*Fortune*, December 2, 1991, p. 59). The considerable amount of preplanning is spent on gaining a consensus among the team members and employees on what the product is—its features, color, shape, price, etc. However, once decided, the company sticks to those specs and implementation proceeds speedily since consensus has already been achieved. As a result, Japanese firms experience far fewer interruptions during development and fewer problems after launch. The Japanese believe in settling on specifications as late as possible and then sticking to them. In that way, people can spend more time planning, discussing, and debating the product's characteristics, and afterward, everyone knows that a change would seriously delay the project. Conflict resolution is accomplished by broad consultation prior to decisions and at lower levels of the organization for successful firms. In other words, lots of up front time spent researching, analyzing, and building consensus leads to an accelerated development and production schedule since almost all potential conflicts have been resolved in advance.

As a result, the average Japanese company receives 44 percent (versus 28 percent for a similar American company) of revenue from its new products (defined as less than five years old). Adherence to proper etiquette (form) often can be equated with morality and sometimes takes precedence over truthfulness and intellectual honesty (function). The Japanese focus on customer satisfaction is also evident in their search for product improvement and development. They continually survey their product users to target problems or newer features their customers want. The Japanese also test their products on potential adopters to evaluate what is needed from the customer's point of view. This zero feedback time allows the Japanese to determine customer satisfaction with their products and act on the improvements suggested by the feedback. The Japanese also use zero improvement time, which allows them to improve their products on a continuous basis, so their products will remain the leader in the market segment. The frequency of engineering changes in the typical American firm is as much as twice that of a Japanese company. This has negative implications for the American firm since engineering change orders are increasingly disruptive to higher volume production.

Due to fierce competition, Japanese companies use multiple-track development. They are reluctant to pin their hopes on one technology or product. Japanese corporations will often fund several groups, both to stimulate internal competition and to devise fallback positions. It matters little if the first generation of a product is perfectly efficient what matters is getting the fourth or fifth generation right and getting a product out the door quickly. The speed with which the Japanese respond is geared to the economies of scale they gain (Makino, 1987). The Japanese bring out a new product in half the time it takes their American competitors and in one third the time it takes Europeans. The Japanese company deadline for abandoning a new product is the first day it's marketed—the ultimate in creative obsolescence. This is called parallel development: developing second- and third-generation products along with the initial version. The theory is that as soon as the pack catches up, the replacement product will be ready to go. Time-based innovation first appeared in the early 1980s, when Yamaha challenged Honda's position as the world's premier maker of motorcycles. Honda responded by introducing or replacing 113 models in just over eighteen months, the equivalent of turning over its entire product line twice.

Although this looks wasteful by American standards, the end result is that Japanese companies develop new products in a third to half the time spent by their Western counterparts at a quarter to one tenth the costs. Many Japanese companies work to have the next generation in development before introduction of the initial product with improvement targets of 40 to 50 percent. Cycle times, instead of being four or five years as used to be typical in Western industry, are reduced to eighteen to twenty-four months. Nissan envisions that in the next decade product modularity will allow it to provide the service of developing, producing, and delivering a completely customer designed car in three days.

In 1977, the development of new products overtook cost reduction as a management goal in Japan; in 1979, it overtook expanding market share to become the top priority. By 1982, the ratio of new to traditional products had reached at least 40 percent among many manufacturers. In 1985, nearly 20,000 new products went on sale in Japan, 12 percent more than in 1984 and 33 percent more than in 1983 (Kilburn, 1986). Mitsubishi Research Institute (MRI), Japan's largest research company, has been researching new product introductions since 1973 and has found that the majority of new products are improvements. Truly new products, based on totally new ideas are only 1 or 2 percent. Intense market competition, continual product improvements, and rapid technological change are all helping to shorten product life cycles. MRI estimates that new food products have a life of only a few months, toys three to six months, and electronics several years. Companies must aim to launch, compete, succeed, and move on all within a short time. It is no longer a question of how many can be produced but how few, to avoid overstocking and leftovers. And if the product becomes an unexpected hit, how quickly can production be expanded to meet demand?

The money spent on developing a product or process is not an investment to the Japanese, it is sunk (fixed) cost. Cross-functional teams strive constantly to improve processes. Managers are coaches, cheering on communications and unceasing efforts to improve. The Japanese niche is in mass production of low-cost, high-quality standard goods and services. Japanese companies adopted this method in order to develop new products rapidly and with maximum flexibility. Or, rather, they were forced to do so in a severe competitive environment of product development. They found, however, as a result of learning-by-doing that phase overlapping is an essential linkage mechanism of networking.

In the Japanese research system, the product development group essentially contracts with the research group for certain technologies and product development priorities. This builds such a strong link that research flows directly into products, into applied uses of the technologies. Many Japanese companies, like Hitachi, encourage researchers to take the long-term view by building additional funds and time into each contract from a development group; the time and money can be used however the research team likes.

One reason Japanese companies are successful in introducing new products is that they use a team approach, which involves more horizontal communication across functions and helps stimulate inventions through cross-fertilization of ideas. Japanese employees form diverse functions that are often teamed to move a product from the idea stage to commercialization. This team can be temporary or could become permanent depending upon the product and its success. This approach helps maintain control until the goal is achieved. Small incremental improvements are perhaps best made by a team (Hull and Azumi, 1989). Multifunctional teamwork is likely to vary in appropriateness by the stage of the technology life cycle. Multiple functions do not need to interact as much upstream at the basic research stage because the commercial implications are unclear at best. Therefore, such interaction is likeliest to be highest when upstream activities need to be transferred downstream (Kodama, 1991).

Japanese companies also excel at catalog design. Instead of designing each component of a new product from scratch, Japanese engineers are trained to use the parts catalog, use off-the-shelf products whenever possible, and even use items found in other products. A more expensive and reliable component would only be used if designers were able to prove that the savings in warranty expenses exceeded the increase in component costs. Changes were not made unless a favorable cost-benefit ratio could be demonstrated. As a result, the Japanese engineer tends to consider the impact of the design on cost or manufacturability, whereas the typical American engineer simply wants to know whether it can be done from an engineering point of view. The final performance may be only 90 percent of the American product but at half the cost.

Competitive benchmarking is also a typical Japanese corporate practice. The idea is to obtain models from one's competitors and then set production targets based on the features, options, and price of the competition. In a benchmark study of Japanese processes, Xerox found that production lead times were kept low by using a selected supplier base, paying attention to their design suggestions, and eliminating time consuming price quotes. Quality was kept high by getting vendors to commit to excellence and then training them as needed. Tooling costs were controlled by avoiding expensive redesigns and hand tooling. Benchmarking, though, has limitations. In Japan, benchmarking has traditionally taken on a "copycat" form. As a result, in an environment with changing market conditions and increasingly cut-throat competition, successful benchmarking has ceased to be a successful business practice. In a mature market, launching a catch-up product, a "me-too," is typically not a winning strategy (Ohinata, 1994).

The Japanese are especially enamored with the use of prototypes. Many companies, especially the automakers, use prototypes as a way to structure the design process. Prototype testing and evaluation provides a way to manage the design process because each prototype stage is an opportunity to review the supplier's performance. The first prototype from suppliers are usually fully functional and complete in appearance. Suppliers who miss prototype delivery deadlines face severe penalties, such as reduced future orders.

Japanese corporate prototyping practices differ from those typically found in America companies. An American firm does not make a prototype until all the problems its engineers can think of have been discussed and resolved. The Japanese slap together a prototype as soon as possible and then use its failures as a learning tool (i.e., trial-and-error learning). Specialization in Japan, under these conditions, is not necessary; the practice is just to watch what happens and then tinker. Benchmarking also has problems—it provides a picture of what was and what is, not what will be or can be.

Reasons for introducing new products in Japan include to match changing customer demand, to grow, and to win share. Product success factors include a product that is matched to customer needs and is superior in quality, reliability, value, and design. Factors contributing to failure include not understanding customer needs, high costs, insufficient prelaunch, and lack of a differential advantage. Most products that succeed are generally considered to embody the concept of *keihakutanshoka*—light, thin, short, and small, as in light in weight, thin in width, short in length and operating time, and as small in size and cost as possible. The objective is to economize on energy, raw materials, time, and space. Any successful product has some elements of each of these four components. In addition, the simplicity, compactness, power, and elegance of the Japanese tea ceremony and flower arrangement often find expression today in many Japanese products (cars and cameras being examples).

The success of Japanese new product programs is related to the level of R&D and marketing integration (sharing of information, working together on specific new product development tasks, organizational structure, attitudes) in Japanese firms. Japanese methods of organizing new product activity are influenced by corporate culture, which accomplishes the necessary factors. In the successful Japanese firm, a common commitment to the long-run success of the firm binds R&D and marketing employees together. Interfunctional cooperation is based on this shared commitment and is reinforced through participative decision making, job rotation, and the use of joint reward systems (Song and Parry, 1993a). When R&D-marketing relationships are harmonious (each party has great professional regard for the other, each feels that the other is competent, each feels dependent on the other, each feels trusting and open to the other), new product projects tend to have greater successes. By their very nature, Japanese companies produce this harmonious interaction. Employee interactions typically involve all these factors; their importance can be traced to the fact that the ability to work well with fellow employees is the most important criterion for promotion decisions in Japan.

Employee participation in new product development, product modification, and product deletion is high, as is expected in a participative decision-making, bottom-up process. R&D and marketing are involved early in the process. Japanese management tends to be decentralized in more successful firms. Highly integrated and successful firms tend to have a greater emphasis on role clarity (i.e., written performance standards and written documentation of duties, authority, and accountability), than is usually perceived for a Japanese firm. The most frequently used method of organization in Japanese firms is the R&D manager directing new product development. Venture teams are rarely used in Japanese high-tech firms.

TARGET COST

Japan's system of forecasting, monitoring, and interpreting costs is fundamentally different from that of the West. This system guides and motivates planners to design products at the lowest possible cost and gives them considerable freedom in introducing new products and getting them to market quickly. The critical feature of the Japanese system is its focus on getting costs out of the product during the planning and design stage. The Japanese engineer tends to consider the impact of the design on costs or manufacturability; the American engineers want to know whether it can be done from an engineering point of view. The price at which the product can succeed in the marketplace is determined first, and then the costs required to make a necessary profit are targeted and allocated (thus the term *target cost*). Instead of designing a product and then determining its costs, target costs are based on what the marketplace will bear, and these are allocated to each component of the product and to suppliers responsible for these components. The team in charge of bringing a new product idea to market determines the price at which the product is most likely to appeal to potential buyers and the price the market is most likely to accept. From this crucial judgment, all else follows. That is the point at which virtually all subsequent costs are determined, from manufacturing to what customers will have to spend on maintenance. Figure 5.1 shows the target cost concept and how it differs from the product design philosophy used in traditional Western companies.

This target cost is based on the price that is most likely to appeal to buyers minus the desired profit. After deducting the desired profit margin from the forecasted sales price, the planners develop estimates for each of the elements that make up a product's costs: design and engineering, manufacturing, sales and marketing. Each of these is further subdivided to identify and estimate the cost of each component that goes into the finished product. Every part of the function is treated as a component, and each is assigned a target cost. Then intensive negotiating processes begin between the company, its outside suppliers,

Figure 5.1
Target Costing

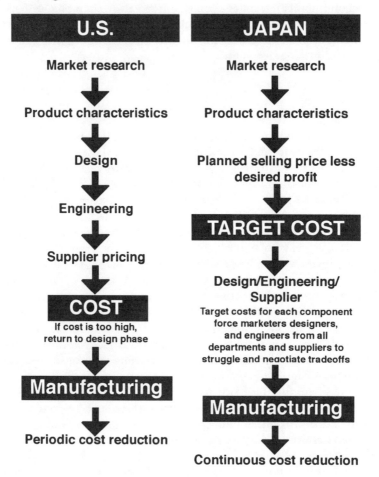

and internal departments. Compromises and tradeoffs by product designers, process engineers, and marketing specialists produce a projected cost that is within close range of the original target.   In other words, the Japanese typically work backward to make sure they can achieve the desired cost. The emphasis is on meeting cost specifications no matter the effort.   This is the essence to the concept of target cost, determine up front the desired price and hence profit, then work backward to calculate the cost the product must have in order to meet the price and profit goals. Once that cost has been determined, do what it takes, whatever it takes, to meet that cost goal.

They then direct designers and engineers to meet that target. Everyone from designers to engineers to purchasing must struggle to meet the cost and make the necessary tradeoffs to meet the cost chosen. Then manufacturing, once the product is in production, works on continuous cost reduction. This system, almost entirely the reverse of what is typical in Western companies (see Figure 5.1), encourages managers to worry less about a product's costs than about its market role. Compromises and tradeoffs ensue until target costs are met. The focus then is on reducing that cost with each new product generation. Long-term supplier interdependence means that companies work with their suppliers to achieve target costs and reductions over time and are willing to support them with engineering help and process innovations.

The Japanese also use target costing to make existing products less expensive in what is known as teardown analysis. Japanese companies often establish target costs for product components on the basis of comparative studies of competitors' products. By tearing down competitors' products, the materials, process, and production and hence the product's probable costs are analyzed. Engineers methodically take apart competitor products, analyzing materials, techniques, and features. Then they determine the product's probable costs and set this as their own target cost. Japanese engineers set target costs in expectation of what competitors' costs may become in the future. The Japanese company then usually adopts the lowest of all its competitors as the target cost for its own similar product. In the United States, this is called benchmarking and reverse engineering. The Japanese do it routinely as an integrated part of target costing programs. When they discover that a competitor has cut the cost of a component, they rush to match or undercut it. By so doing, they set their sights on tomorrow's marketplace, not today's. The Japanese know a competitor is going to come along and bring out a better product at a lower price, so they constantly strive to be the one to do it, instead of their competition.

Hence, what matters for many Japanese companies is not the apparent profit an individual product can earn but the profitability of portfolios of products. This allows the companies to offer marginal products for small niches without worrying about profitability—the higher margin profits will carry the marginal products. If the Japanese believe it makes competitive sense to carry a product, they will, regardless of whether or not it is profitable. In addition, sometimes these peripheral products do result in hits and are products that would never have been launched if the company had based its decision strictly on the product's standalone profitability. By producing so many products, the Japanese company allows the market to determine which are winners and losers, instead of a biased company task force doing so.

ORGANIZATION

Japanese companies make sure that employees understand how their work is translated into the numbers that represent the company's performance. The people responsible for projecting and measuring product costs are not narrowly schooled accountants , as in the West, but typically cost engineers who have rotated among several departments before taking on a cost planning job and thus have broad perspectives. Managers rely heavily on those direct performance indicators that employees can readily grasp and do something about: the time it takes to set up the manufacturing line to produce a particular batch of products; the amount of materials that must be scrapped because of worker error; the percentage of purchased parts that are rejected because they do not live up to specifications.   This typically provides the company with broad perspectives that give them unique abilities to reduce costs.

Finance and accounting functions focus not on external financial reporting but on manager-useful information as well as worker-useful information. Japanese companies tend to use accounting systems to motivate employees to act in accordance with long-term manufacturing strategies than to provide management with precise data on costs, variances, and profits. These practices result in sound decisions, both long term and short term. Japanese management is free from the short term pressure of steady improvements in earnings per share seen in U.S. companies.   Achieving market share through introduction of new products will result in growth and profitability. The Japanese accounting system encourages managers to worry less about a product's cost than about the role it could play in gaining market share. In the West, obsessive attention to allocating expenses from labor to overhead against each product often consumes effort that could be better spent on systematic efforts to drive costs down. A long-term investment in capital, people, and technology is required to maintain strategic competitiveness, not shortsightedness. Japanese companies pay special attention to their core competencies that mean success in the marketplace. The detrimental effect, however, is that stockholders may be ignored along with short-term financial results. The Japanese target market share with gains.

The majority of Japanese R&D personnel are recruited directly from undergraduate or master's degree science and engineering programs. Much less attention is paid to a recruit's formal academic training. Japanese companies usually do not look for the most intelligent, the most ambitious, or the most energetic employee candidates (these may not fit into the company system); rather, employers seek young people who do not have strongly held opinions or ambitions and can be molded into what managers regard as company soldiers, people who will adhere strictly to the hierarchy of the company, obey rules without question, and devote their lives to working diligently and rising slowly in the ranks. Throughout Japan, the hunt is continually on for such workers; unfortunately, the criteria almost always forgets creativity, originality, individuality. The presence of these characteristics, although vital to research, have been known to create conflict and strife in the workplace; in Japan, harmony is so essential, the trade-off is obvious: a smoothly running workplace is far more important and desirable than an original one.

In Japan, individuals are typically assigned to interdisciplinary teams. Assignments are given that often do not directly relate to a recruit's background or academic training. Thus, employees learn to work together and learn from each other. Learning, therefore, is a constant process that Japanese employees and companies must pursue (often it becomes the individual's responsibility at his or her own free time to learn the new job). Japanese R&D also benefits from the long-term employment and low turnover typical at large Japanese firms. Three quarters of Japanese engineers will have only one employer during their entire career. A firm therefore retains its human capital investments. This lack of job hopping among Japanese engineers also limits leakage of information to competitors; although it also increases considerably technology transfer between sister divisions or sister *keiretsu* companies. Lifetime employment is also a powerful impetus to innovate; increased competition constantly threatens the firm, and new business opportunities must constantly be found (Worthy, 1991). In Japan, engineers thus enjoy high status, equal to that of scientists. Process (production) engineers, especially, are highly valued in Japan.

The corporate evaluation and reward structure is different in Japan from the United States. Evaluations are based on daily observations by managers. This is typically informal and is carried out with minimal direct feedback to the employee. Annual face-to-face evaluations are not provided in Japan. Employees are required to give to their managers an annual written self-assessment, but the employee receives no formal feedback back in return. This works well if there is a strong, trust-based relationship between employee and manager. Nonetheless, frustration levels are growing in Japan. Companies have been traditionally reluctant to provide merit pay. Job performance typically has little impact on salary and bonuses for the individual researcher. One of the most significant rewards and incentives is to be assigned to interesting and potential important projects. But these are firmly controlled by research managers.

FACTORY-R&D INTERACTION

In Japan, R&D scientists and engineers are integrated with factory workers and are not distinctly separated, as is favored in the West. Multidisciplinary research teams are the cornerstone of Japanese policy and contain between five and fifteen scientists and engineers. The emphasis is on collective, not individual, effort. This leads to team building and project formation. Consensus decision-making, however, can lead to corporate group think, which mutes the expression of new ideas and leads to overwork and burnout; this may explain the Japanese inability to pioneer radical discontinuous innovations.

The R&D lab and the factory are linked and integrated. R&D takes place both at the central lab, where both development and high-end basic research takes place, and at the product development centers located adjacent to the factories. The latter focus on developing new products and processes. Most factories also have their own engineering staff, whose main job is to upgrade those products and manufacturing processes used in their particular plant. Constant communication with manufacturing and the plants occurs in the Japanese R&D organization. Central lab personnel tend to communicate far less frequently with sales and marketing than with development centers. This is because the engineers know that later in their careers they will eventually move to manufacturing positions and, thus, they must develop good relationships with the manufacturing units.

In Japan, when a product development project is approved, research and project engineers are joined by a small number of manufacturing engineers, industrial designers, etc. As the effort continues, more manufacturing engineers are added to focus on design, machine setup, and assembly. Tool engineers are then brought in to develop the special instruments and machinery necessary for manufacturing. Suppliers become team members as well at this stage. Representatives of each group remain with the project until early production runs are successfully accomplished. This functional integration facilitates knowledge sharing and learning-by-doing. Having hands-on personnel involved at the early stages ensures that the design staff does not develop plans that are too difficult to implement. This process is reinforced by the career cycle of Japanese R&D scientists and engineers. Transfer from R&D to manufacturing is common. Japanese researchers spend the first decade or so of their career engaged in long-term research at central labs and then are deployed to a divisional laboratory or engineering facility or to manufacturing sites where they function as members of particular projects and thus transfer technical knowledge. This is not temporary but is part of the permanent reward structure in a career path toward line management. At NEC, approximately 50 percent of all research personnel are transferred to the operating division during their first decade of service, and 80 percent are transferred within twenty years of service.

PROCESS ENGINEERING

The Japanese distinguish between productive and unproductive time: operational efficiency is about productive time—time during which material is being transformed by machining operations. Process efficiency includes both. Unproductive time is the time materials spend in inventory or other nonoperational activities. Operational throughout is measured in terms of productivity per labor or machine input hour. Process efficiency is ratio of the time a product is being transformed to the time it is in the production system. Operational efficiency focuses the attention of management on increasing the productivity of workers and machines; emphasis on process efficiency focuses attention on activities that absorb unproductive time. The Japanese focus on process engineering—the reduction of time required to move materials from plant entry to plant exit; the time required to transform new product ideas into products. Long runs tend to be operationally efficient but process inefficient. Short runs enhance process efficiency by reducing the time that materials are stored and leveling out production runs. The barrier to short runs is changeover. Long runs minimize changeovers.

The Japanese minimize changeover times to allow small batches to be run with minimal interference, in minutes rather than hours. JIT depends on and is a consequence of flexible production based on short runs and changeover times. Machine breakdown becomes an opportunity for improvement in the process; the worker becomes an active force in the continuous upgrading of the productive system. Teamwork and cooperation between team members are emphasized in a Japanese factory.

For the *kanban* system to function smoothly, the production steps must be tied closely together. The process layout must be like a tree and its root system, in which final assembly is the trunk and subassembly and fabrication flow smoothly into the trunk like roots. Balance must be achieved. Changeover time must be kept to an absolute minimum. This is a pull system whereupon the production schedule results in material being pulled into final assembly. The MRP (Material Resource Planning) systems that predominate in the West are push systems, in which the computer as master scheduler determines the production schedule based on forecasts and availability of parts. The key elements of the *kanban* are small batch sizes, reduced material handling, level scheduling, low inventory levels, and production control by *kanban* cards. These enhance the productivity and performance of a factory. The factory is becoming an environment of ongoing experimentation and continuous innovation, a place where new ideas and concepts are tested and actualized. Factory workers and technicians are constantly consulted about the ability to produce with the new technology, and they suggest how to upgrade and improve both the quality of the technology and the manufacturing process. Continuous involvement and interaction leads to continuous improvement.

Total process efficiency in production results in low overhead and bureaucracy, low total costs, high production flexibility, elimination of waste, low inventory carrying costs, greater variety at lower costs, integration of thinking and doing, continual process improvement, high utilization of and investment in worker skills, sense of community, optimum quality, and high labor productivity. This results in continual improvements, eventual technological superiority, integration of innovation and superiority, low costs and short cycle times, better fulfillment of customer wants and needs, frequent process innovations, and mutually beneficial relationships with other firms. However, a lack of breakthrough innovations is also a result as is a demanding, stressful environment.

In manufacturing technologies, Japan leads the world with a highly efficient two-tiered production process: process automation and factory automation. The reasons are the key to this are that Japanese companies are typically very quick when it comes to introducing new machinery. Factory workers, engineers, and accountants are flexible when it comes to change. The Japanese have responded quickly in establishing economies of scale. The introduction of computers in Japanese factories has been rapid, and excellent uses have been made of them. In addition, Japan has 5,000 technical workers for each million people, compared to 3,500 for the United States and 2,500 for Germany.

Much of the Japanese advantage in quality stems from successful management of the production process. Strict control limits have been established using statistical techniques that handle damage, worker inexperience, and other sources of variability. Large numbers of inspectors monitor the process and report on unexpected deviations; quality information is widely distributed; and quality control centers are given the authority to analyze and address quality problems. The result is a tightly controlled manufacturing process with few defects stemming from process-related problems. Japanese quality departments serve mainly as coordinators, consultants, and information clearinghouses, processing and interpreting quality data for other groups within the company. The final responsibility for quality is the worker. In addition, Japanese firms are now moving from total quality management to zero defects management. More obsessed than ever before with quality, Japanese auto companies are proceeding aggressively from *atarimae hinshitsu* (quality that is taken for granted) to *miryokuteki hinshitsu*, quality that fascinates.

QFD (Quality, Functionality, Dependability), is an approach pioneered by two Japanese scholars (Professor Yoji Akao of Tamagawa University and the late Shigeru Mizuno) in the 1970s (derived from the joint efforts of Bridgestone Tire and Mitsubishi Heavy Industries) and is the next buzzword and level in the quality chain. With QFD, designers use a detailed matrix (House of Quality) to help them take account of consumers needs and wants. On the left hand side, designers list every market expectation they can identify; this information is drawn from salespeople, market research, and customer interviews. Each of the general features then is broken down into more specific requirements and then split into even more exact ones. Each requirement is ranked in order of importance, and the completed list represents the product's true quality because it represents what consumers really want. Across the top of the grid, designers list every conceivable product characteristic. At points on the grid where the vertical and horizontal features intersect, the developers assign a degree of correlation between the market need and the product characteristic. The completed chart provides supposedly foolproof guidelines that designers can use to develop the most appropriate product.

Mass customization is the ability to offer highly responsive and flexible production methods, and thus to offer potentially millions of variants which differ and which can be ordered one at a time. Japan, with its flexible manufacturing systems, has begun to work on this new phenomenon. This joins cost leadership with differentiation. The Japanese stand to gain the most from the rapid introduction of customized, mass market products. Their well-developed subcontractor relationships and *keiretsu* networks, which link sales, assembly, component, and raw material suppliers, will be even more potent sources of advantage when flexibility and variability are extended back into manufacturing (Westbrook and Williamson, 1993). Mass customization calls for flexibility and quick responsiveness. In an ever-changing environment, people, processes, units, and technology reconfigure to give customers exactly what they want. Managers coordinate independent, capable individuals, and an efficient linkage system is crucial for low-cost, high-quality customized goods and services. Mass customization involves seeking the wants and needs of individual customers, reducing product development and life cycles, fragmenting market homogeneity, and using the new processes. To do so, processes must be able to be linked together as quickly as possible; linkage systems must add as little as possible to the cost of making the product or service; and everything must work together well; with no friction because there is no time for team-building efforts.

Suggestion systems are a formal mechanism used to harness workers' knowledge in Japan. Toyota's suggestion program yielded nearly thirty-three suggestions per worker in 1982. Nearly two thirds of all Japanese employees submit suggestions for increasing efficiency, reducing costs, or improving morale, in contrast to only 8 percent of Americans. Japanese employees submit nearly twenty-five suggestions per year on average, versus 1.3 suggestions in the United States. Japanese companies accept some 80 percent of their employee suggestions versus the American adoption rate of 25 percent. Although suggestions are not mandatory for Toyota personnel, workers who do not contribute are criticized and may receive smaller bonuses. Of the number provided, how many are trivial suggestions provided by workers to appease management?

The new era of flexible specialization in manufacturing entails the transformation of traditional mass production by information technology, which results in less labor-intensive, more efficient production processes and makes it easier to switch workers around. When automation is used to produce small batches of specialized products, greater worker intervention and skill are required (Kennedy and Florida, 1989). Team performance is crucial as well as increased flexibility. In Japan, work teams, job rotation, learning-by-doing, and flexibility replace the functional specialization, task fragmentation, and rigid assembly line production of Fordism. Job tenure as in the lifetime employment system, provides high incentives for workers not to resist automation and work redesign. Since job protection is no longer an issue and wages are largely based on seniority, there is less need for an elaborate job classification system. Rotation can be be used to upgrade skills and increase interaction and information transfer among workers. Because employees stay with one company until retirement, investments in human capital have long amortization periods and remain internal to the enterprise. Wage determination through seniority allows workers' incomes to fluctuate with corporate performance through the size of the bonus.

Few job classifications exist in a Japanese company. The work rules overlap, and production is organized on the basis of teams. Workers can cover for each other and experiment with new allocations and machine configurations. Considerable shop floor learning exists, which results in increased productivity and reduced worker alienation. The Japanese worker has a broader view of the production process and is more integrated into the production system. The term for this is humanware. Learning-by-doing is an essential part of the Japanese employment process. *Kanban* (just-in-time) is used to squeeze more productive labor out of workers via increased technological efficiency, minimal scrap or rework, and decreased inventory. This system allows massive use of information technology to transform traditional manufacturing. A linkage of innovation to production is part of the process and provides new ways of organizing demand and channeling consumption.

New manufacturing techniques, such as flexible manufacturing systems, mean that flexible machinery are merely reprogrammed, not replaced, when a factory is switched over to a new product. Flexible manufacturing systems (FMS) in Japan are complemented with significant worker reskilling. FMS requires development of higher precision in mechanical technology, the electronic revolution (microprocessors), robot technology, and quality control technology. Only when all four were present did FMS take off. The reason FMS has been applied so successfully in Japan is that the Japanese industry urgently needed and was looking for a means of small batch production of a diversified range of products. Small companies are bound by contracts to producing a wide range of products in small batches. This spurred the development of FMS. FMS incorporates process accuracy, quality control, reliability, maintenance, and worker skill requirements.

KEIRETSU CONTRACTING

In Japan, many large companies, like Toyota, have uniquely tight relationships with suppliers and subcontractors that make up their horizontal *keiretsu*. People, cost data, and technology move freely among these companies and their suppliers, so products can be developed and put on the market faster and more cheaply. Japanese manufacturers share plans with suppliers and hand over proprietary know-how. The big firms also use this arrangement to their advantage to bludgeon suppliers into meeting difficult target costs.

The Japanese supplier system is organized according to a pyramidal structure of first-tier, second-tier, third-tier, and up to tenth-tier suppliers surrounding a central hub company. The typical Japanese major company regards only a handful of its (usually no more than a dozen) suppliers as partners (first-tier suppliers) and assigns a more limited role to the rest. Most companies do not work with all their suppliers in free-flowing product teams but rather the companies structures their development programs tightly and use carefully considered targets (for price, delivery, performance, and space constraints) and prototypes to keep the lower tier suppliers in line. The elite first-tier suppliers coordinate the activities of the second tier, the second tier coordinates the third tier, and so on down the hierarchy (Kamath and Liker, 1994).

The core company structures linkages and coordinate flows within this network of producers. Suppliers are located close to the assemblers, interact constantly with them, and are frequently partly owned by them. The core company delegates out much of the work. In Japan, as much as 70 percent of the components are provided by loyal suppliers. This allows the core company to remain strong in good times and bad; during recessions, any layoffs will either take place in the tier suppliers or personnel will be reassigned to the supplier companies. Toyota and its Toyota City production complex provides the classic example: In 1980, Toyota controlled ten important subsidiaries and 220 primary subcontractors, 80 percent of which had plants within the production complex. These were served by 5,000 secondary subcontractors and approximately 30,000 tertiary subcontractors. The Japanese subcontracting system allows the parent firms to reduce both costs and risk by developing a hierarchy of production. Often the large parent core companies apply not-so-gentle pressure to coerce their suppliers to innovate, cut prices, and share proprietary data, information, and technology with one another for the benefit of the entire complex (i.e., the core firm). Because of the *keiretsu* relationships between manufacturers and contractors, pressure can be brought to bear on the subcontractors to meet the cost target.

Japanese manufacturing is remarkable for its high proportion of small and medium-sized firms; in 1982 these accounted for 99.4 percent of all manufacturing establishments, 81.4 percent of all employees, and over half of all shipments. When a subcontractor accepts its first contract, probably from a small subsidiary of one of the giant companies, it gives up its freedom. It is told what product to make, when to put it on line, and what price it will get on delivery. If the company that placed the order feels a profit squeeze, it can easily order the subcontractor to reduce its final price. If hard times continue, the larger company can demand another cut. If the subcontractor loses money on each unit it produces and already has cut expenses and streamlined production, the parent company could require the subcontractor to buy a new piece of equipment to increase productivity, even if the subcontractor does not need or want the equipment. If it refuses, the flow of orders from the parent companies will dry up overnight and its business will be gone (Sasaki, 1990).

Supplier networks are made up of autonomous firms that gathered around the lead manufacturer's plants. Proximity brings many benefits, including shorter delivery time, lower inventory carrying costs, lower transportation costs, and improved communications. Each supplier knows that it cannot survive on its own; its survival is a function of how well it can coexist with others within the network. A company's new product development project benefits from the existence of an interrelated group of specialized suppliers and its network. A supplier network facilitates learning. Nonetheless, numerous drawbacks exist. Most subcontracts are small and within walking distance of each other's factories. These subcontractors are almost wholly dependent on the firm and therefore, by necessity, extremely responsive. The larger Japanese companies will make certain that their smaller suppliers remain in business but sometimes at a minimal profit.

A dual pay and benefits structure exists between first-tier and lower order firms: The differential between firms with over 1,000 workers and those with between ten and twenty-nine is on the order of 100:60, even within the same industry (Dore, 1989). From the employee's point of view, a lifetime employment system implies a considerable restriction of freedom of choice. In an individualistic society, such long-term commitments are more likely seen as a surrender of desirable freedom than as a gain in security and sense of belonging. Mobility is good for an economy because it diffuses knowledge and acts as a means of adjustment (Dore, 1989). The Japanese supplier network provides manufacturers with substantial advantages in product and process development as well as in production itself.

Kyoryokukai are formal associations of cooperative part makers, informal understandings, and shared network norms. The lead manufacturer becomes the legitimate leader, and the cooperative suppliers are support system. Japanese automakers deal with few part makers: 100 to 300 versus thousands. Toyota deals with 300 component suppliers, which in turn deal with 5,000 second tier suppliers, which in turn coordinate 20,000 third- and fourth-tier suppliers. Smaller contacts mean more intimate personal contact and relationships.

The suppliers to a large Japanese company know that there is a small window of opportunity in the concept stage, before the release of specifications when it can suggest new technology and try to introduce new methods. Outside that window, suppliers must focus their overall efforts on incremental cost savings improvements that will not involved the redesign of parts. If a technological breakthrough occurs at a time that does not coincide with one of these windows, the supplier must simply wait until the next window comes along—the next model change. It is a highly structured and routine product development process. Japanese suppliers know exactly where they fit in and when; this arrangement allows them to be innovative and creative without being disruptive (Kamath and Liker, 1994).

CULTURAL RATIONALE

The reason so few defects in Japanese products exist and that breakdowns are so rare is that Japanese companies regard such problems as a matter of shame, reflecting on company honor. Not only top management, but department and section heads as well feel an extremely strong sense of responsibility for the quality of products they turn out. In Japanese society, everyone is part of a group. What the Japanese detest more than anything else is to have members of their group criticize them behind their back. As a result, casual acceptance of defective merchandise or faulty products is out of the question. This strong Japanese dislike of defective goods also comes from the fastidiousness which is part of their Japanese character. The slightest blemish makes them uneasy, and they naturally aim for perfection. Breakdowns of just-invented products are unacceptable. Industrial products were conceived in the West and entered Japan only after they had reached a state of relative perfection. When breakdowns do occur, complaints are made directly to the manufacturer. The manufacturer must jump to repair the defective merchandise at once. Thus manufacturers do everything in their power to produce sound and reliable goods. If the service a company offers is no good, customers will simply stop buying its products.

Kaizen works because of the structural and social changes it brings about in factory work. Workers are no longer viewed as either operators or nonoperators. Both roles are combined, and workers become producers and monitors of production at the same time. They are doers, information collectors, analyzers, and change agents all rolled into one. In Japan, even the top engineer goes to the production line to learn from the manufacturing process. The Japanese tend to be assigned their jobs as part of a company job rotation plan. Japanese are sent to research, design, development, production, and marketing more frequently than Americans and thus, develop breadth. Americans play poker; Japanese play chess. Americans calculate probabilities and risk, but Japanese apply tried-and-true general rules to most situations. Japanese executives resist creative leaps to new but risky ideas. Like chess masters, they have a repertoire of moves and choose from them.

FASTER PRODUCT DEVELOPMENT

Japanese corporations are attempting to bring out a new product in half the time it takes their American competitors to do so and in one third the time it takes Europeans. They are trying to do this by reorganizing their R&D so that a single team of engineers, scientists, marketers, and manufacturers works simultaneously at the three levels of innovation and simultaneously produces three new products. They do this by starting out with a deadline for abandoning today's new product on the very day it is first sold—creative obsolescence with a vengeance. At the lowest level, they seek incremental improvements of an exciting product—*kaizen*—process improvement, whereupon the corporation's employees work on improvement of the product with specific goals and deadlines (e.g.,10 percent cost reduction within fifteen months).

The second track is leaping—developing a new product out of the old, trying for a significant jump, such as Sony's move from the microtape recorder to the Walkman. The third track is genuine innovation. It is the Japanese corporation's goal to pursue all three tracks simultaneously and under the direction of the same cross-functional team. The idea is to produce three new products that will replace each present product with the same investment of time and money, with one of the three then becoming the new market leader and producing the innovator's profit. In Japan, operators themselves rather than the engineer take the initiative in studying the task, organizing the work, and creating the needed tools by using computer simulation. Sony Chairman Akio Morita argues that whereas American companies struggle to create a vision for the next quarter, Japanese companies have a vision for the next decade.

This overlapping product approach has its merits and faults. Advantages include faster development, increased flexibility, and information sharing. On the other hand, the burden of managing the process increases exponentially. This amplifies ambiguity, tension, and conflict within the group. The burden to coordinate the intake and dissemination of information also increases, as does management's responsibility to carry out ad hoc and intensive on-the-job training. This approach requires extensive social interaction on the part of all involved in the project as well as the existence of a cooperative network with suppliers. Mutual exchange and openness about information work to enhance flexibility. This creates linkages between people in different functions and between different firms by a commitment to joint partnership.

Japan's traditional approach to product development and testing and market research was to make the products, get them to market, and watch which succeeded and which failed. Japanese companies view new product development as a trial-and-error process (learning-by-doing) and resort to a considerably looser format of phase management. Product development is undertaken by a team of nonexperts (generalists). Everyone participating in the development process is engaged in learning. Product development in Japan also acts as a change agent for reshaping corporate culture.

For example, Japan's electronics supermart in Tokyo's Akihabara District has hundreds of small shops stocking hundreds of latest models. At a typical electronics store in Tokyo, consumers can choose from more than 250 varieties of Sony Walkman-type products, and almost as many coffee makers. Old models often less than one year old sell for discounts of between 30 and 50 percent. This is how manufacturers experiment. The winners will be sold nationally and then internationally, and the losers will be withdrawn from the market. This has created a tough proving ground for new products, and only the best make it to the American market. This is a testimony to the ability of the Japanese to produce endless varieties of products with breakneck speed.

This supply of products has flowed continuously for nearly forty years, with new features and new designs appearing (and disappearing) daily. Japanese companies typically first launch a product that is good but which is one or more iteration away from gaining full customer acceptance. In high tech, by introducing new products before the learning process is complete on the technology of the preceding innovations, new devices drive their predecessors completely out of the market within six years of introduction. The rate of return has become obsolete as a decision-making tool for many Japanese companies. Merely to stay in the game for one more round, companies must continue to invest and invest heavily. It becomes a game of chicken as all stay in and continually raise the ante as they mutually head for oblivion.

Japanese companies have a tendency to pursue every strategy to the maximum, and every company pursues the same strategy at the same time. No company therefore gains permanent advantage against its domestic competitors. Historically, Japanese companies have been notoriously poor marketers. They substituted a scattershot approach to production for the hard work of marketing. A Japanese company would develop a line of products, throw it against the wall and see what stuck, drop the losers, push the winners and look like a great marketer. As long as cheap money existed and consumers abounded, it made little difference.

Time-based competition emerged in Japan during the 1980s. Speed became essential and was pursued as an end in itself. Time to market, new product development time, time elapsed between order and cash, and real-time customer responsiveness became critical as measures of a company's performance versus competitors. Time defined a new way to practice. The Japanese took this to heart. However, a dark side to time exists. Time became a trap, a strategic treadmill on which companies were caught, condemned to run faster and faster but always staying in the same place competitively. Companies had to commit more and more human and financial capital at an ever-increasing pace to bring out more and more varieties of products, without any prospect of achieving competitive advantage, higher margins, or more attractive profits. Managers and workers were therefore exhausted by the relentless pace. The cycle became self-destructive. Supply flowed continuously, with new features and new designs appearing almost daily. But it is not profitable. As a result of this constant battle with time, neither manufacturers nor retailers make much money.

The Japanese companies interpreted time-based competition to mean speed, but speed unconnected to any strategic purpose. Faster and faster they brought out new products, but never connected to customers or workers. Time compression does yield cost reductions and quality improvements and frees up valuable human and capital resources. This can become addicting if companies push it to the limit. The capabilities of time-based competitors enabled them to produce smaller and smaller gradations of innovation, which were launched faster and faster in the market. By doing so, they failed to invest the time and energy in searching for new ways of doing business with customers.

In the scenario when all competitors are using time-based manufacturing, no single company makes money. If all companies are time-based, then time becomes a commodity that offers no advantages and no differential performance. Japanese companies acting in near lock-step unison have achieved uniform variety and as a result, have incurred the costs of the time-based competition without the benefits of differentiation (and the higher margins that come with it). They took a strategy based on variety and made it produce commodities. They have relentlessly pursued the use of time as a source of competitive advantage, but with every company following the same strategy, thereby nullifying any advantage for any one company. A strategic tool designed to create differentiation through increased variety has reduced everything to a commodity. This approach has produced efficiency, but efficiency does not meet or create needs for any customers. By translating time-based competition into an internal exercise designed purely to streamline the company's operations, the Japanese have lost sight of the real value of competing on time. This creates a closer, tighter feedback loop between the company's customers and the company's employees. Used correctly, time-based competition can erode the boundary between the external and internal environment and bring customers' needs and wants and companies' capabilities and offerings into closer, more immediate contact.

As a result of just recently recognizing the dark side of time-based competition (in the early 1990s), Japanese automakers announced that they were stretching out their new product introduction cycle from four to five years and cutting back on the variety of their offerings. Consumer electronic firms began eliminating dozens of models of VCRs, televisions, and fax machines. Kao trimmed its product line from over 600 to less than 550, whereas its main rival Lion announced plans to reduce its product lineup by 30 percent. Nissan at its zenith used 110 different radiators and over 300 types of ashtrays. As its small subcontractors tooled up to produce ever tinier lots, their break-even points rose. As a result, they suffered huge diseconomies of scale. Now that the Japanese carmakers' sales have fallen, the Japanese are paring part variations by 30 to 40 percent. In either case (too many or too few versions), the firms hurt the most will be the small subcontractors. Many companies are reducing variety to the 20 percent of models and product variations that generate 80 percent of their sales and profits.

The "lean" and fast approach favored by Japanese firms in the eighties have yielded in the nineties as the limits of "lean" were reached. A true JIT (*kanban*) system can only work in theory if suppliers are geographically proximate. It does not work well in congested urban areas. With the spread of plants to the other islands in Japan, throughout Asia, Europe, and the Americas, rethinking of the kanban concept is mandated. Cooperative and reliable suppliers and cooperative and skilled blue collar workers are also required for the system to work. As Japanese companies are forced to accept more parts from non-Japanese firms, the nature of this relationship necessarily changes. Demographic changes at home in Japan have led to blue-collar worker shortages as there are not enough young Japanese men (women are still not permitted to work in most Japanese assembly plants) interested in such low occupations, let alone motivated and cooperative as required in the "lean" approach. And lastly, the cost of new model development and model replacement has become apparent now that money is expensive in Japan (Cusumano, 1994).

In the future, one can expect longer product life cycles and a more carefully planned product development cycle as the dark side of time-based competition becomes evident and international competition comes to domestic Japan. The other constraint to product development is the soaring cost of doing leading-edge research. Each generation of technological advance raises significantly the ante for a company to continue in the industry. To develop the next-generation chipmaking method, which will use X-rays instead of lithography to print circuit patterns on silicon, IBM alone is spending nearly half a billion dollars. The number of entrants decrease in each cycle as the ante keeps climbing.

Therefore, the Japanese approach to product development has numerous limitations (Imai, 1992a) including the following:

1. It requires an extraordinary effort on the part of all project members; 80-hour weeks are not uncommon.
2. It may not apply to breakthrough projects.
3. It may not apply to mammoth projects, in which extensive face-to-face interactions are limited by the sheer scale of the project.

Chapter 6

Cultural Reasons for Japanese Innovation Styles

RICE AS A CULTURAL ORIGIN

The Japanese climate is warm and humid and its geography is characterized by steep mountain ridges enclosing narrow plains. Such terrain is not suited to herding but to paddy-based rice cultivation. Rice has dominated Japanese history and civilization, so much so that the Japanese word for rice is also the same symbol as for food. Flooded-field cultivation exploits the nutrients carried by waters, so fields can be cultivated year after year and harvest yields are high. Such cultivation is extremely labor intensive: The field must be leveled so it can be flooded, slopes must be terraced, and channels must be built and maintained. In a village, there are two times of year when rice farmers desperately needs help: when the rice seedlings are transplanted to the fields in late spring, and again in the fall for the harvest. They depend on the cooperation of their village and neighbors. Without that cooperation, they are ruined. So they must strive to maintain positive relations with everyone around them.

The continuation and success of an irrigated wet-rice growing culture has had a long-term effect on the Japanese social system and lifestyle—patience, perseverance, diligence, cooperation, passivity, conservative, fatalism, energetic, courageous, self-reliant, tenacious, patient, humble, and law-abiding—because this kind of farming required elaborate irrigation systems that could not be easily built and maintained or protected by single families; communities had to work together in large units in order to survive. Through centuries of agrarian experience, the Japanese have developed customs of mutual help, collective coordination, risk sharing, and flexible adaption to continual and incremental environmental changes. The two Japanese gift giving seasons stem from the practice of offering gifts to fellow villagers who have helped with the rice crop, to thank them for their help and to ensure that they will help again. This communal living, working together diligently, and group loyalty instilled in the Japanese a spirit of cooperation, acceptance of discipline and regimentation, for one could hardly survive without group membership. These characteristics are now viewed as characteristics of modern Japanese factory life. In this society, the individual hardly exists as a distinct entity: in almost every aspect of life, the individual is tightly bound to a group and is allowed few primate emotions and virtually no freedom for individual action. The group imposed the norms of conduct on the individual, whose lot is to conform. The individual who does not conform is quickly ostracized to protect and sustain the group.

Cultivating rice fields, families tended to stay together and perpetuate themselves for generations. The entire settlement took on characteristics of one large family. Intimacy has evolved from the dictates of collective farming—little available land space and the need to construct homes that offered little privacy. Several aspects of village tradition are still evident in Japanese culture: leisurely and task-oriented teamwork, which grew out of planting, cultivating, and harvesting rice; consensus decision; and equality among coworkers and members of the organizational family. The process of rice farming was prescribed down to the last detail. This has evolved into present-day *kata*, the institutionalized processes of everyday Japanese society that prescribe practically one's entire existence in minute detail.

Ningen kankei, human relations, is at the heart of the Japanese society. Commonality is a large component of *ningen kankei*. It is therefore not surprising that the history of common experiences or associations is also the foundation of business dealings in Japan: a shared childhood, high school, or college classmates; growing up in the same neighborhood, hometown, or prefecture; working in the same company or group, or being in the same sports club are all bonding elements. These ties are essential in building business relationships in Japan, and few foreigners can share them. For the Japanese, death is preferable to going against the expressed wishes of the group. Falling out of favor with the villagers meant that one would not survive; as a result, in modern-day Japan, the Japanese are discouraged against going against the group's wishes.

Japan is a non-consanguineous society (i.e., people who are not related by ties of blood can form bonds as strong as those only formed between blood relatives in the consanguineous societies of the West).

The traditional Confucian values of loyalty and commitment can be found in large Japanese companies, which in a sense are similar to tribes. Members accept the authority of their leaders, who in return protect the member and the member's family. Members work together willingly to strengthen their household. The Japanese language, with its military-like recognition of rank and hierarchy, smooths the interpersonal barriers which exists to communication (Campbell, 1985). Thus loyalty and commitment to one's firm is the norm in Japan. Job security and a feeling of belonging to the tribe (i.e., company) is important and creates a psychological as well as an economic bond between the employee and employer.

JAPANESE CULTURAL ATTRIBUTES

Collectivism

The group is the primary unit of social organization in Japan. An individual's social status is determined more by the standing of the group to which he or she belongs than by his or her individual performance. In traditional Japanese society, the group was the family or village; today, the group is the work team or business organization to which an individual belongs. This relationship often evolves into a deeply emotional attachment in which identification with the group becomes all important in one's life. Strong identification with the group creates pressures for mutual self-help and collective action; if the worth of the individual is closely linked to the achievements of the group (the firm in Japan), a strong incentive is created for the individual members of the group to work together for the common good. This ability to cooperate is apparent in the widespread utilization of self-managing work teams within Japanese organizations. Cooperation is driven by the desire to improve the performance of the group to which individuals belong.

In Japan, when something goes wrong, the person in charge takes the blame. In the United States, decision making is centralized and responsibility is diffused; in Japan, decision making is diffused and responsibility is concentrated. The level of competitiveness that individual Japanese may show often surprises Westerners. Even when alone, Japanese employees know that they have their group behind them, and this group support seems to propel them forward with unbelievable energy. In Japan, one of the highest goals in life is to be able to contribute to the group against the group's competition. If individuals do not measure up in terms of putting the group first, maintaining harmony, and demonstrating a fighting spirit on behalf of the group and company, no matter how hard they may actually work or how talented they are, they will receive low marks, which will likely result in their being outside the mainstream of their company.

In Japan, corporate success and company goals are achieved through the result of group effort and not through the exceptional activities of individuals. Ideally, there are no production heroes in a large company. Instead, there are workers whose work groups, teams, or departments have improved their productivity and have excelled beyond their quotas. Sacrificing one's personal life for the good of the company is expected. This often results in giving up accrued vacation time or controlling one's inclination to confront others for the sake of maintaining harmony (Rosenberg, 1986). *Tatemae* (face, or facade) is a term used by the Japanese in reference to masking one's own thoughts or intentions. *Honne* means the honest voice, the real intentions, one's personal feelings or beliefs. These contrasting principles are used to cloak the truth or reality of situations that might be inconvenient or embarrassing to acknowledge publicly.

Competition is not between individuals but between groups, and it can be extremely fierce. The Japanese are integrated mentally, based on the principle of interdependence in both formal and informal human relations. What motivates members is not an economic contract. They have a tacit agreement to cooperate interdependently. They feel strongly that they belong to the community and come to have a sense of solidarity only when they work at the same jobsite or in the same company. Individual employees in a given Japanese firm may be likened to individual players in a volleyball team competing against another team. Each individual's position and expected role at any given point is determined and understood by his or her teammates. The team's overriding goal is to beat the opponent according to the rules of the game. To attain this shared goal, individuals are encouraged to exercise discretion and to deal with emergencies. When the team wins, the victory belongs to everyone. The size of the team is small enough to permit intimate face-to-face communication among team members. Although individuals are expected to develop their own expertise and special plays, they rotate not only the server's role but also the defense positions. By practicing together and by sharing both personal and team lives, the members get to know one another so well that their mode of communication takes on implicit phrases and expressions, rather than explicit verbal discussions (Tsurumi, 1976). In Japan, it is the non-verbal, the implicit, how something is said, that is more important than the verbal, what is said.

Japan is like a group of people on a train. Everyone goes in the same direction. The train cannot stop for one person. The United States is analogous to the automobile: when one wants to stop, one does so. In Japan, no amount of individual sacrifice is too great for sake of the family or nation-state (as shown by the ultimate sacrifice of their lives by thousands of *kamikaze* pilots during the final stages of the Second World War). *Kojin shugi,* the Japanese word for individualism, has negative connotations and traditionally has been equated with selfishness. In Japanese society, it is considered brash for an individual to make decisions or even to urge the acceptance of an individual opinion. The individual Japanese tends to be not an autonomous whole but a fraction of the whole. Group welfare and security has been and still is considered more important than individual welfare and autonomy.

Groups are held together by two means: a natural feeling of solidarity between group members and internal organization. The solidarity between group members is emotionally based and carries with it an us versus them attitude. It becomes difficult for the group members to transcend the group and act individually. Social groups demand exclusive allegiance from their members, and individuals must be primarily absorbed in the group from which they derive a livelihood. The emphasis is on vertical rather than horizontal structures. Strong departmentalism constructed along vertical lines is latent in all social groups and shapes not only attitudes and behaviors but overshadows everything. This is most prevalent in large, older, and more stable Japanese groups. In such groups, all group members are collectively responsible for each other's actions. All members therefore can be punished for the transgressions of any one member. This creates a family consciousness and fanatical loyalty to the group, a high degree of passivity, and the tendency to move as groups in unison. In Japan, it would not be an understatement to say that an individual who is not a member of a recognized group literally does not exist.

In Japan, an individual is also an integral part of the environments of all others as well. This results in the doctrine of shared responsibility: All groups members are responsible for all of the group's actions; there is permissiveness toward others' failures, a stress on group harmony, a preference for shared common feelings, and a strong loyalty to the group. A Japanese person draws sanction for his or her acts from the approval of the community, his or her participation in it, or from his or her ancestors. (Buddhism, as adopted by the Japanese holds that everything in the universe has life, every living thing follows a path of cyclical existence and all are interdependent. The natural law of cause and effect holds and a person's life descends from and is influenced by all of his or her ancestors' doings.) Ostracism— *mura hachibu*—is the worst possible fate for a Japanese. The *ronin* (masterless samurai) was a sad fate, signifying a man who had lost his feudal leader. The Japanese story of forty *ronin* is not a story of one man's popularity but of forty men fulfilling a feudal duty. This groupism often leads to the inability of Japanese to think of themselves apart from their particular group. Most Japanese have abandoned their efforts to express themselves as individuals since most organizations are much too solidly organized to permit single persons to express their individuality.

One reason for Japanese collectivism in organizations is the cooperative nature of the Japanese decision-making process. A general consensus is emphasized. This may mean that the most creative and rational ideas are sometimes rejected to pursue a general consensus and maintain group harmony. Any sign of superior ability provokes negative behavior. Conformity is demanded in Japan; one is supposed to think and act alike and be equal in ability. The more able are expected to behave as if they were no more talented than others. One does not want to be singled out from other members of one's group. The Japanese hesitate to change conservative ways of thinking and management or to adopt improvements which make rapid progress from traditional ways. The tendency is to choose conservative- and compromise-oriented plans (Watanabe, 1987). Taken to the ultimate, the tendency is to choose the mediocre man as the leader because he will not create envy or upset the *wa* (harmony) of the group.

The Japanese value motivation more than ability as a precursor to success. Good employees are diligent; if they are diligent they will develop as a person. If they develop as a person, they will help the company be successful. Good employees work hard to cooperate with others. Their group's success is the individual's success. The primary concern is to maintain good personal relations (harmony) first and then solve problems later. The person responsible is not simply an individual but a member and a representative of a group and system; it is this group harmony which has priority over all other issues and is paramount in any problem's solution. The Japanese value system includes an absolute obsession to avoid bringing shame to themselves, to their families, to their company, to their immediate work group, or to Japan itself. Nothing must ever be done which will cause disgrace and tarnish the reputation of oneself or of others. A culture of shame implies a society in which the esteem of others and cohesion of the group are the criteria for one's behavior.

Japan can be characterized as collectivist in comparison to other industrialized countries but as individualist in comparison to other Asian and Third World countries. Countries with an individualism score below Japan are developing or undeveloped countries whereas those above are industrialized, rich countries. Evidence exists that individualism increases when wealth increases. However, one must note that Japanese capitalism was fostered by the state and did not arise from individual initiative and competition, as in Great Britain and the United States. Japanese society is built on lineal families, not extended families, as in China; younger sons have to leave the parental home and are forced into other activities, which makes Japanese society considerably more dynamic than Asiatic societies based on expandable, extended families.

In Japanese group psychology, social groups control the ethical behavior of their members, with the individual ignoring his or her own ethical impulses for the sake of the group. Society is viewed as comprised of three tiers: the inner circle, the outer circle, and those with which you have no relationship at all. Superiors do not give orders, but their subordinates are sensitive enough to understand exactly what they want and act accordingly. In this relationship, no room exists for an individual to express his or her own personal feelings or lifestyle. All employees are forced to share the same set of attitudes and values. Everyone believes that the development of the corporation is for the social good, and the accomplishment of the work of the company is a goal of society. If something is for the good of the corporation, one can ignore the expectations of others outside the company and even break laws, if necessary, to achieve one's goals. Work is a sufficient excuse to ignore family. Everything is evaluated in terms of whether it is good or bad for the company community. To be a good employee, one must belong only to the workplace.

Competition between groups is valued as a means of encouraging unaniminity of effort within the group. Responsibility is diffused within the group; each group member shares the responsibility of every other member. The emphasis is not on mobility but is on maintaining one's own personal relations. Fear of isolation leads to a conservatism which dislikes change and avoids initiatives. The Japanese are often resigned to irresistible realities. Life is conducted without independent thought and is accompanied by a deferment to the status quo. Maximum individual freedom is obtained when a Japanese is very young (a time of no shame) or very old (a time when obligations to society are small or none). Personal relations are characterized by a deep-felt need to be nurtured in a sympathetic, understanding, and harmonious environment and an outward fear of incurring or creating unnecessary obligations. A preference exists for protection provided by a group. Friendships within the group are marked by high emotional content and extend into private lives. The work ethic is characterized by perseverance, discipline, and curiosity. Obligations arise from a worker's decision to take on the work.

The desire for peer approval encourages a group orientation and thus the downward dispersion of authority. In effect, Japanese society has become optimized for standardized mass production. This has enabled Japan to achieve the world's highest levels of manufacturing prowess and competitiveness in its mass production industries. In technology fields like aerospace, which produce complex products in small volumes, and in the information and distribution industries, the labor rigidity and group orientation of Japanese-style management are at the very least a disadvantage because these fields require rapid decisions and diverse creativity. Another reason which may explain Japan's weakness in basic research is a national character trait that shuts out anyone with a marked individuality in favor of a bland groupie person. This philosophy is well suited for manufacturing but not for research. Whereas the Japanese attach supreme importance to production, they accord research less status. Members of a group must cooperate with and trust each other.

One must sometimes subordinate the truth to maintain group harmony. The group's survival is keyed to long-term behavior and hence, once accepted, it is for life. The power of the group is immense, since as soon as an individual is rejected by a group, he or she loses social identity. Promotion of group harmony means that one's individuality and originality must be subdued. The Japanese have a saying that "a nail sticking up is meant to be hammered down," which means that being different is frowned on and is therefore to be avoided whenever possible. The Japanese find themselves bound in a web of obligations and debts that affects their every action. The Japanese are forever in debt to parents and this debt extends to all who have done you any favors, from teachers to society in general. The Japanese take these debts seriously and cannot act without considering the implications of their actions on those who are owed. Success for the Japanese individual is viewed as flowing from the kindness and cooperation of many other people.

In the networks of large numbers of mutual dependents, one cannot conceptually differentiate the self or ego from others. The self merges into the totality of mutual dependence. One always needs to justify one's existence on the grounds of some type of social unit—the nation, a company, a family. This becomes the existence of the individual, who is dependent on the existence of the totality. No concept of a private domain exists in Japanese society. The social attitude which enables individual members of a private company to see themselves as members of the same clan also motivates management and financial backers to see their company in the same light. This attitude is rooted in Buddhist philosophy and produces a tendency to regard broader human relations in the context of quasi-blood relationships, so that senior members of a company have a quasi-parental relationship with the other employees.

In Japan, the employees of a company have formed a team which acts as a united body in competition against teams from other companies; successful companies distribute the profit gained to all members of the team in the form of a bonus. The national spirit also is strong, with employees of companies constituting a national team of Japanese industry in competition with their foreign rivals as a single united body. The Japanese emphasize consensus as the source of legitimacy in decision making; a decision isn't quite right until all agree. Certain accommodations must be made, conflict must be avoided, and when one cannot avoid it one must keep it personal rather than making it public. This repression of conflict makes agenda setting difficult. When whatever the group is doing does not seem to be working, people must edge warily toward a new consensus, eying each other all the time. First must come a general willingness to admit the old course's failure, and then the whole group must somehow find a new course that almost everyone is willing to follow. Often, the group will sit until action is forced. In the competitive arena, groups often rely on outside competitive selection systems to set the agenda; then they run with it (this explains the follower role, which dominates the Japanese style of innovation). A lack of emphasis on the profit motive tends to result; one's duty to nation and service in the private interest come first. Industrial paternalism, a seniority-based reward system, and lifetime employment result. Japanese organizational structure is defined in terms of groups of people and not in terms of individual positions. Responsibilities are defined only in general terms, with a view that tasks should be performed only through the cooperative efforts of the members of an organization.

One example of differences in culture is the importance attached to the group versus that to the individual: In Japan, the impulses and needs of the individual tend to be subordinated to the good of the group; in the United States, any intrusion by the group on the rights of the individual is regarded as unwarranted. In Japan, there is a concern for minimizing differences, preserving harmony, and reinforcing group loyalty; these customs are derived from ancient Japan, in which a nation short on resources but long on people required the participation of all its members in an orderly manner if survival were to result—hence a heavily collectivist tradition evolved. In the United States, the prevailing customs tend toward maximizing difference, confrontation, and compromise. This individualistic approach may be derived from the frontier days, when one's nearest neighbor was miles away and one had to be driven, self-oriented and individualistic. The aim of decision making in one is to avoid discord in pursuit of consensus, whereas in the other it is to promote competition among ideas in pursuit of objective truth. Despite equally pragmatic goals, decisions in Japan tend to be based on mood but in the United States on arguments. These are vastly different philosophies but are equally reasonable based on their own respective geographical limitations and history.

In Japan, it is unusual for an individual (alone or as part of an entrepreneurial team) to set out on his or her own, raise venture capital, and establish a new company. An individual who would leave an established company to start a new firm would be considered an eccentric and a social outcast in Japan, not a hero, as in America. In the Japanese culture, no role model equivalent to Horatio Alger or Steve Jobs (founder of Apple Computer) exists. The occasional Japanese entrepreneur succeeds not because of the system but despite it. The risk-taking entrepreneur in Japan has social pressures as well as financial obstacles on the way to success. It is risky to leave one's group, to dare to be different. The Japanese system appears to promote imitation and adoption of process innovations at the expense of radical innovations.

Wa

W a (harmony) tends to be result in nonconfrontational behavior, using ambiguity as a security device to avoid taking a weak position until a majority position emerges. The Japanese tend to view any threat to harmony as a matter of life and death and will do whatever is necessary to protect and maintain the *w a* of the group. The Japanese are obsessed with information gathering and endlessly asking for advice from experts and authority figures. The decision process in Japanese organizations, due to the consensus approach to management, is a long one, but the consequent advantages of such decisions enable fast and smooth implementation. This may not be conducive when thinking and decision by individual scientists and engineers is more desired.

A harmonious working atmosphere, in which workers are genuinely concerned about their company's welfare and the spirit of consensus, makes for efficient production and for effectiveness in some aspects of research and development. Innovation, however, in such a society as Japan's where individualism is not appreciated, tends to follow a linear rather than an interactive pattern. Too ready an acceptance of consensus can inhibit vigorous discussion and dissent. Japanese innovation has been most successful in linear development, when there have been agreed-on objectives to work for.

The Japanese differ because of pseudo-harmonism, eclecticism, and exceptionism. Pseudo-harmonism is the Japanese ability to agree to disagree. In the conduct of business, the Japanese can tolerate significant levels of latent conflict while maintaining a surface harmony. Eclecticism is the maintenance of harmony while keeping constantly attuned to economic costs and gains. Thus, rather than selecting any single course of action, the Japanese select, adapt, and blend toward a moderate solution. Exceptionism is the ability to make constant and frequent exceptions in marketing practice, which tends to make the Japanese flexible and adaptable (Lazer, Murata, and Kosaka, 1985).

The Japanese quest for freedom for individuals is subordinate to a prevailing societal emphasis on order and harmony. This leads to the much more intrusive role of government in Japan. Fierce competition exists between companies, but the competition is expected to remain within the context of harmony and national interest. The Japanese people view government as having the responsibility to ensure that companies operate within this context. Japan is highly regulated relative to the rest of the industrialized world: Over 24 percent of its industries are strongly regulated. Most of the regulations involve entry barriers or price controls. Mining, construction, finance, utilities, transportation, communications, and agriculture are almost completely regulated in an attempt to secure "fair" competition and protection of established firms through the creation of oligopoly conditions.

Order and harmony take precedence in Japanese organizations. The individual's behavior within and even outside the organization is specified in great detail. What is more important than an individual's performance is working together harmoniously to accomplish the goals of the collective. The purpose of the Japanese education system is to provide highly socialized and effective employees who can mesh well in a management structure molded to traditional Japanese values. A high level of conformity to specified patterns of behavior is expected, in everything from punctuality to exchanging greetings to seating and speaking order. Even after work hours, employees are expected to conform to stands of public conduct consistent with their membership and position in the organization.

Sincerity is another key concept in Japan: one should never deceive one's self or others, one is expected to promote harmony, to follow proper etiquette precisely, to adhere faithfully to all expected behavior, to take no actions that would result in others losing face, and to embrace actions that reflect the will and need of group. Japanese business managers believe that sincerity takes precedence over all other values, whereas Western managers consider fairness the most important value. Japanese baseball is an excellent example: In the Japanese version of the game, it is not how well you play but how well you train and how you play that is important, as well as whether you are sincere about trying to perform your best.

Konosuke Matsushita, widely regarded in Japan as the supreme master of the Way of *w a*, codified his *wa* approach to management in these seven objectives:

- •National service through industry
- •Harmony
- •Cooperation
- •Struggle for betterment
- •Courtesy and humility
- •Adjustment and assimilation
- •Gratitude.

What the ten commandments are to the West, these seven objectives are to the Japanese.

Amae

The other major aspect in that defines Japanese collectivism is *amae*. *Amae* is indulgent love as in the infant utterly dependent on mother and the mother totally forgiving of the infant's activities. It is the obligations and lifestyles, the strict guidelines for social relationships, the *kata* that every Japanese knows his or her place and acts according to a prescribed form. The Japanese tend to prefer dependence over self-reliance. Mutual dependence is simply taken for granted. The desire for belongingness is a necessary basis for establishing identity and is fueled by the fear of being left alone or ostracized by the group. The ultimate punishment in Japan is to be left alone, to be ostracized by one's group.

People in collectivist societies typically are born as members of in-groups, of which they are supposed to remain an integrated member throughout their lives; their individual fate is to a large extent determined by the interest of their in-group. They sacrifice individual interests in exchange for protection by the in-group. They are not supposed to have private opinions different from the opinion of their group. People expect their private life to be invaded by the groups to which they belong. The penalty for not maintaining the proper relationship with the group is a feeling of shame, a loss of face. People let their attitude to others depend on whether the other belongs to their in-group or to an out-group (particularism). Japanese capitalism was fostered by the state and did not arise form individual initiative (in most cases) and competition, as in the West. Japanese employees show a much stronger loyalty to their firm than in the West.

Group cohesiveness, discipline, and consensus have helped Japan excel in applications—allowing process innovations and step-by-step innovations (evolutionary innovation) to flourish. In Japan, this cultural tendency toward group working and group solidarity has contributed to the Japanese emphasis on mass production and total quality control, but these same factors have inhibited entrepreneurship and individual creativity. The Japanese are typically unwilling to differentiate themselves by stating new ideas or using different methods (Rosenberg, 1986). Hence, the acceptance of misfits, geniuses, entrepreneurs, and the ability to be different, which is a catalyst to the pursuit of inventions and radical innovations, is lacking in Japan but is readily apparent and available in the United States.

Giri— Obligations and Expectations

Giri is the moral force that compels the Japanese to engage in socially expected reciprocal activities even when they are not naturally inclined to do so. The consequence of not fulfilling these expectations is the loss of trust and support not only of the person directly affected but of any observers as well. Every favor is remembered by both the giver and receiver, and they both calculate the appropriate response. Few things can bring greater shame on an individual than the failure to repay an obligation. Once, in Japan, it was illegal to save a stranger's life because of the intense obligation and repayment owed to the rescuer. It was viewed as better to have died than to have to try to repay a debt continually which could never be fully paid. The social sanction used to enforce strict obedience to the life obligations of the Japanese was the concept of shame, which sometimes became so intensive and overpowering that the only acceptable recourse was suicide. Social harmony based on following proper etiquette in daily behavior and threat of ostracization remain the guiding principles in all Japanese relations.

The most desirous end state is that in which the incurrence of obligations is minimized and the flexibility in fulfilling obligations is maximized. Americans may feel obligated to others who have done favors for them. In Japan, obligations are a critical influence in daily behavior. For many centuries, the Japanese were taught not to become involved with others, particularly strangers, because by doing so they might incur obligation and thereby complicate their lives. This historically conditioned fear of incurring unnecessary obligations or making others obligated to oneself when they might not wish to be causes the Japanese not to make friends easily or quickly among themselves. Many Japanese tend to avoid even casual acquaintances for fear of being put under some obligation. Most Japanese, however, will go out of their way to seek the acquaintance of Westerners because they know that the foreigners, not being members of their society, are not likely to put them under any undesirable obligations. *On* is the deep sense of obligation which lies at the center of interpersonal behavior in Japan and refers to the debt one incurs upon receiving a favor or gift from another person. The social rules of obligation must be obeyed or severe losses in face, in trust, and social status will be incurred (Black and Mendenhall, 1993).

Uchi and *soto* refer to the perception and structure of in-groups (*uchi*) and out-groups (*soto*). Japanese society has extremely rigid boundaries, and it is much more difficult to move between in-group and out-group status in Japanese organizations than in U.S. organizations. In Japan, there are no expectations of being treated equally despite differences in rank and status. Some of the boundaries in Japanese society include age, university attended, rank/title, seniority, gender, and family. The Japanese believe that one can expect much more slack, understanding, acceptance and flexibility in interactions with in-group individuals. One can also expect in-group individuals to recognize and honor obligations they incur whereas the same confidence cannot be placed in out-group individuals. *Omote* refers to the behavior, expressions, words, and policies an individual or firm expresses to the public—the formal, legal self. *Ura* refers to the behavior, beliefs, attitudes, and policies that are privately allowed and tolerated—the informal, flexible, private self. Note that an out-group individual is not necessarily a foreigner; the Japanese view any person, Japanese or otherwise, not associated with his or her own group as a *soto*.

Power, Status, Hierarchy, Seniority, Acceptance of Authority

Until 1868, any samurai was legally permitted to kill on the spot any commoner guilty of breaking a law or behaving in a disrespectful manner. This provided a great incentive for the average Japanese person to obey the law exactly. In Japan, a right way for every facet of life exists, the *kata*. The proper bow is determined by relative ages, personal or professional relationship, past experience, purpose in meeting, etc. A marked parallel between aspects of the Japanese management system (such as senior wage and advancement system, high interjob mobility within each firm and the intrafirm welfare system) and an autonomous ranking hierarchy characterizing the traditional principle of the samurai.

The power-distance norm is reflected not only in the values of the leaders but also in the values of the followers. In large power-distance countries, most of the powerless people actually prefer to be led by powerful (autocratic or paternalistic) leaders. In small power-distance countries, people like a mutual dependence between leaders and followers. Countries with large power distances show centralization in work organizations, many levels of management, and privileges for managers. Countries with smaller power distances tend to have work organizations with decentralization, flatter organizational pyramids, and forms of worker consultation of representation (i.e., worker representation on the company board). Japan's average position on the Hofstede power-dimension reflects the coexistence of a strong sense of hierarchy with the consultation of subordinates and consensus decision making. Inequality is more accepted in Japan than in the United States. However, the power of the superior is not absolute. Loyalty in Japan is directed toward a position rather than toward that position's occupant (i.e., institutional power rather than personal power).

Japanese society is organized and functions according to military tenets: a strong hierarchical structure, insistence on following the chain of command, daily acknowledgment of differences in rank between individuals, an obsession with loyalty, deep personal attachments, emphasis on the performance of the group, willingness to make both individual and group sacrifices to reach a major objective, strong feelings of identity with and loyalty to those with the group (clearcut lines between insiders and outsiders), and a belief that the organizational objective is the reason for existence and strategic ways of thinking (Hall and Hall, 1987). A person's primary obligations are to his or her superiors, the secondary obligations were to his or her subordinates; few rules exist governing relationships with equals.

If an employee were to leave one company for another, the employee would lose the human connections and relations previously established in the first company. Also lost would be the reputation and achievements accumulated over time by the employee. One must usually be wiling to accept negative impacts on salary, retirement pay, and rank if such a change were to be made. Reputation outside corporations is secondary. Achievements are evaluated and promotion depends on senior officers. Status is influenced by educational background, size of company, length of service, and finally whether one has reached the executive level. The higher the salary, the more fringe benefits and the higher the prestige.

In Japan, putting in time until one earns seniority is the way to advance up the job ladder. Traditionally, a worker could not move easily; job hoppers were mostly seen as pariahs. Immobility, however, can breed complacency: A scientist who sits tight and doesn't push controversial ideas has his or her job until retirement. Lifetime employment also prevents labs from hiring short-term help, so scientists are typically diverted to doing mundane tasks that lesser trained technicians do in the West. Scientists have fewer support staff to help them; the ratio of technicians per scientist fell from 0.85 in 1965 to 0.31 in 1985. Learning to avoid boat rocking and controversy is necessary for so many people on so small an island, but it also forces Japanese scientists to eschew public argument and scientific debate. Scientists must apply months ahead for government consent to leave Japan, even on vacation. Upon returning, they submit photocopies of their passports to prove that they went only where they applied to go.

The godfather or *oyabun* human relationship, or *oyabun-kobun* (godfather-godson), is a key relationship in Japanese relations. The circulation of the *ringi-sho*, or decision proposal, with a strict hierarchical order from the original drafter to assistant section chiefs to deputy department heads is the daily confirmation of the strict pecking order of the system. This decision-making process contributes to the diffusion of responsibility throughout the organization. Once the plan becomes official, no individual can object without risking ostracism from the organization. This also blurs the sense of responsibility with the result that it becomes impossible to put the blame on anyone because it is not possible to determine who is responsible.

The work environment in a Japanese enterprise resembles that of life in a small and traditional rural community. In the tightly knit web of human relationships, one's position in the organization becomes secure. The organization gives the individual an identity by providing security, a source of income, and a pecking order in the vertical hierarchy. An introduction without the name of the company (the basic unit, in-group, in which a person's existence as an individual is defined in a mutually dependent, human relationship), is without meaning. For a Japanese university graduate, the choice of a place to work is the choice for the type of life the student is to lead henceforward. Once employed, his or her human relations rarely extend beyond the scope of the company. Often, the employee's family's residence is provided by the company for a nominal rent; vacations are spent in recreational facilities owned by the company. Japanese men spend their evenings out with their company colleagues drinking or chatting. Such extensive personal involvement in the company village is the major source of loyalty and devotion of Japanese workers to their company.

The seniority principle of wage and status determination also derives from the company village. The egalitarian aspect of the seniority system, that an individual is promoted to a certain position as the employee's seniority accumulates, contributes substantially to the strengthening of community among members of the organization and provides a rigid vertical hierarchical order. Japanese managers are motivated by rank, relative values of sales, or market shares. This rank consciousness is well demonstrated by their unusually strong interest in the ranking of foreign companies by *Fortune* magazine.

Specialists have usually been treated as being apart from the vertical hierarchy, and it is implicitly assumed that they will not be promoted to any prestigious position within the organization. In a vertically structured organization centered around mutual dependence of godfather-godson relationships, technical expertise can always be accommodated. Therefore, job rotation must be continual. Those who have stayed in the same position or even in the same type of position for more than a few years can come to be regarded as specialists and eventually drop out of the promotion race for top executive positions. This is not suitable for high technology—specialists rather than generalists are needed for radical innovations.

Formidable societal obstacles within Japan litter the road to a truly innovative way of doing things: a stifling seniority system that equates age with wisdom, a tradition of subordinating the individual to the group, schools that turn out drones singlemindedly programmed to pass college entrance exams, a national disdain for "eureka"-style imaginative leaps rather than the *ipo-ipo* (little-by-little) approach to problem solving. Japanese education tends to place limited value on conceptual thinking, which is essential for everything from doing pure science to writing software (Bylinsky, 1987).

Avoidance of Risk and Nonconfrontational Behavior

Japanese managers are generally conservative and risk averse. Traditionally, they were not rewarded for successes as much as they had been penalized for failures (the exact epitome of bureaucratic behavior). The Japanese are trained not to make a mistake, even if this means that nothing spectacular is achieved. However, if everyone makes the same mistake together, is not a mistake. In science, aversion to error can suffocate knowledge. In Japan, criticism tends to be taken personally and even viewed as an act of antagonism. The Japanese do not like openly adversarial bargaining relationships, which are low-trust relationships. Most Japanese feel more comfortable in high-trust relations of friendly give and take, in which each side recognizes that each has a stake in the other.

Open debate is nearly impossible in Japan. Actions that cause enmity and break social ties are dangerous to everyone and threaten the peace, the *wa*, the harmony of the group. In Japan, only one right way of thinking, one acceptable way exists to perform various activities. Every action is either right or wrong, natural or unnatural. When a Japanese is confronted with a new, unfamiliar situation that does not have its own *kata* (the prescribed way to behave), he or she becomes either incapable of action or takes action that is often the opposite of common sense. *Kata* is paramount to the Japanese; practically all of their existence is inscribed in cultural rules so that little is left of chance or personal inclination. This has been necessary to avoid conflict, to avoid harming the *wa* of the group. The Japanese fanatically pursue conflict avoidance. To the Western mind, conflict avoidance and harmony achievement are mutually exclusive. For the Japanese, harmony, conflict resolution, and conflict avoidance are all means to another end; they are not a desired end state in and of themselves. In fact, subjectivity engenders conflict and the objective test avoids it. To the Japanese, fairness is the paramount concern.

The oral commitment often counts far more than the written contract (the Japanese language is so vague that more written communication problems will be caused than solved). The Japanese tend to apologize in advance because apologies carry considerable moral weight; a guilty individual who apologies sincerely is often forgiven for relatively serious transgressions. Japan has advantages in staff, skills, and style which stem largely from its implicit culture. The Japanese manager learns to make the most of ambiguity, indirection, subtle cues, trust, interdependence, uncertainty, implicit messages, and management of process. This ambiguity and lack of confrontation is meant to eliminate envy, prohibit individualism, and suppress talent.

A self-assertive communication style is often seen as arrogant, insensitive, egocentric, and disruptive. What you are is how much you say as well as when you say it. Thoughts and ideas are pondered long and hard before people talk. Communication is indirect, with as much emphasis placed on what is left unsaid as on the spoken word. The social ideal is the hard-working low-key craftsman. To maintain group harmony, individualism is downplayed. Individuals must consider the interacting others—their social positions and demeanors. A direct style of interpersonal communication is disrespectful and discourteous. The more acceptable indirect style is non-confrontational. Cautiousness signifies patience, dependability, and sincerity. The Japanese tend to base their understanding of people on intuition and emotionality.

The Japanese language is hierarchical, reflecting the human relationships of a vertical society, and it limits the permissible range of expression according to the status of the speaker. Japanese communication is much more ambiguous, with an emphasis on gesturing, intonation, and protocol. Individualism is more often equated with disruption, insensitivity, and selfishness. Japanese democracy is the process of obtaining the consensus of as many people as possible. Freedom in Japan is a matter of reaching harmony within one's self and one's environment.

In the United States, forgiveness is easier to receive than permission; in Japan, the opposite is true. The Japanese tend to be sensitive about the use of incorrect and inappropriate language, and overassertiveness is avoided. Indirectness and ambiguousness in speaking and a desire to avoid conflict-causing situations are the norm. Confrontation is generally avoided because it often necessitates avenging one's honor; indirection is used to preserve harmony. Conformity is not simply passive obedience.

Overt competition must be avoided as much as possible. Creation of industrial or national consensus is deemed far preferable to a situation in which firms engage in brutal behavior as unabashed competition. Cooperation by government and industry is viewed as natural. As long as cooperation does not lead to gross violations of accepted rules of conduct within the society, it is considered to be an important part of the function of government. The government, therefore, is a sort of guardian or godfather for industry, and the companies and public as godsons accepted its involvement as necessary for the national interest.

The combination of strong uncertainty avoidance and moderate collectivism has created a Japan which produces quality goods. Quality production presupposes a strong sense of order and avoiding the unexpected; moderate collectivism allows mutual help in achieving quality objectives, as we find in the Japanese quality control cycles. A strong uncertainty avoidance value system does not make the average Japanese person flexible abroad; nor does it facilitate understanding among the Japanese public for other countries' values. Those with a high tolerance for uncertainty make the best foreign representatives; however, those people may have a problem communicating with their home base in Japan. A strong uncertainty avoidance society does not treat with kindness its sons or daughters who return with foreign ideas (Hofstede, 1992). The Japanese may have a relative advantage in countries in which the collectivist values prevail. Japan's extreme position on uncertainty avoidance suggest that there are only a few other countries (Greece, Portugal, and Belgium) for which the need for order and predictability in society is as pronounced as in Japan. A high level of pressure for social conformity and a strong inner urge to work hard results. The history of Japan as an insular society can partially explain this. Countries with lower individualism, stronger uncertainty avoidance, and larger power distance have shown the fastest growth (true for the post-Second World War era).

Other societies feel the uncertainty of the future as a threat against which they have to defend themselves (strong uncertainty avoidance). People feel a strong need for formal rules to go by and have little tolerance of deviant ideas and behaviors and what is different is considered dangerous. Nothing should be unexpected, and such societies strive for a known world. They believe in absolute principles and truth. Life is experienced as threatening; there is more tension and a higher anxiety level. People cope with their anxieties by hard work; their need for working hard comes from the inside. These societies also generally allow their members to cope with tension and anxiety by expressing emotions and behaving aggressively, at least on certain socially approved occasions. Japan's extreme position on uncertainty avoidance shows a high need for order and predictability in society and suggests a high level of pressure for social conformity and a strong inner urge to work hard.

The excess competition in Japan makes new products relatively more important. Fierce competition on a wide front forces companies to put more effort into development than basic research, in order to bring out new models and improve old ones. This emphasis has its price: Creativity is often precluded in such an environment. When curiosity is lacking, creativity turns imitative. Coming up with new ideas is easy, but the hard part is to sort the grains of gold from the mountains of sand. In Japan, a preference for benign neglect means that new ideas lie on table and it is left to the *gaiatu* (foreigners) to sort the winners from the losers.

In Japan, the maverick in a group can be isolated, ridiculed, ignored and banished (*mura hachibu*) from the group, as in the traditional village. It is difficult for a maverick to stand against a group or for a creative misfit to gain support. Those who do not conform to narrow guidelines are criticized and pressured until they fall within those guidelines. The Japanese are also less tolerant of deviants. Their educational system tends to place everyone into the same mold, and examination hell tends to nip any geniuses in the bud. No Newtons nor Einsteins can be expected to emerge out of the present Japanese social environment. The Japanese capacity for research that requires group cooperation is great; yet in basic research which relies on individual creativity, Japanese achievements lag (Vogel, 1985).

Aggressiveness, Competitiveness, Achievement, Motivation, and Persistence

The great pressures of preserving honor and face drive the need for the Japanese to achieve, to succeed. In the United States, a mother tends to push independence on her child; in Japan, the mother, once the baby has left the womb, spends most of the rest of her life seeking to foster dependence in the child. The mother is expected to cater to the child's every wish. ("Education Mama" is the term used for these compulsive mothers, who often go to the extreme of even sitting in classes for their child and taking voluminous notes when he or she is sick; this is especially true for male children who tend to be treated as surrogate husbands). Motivation is based on the values of indebtedness, loyalty and obligations. Achievement is oriented toward merit acquired by individual contributions to the goals of the group.

Shogyo soku shugyo means that all work is the pursuit of knowledge. Working with all one's heart at any occupation is a means of training one's character. Work is primarily seen as a means of building character and only secondarily as a productive activity. Time spent without a purpose is disliked, and time spent doing nothing is a waste. For a Japanese worker, a vacation must be filled with some defined activity. Time is time spent doing something. The Japanese work hard and play hard. Motivation arises from a perceived sense of collective social responsibility and obligations to groups both inside and outside the company. Personal success and company success become interconnected. The firm employs the entire person instead of just the labor and takes great interest in its employees' well-being both inside and outside work.

The Japanese are quick to adopt and change for the following reasons:

1. They attain high levels of education (math and science) and a very high level of literacy.
2. They live in a society which is attached to acquiring new knowledge and is therefore information oriented.
3. The Japanese worker's intimate identity with his or her company (loyalty bred by the lifetime employment system) means that the typical Japanese worker has a real impact on innovations in the workplace and is not afraid of change being a negative force on his or her life or lifestyle.
4. The work force is willing to collaborate in innovation and change in production as a means of improving the company's and its own position; workers make suggestions which are often accepted and implemented.
5. The lifetime employment system ensures continuity in company R&D, which is a clear asset in terms of efficiency; moreover, there is less likelihood of know-how being lost by a company through departure of researchers, and this in itself is an inducement for investment.
6. Companies are as information-oriented as their employees and are better equipped than average to anticipate new or changing demands in the marketplace (Healy, 1983).

Nevertheless, not all change is welcome. If a technology or management practice contributes to Japanese well-being, it may be copied perfectly and perhaps improved on. However, if a notion or concept is destabilizing or challenges Japan's long-term interests, it will be screened out.

Industry recognizes that it must continually learn, hone, and develop skills and at the same time be aggressively curious about new knowledge, discoveries, and markets. This is based on a deep appreciation that in order to ensure the survival of the clan, the Japanese must be quicker than the competition to adopt new knowledge or move into new markets. This attitude is reinforced by Buddhist thought, which holds that all facets of life and nature are in a state of constant change. For example, Hitachi turned itself from the workshop of a mine into a massive engineering company with an almost complete range of innovative, high-technology products. Sharp moved rapidly in recent years from making automatic pencils to computers. Cannon moved from cameras to computers. Toray turned an ailing textile company into the world's largest manufacturer of aerospace carbon fibers and is now moving rapidly into biotechnology. Yamaha went from pianos to motorbikes and then to computers. Change is acceptable and even desired in Japan, but within well-defined limits.

Persistence is probably stressed more in Japan than in most other countries. Persistence and will are instilled in Japanese children as an integral part of their education, as reflected in the term *Gambare:*, which means "persevere, endure, don't give up." At work, among the team, *gambare* is a permanent slogan, "work hard and diligently" (Turpin, 1992). Whenever Japanese managers feel that an industry or a market is going to be strategically crucial for the survival and the development of their company, they will launch an all-out effort to capture market share in those industries. Despite continuous setbacks, Japanese companies are unlikely to give up. The samurai origins of Japanese business are strongly influenced by the Confucian values of patience, loyalty, determination, and endurance.

By continually emphasizing a new target rather than gloating over achieving the last one, Japanese firms underscore the value of persistently striving for improvement. They continually tap their cultural energy source instead of cultivating complacency. By strategic accommodation or adaptive persistence, corporate direction evolves from an incremental adjustment to unfolding events. A lack of worries about quarterly profits as well as long term employment and the resulting social responsibilities, serve to reinforce persistence. The three top words for the typical Japanese are *effort, persistence,* and *thank you,* whereas the Western equivalents are *love, family, and fun.*

Chauvinism and Masculinity

All societies reserve for their men primarily the achieving role outside the house and for their women the nurturing, caring role inside the house. Societies differ on the degree of this social role division. In feminine societies, men are supposed to care for children, for others, for the weak, and for the quality of life. Relationships are at least as important as work performance and results. Masculine societies maintain a strict role separation between men and women. Men are supposed to achieve, to perform, and to behave assertively and at times aggressively. Relationships are maintained because of their contribution to performance and results. There is a general sympathy for that which is big, fast, and strong. and a belief in and admiration for supermen. Children are stimulated to excel in their studies. Women are supposed to serve men but dominate them in the home. The traditional Japanese view is that a woman should be like water—able to lose herself in her husband. In a marital relationship, peace is more important than justice, and harmony is sweeter than equality.

Japan's extreme position on masculinity suggests that in no other country is the sex role separation as strict as in Japan. This suggests a strong performance orientation of Japanese men. Japan's extreme masculinity can be traced to the samurai, with its stress on masculine assertiveness, honor, and its absolute sex role separation. During Japan's 1992-94 recession, the situation for career Japanese women worsened as many part-time and temporary workers (mostly women) were released. To work and advance many career women have been forced to work for foreign companies or to move out of Japan altogether to countries which provide opportunity for professional advancement that are often unobtainable in Japan. Japan has no effective legal barriers to sexist questions in employment interviews and its equal employment opportunity law (which bars sexual discrimination) contains no penalty and hence no incentives to change (Cody, 1994).

Confucianism

The key principles of Confucian teaching are are as follows:

1. The stability of society is based on unequal relationships between people. The *wu lun*, or five basic relationships, are ruler/subject, father/son, older brother/younger brother, husband/wife, and older friend/younger friend. These relationships are based on mutual complementary obligations. The junior partner owes the senior respect and obedience; the senior owes the junior partner protection and consideration.
2. The family is the prototype of all social organizations. A person is not primarily an individual; rather, he or she is a member of a family. Children should learn to restrain themselves, to overcome their individuality and thus to maintain harmony in the family (if only on the surface); one's thoughts, however, remain free. Harmony is found in the maintenance of an individual's face, meaning one's dignity, self-respect, and prestige. Losing one's dignity in the Chinese tradition is catastrophic. Social relations should be conducted in such a way that everyone's face is maintained. Paying respect to someone else is called "giving face."
3. Virtuous behavior toward others consists of treating others as one would like to be treated oneself. This is a basic human benevolence which, however, does not extend as far as the Christian injunction to love thy enemies.
4. Virtue with regard to one's tasks in life consists of trying to acquire skills and education, working hard, not spending more than necessary, being patient, and persevering. Conspicuous consumption is taboo, as is losing one's temper. Moderation is to be enjoined in all things.

The values of obedience, loyalty, commitment, and harmony derive from the Confucian traditions. Interpersonal relations were codified and behavior was carefully prescribed to avoid conflict and preserve harmony. Confucian philosophy hence discourages individualist behavior. Because of its reverence for hierarchy and order, Confucianism is a barrier to change. Confucianism has nurtured the conservative nature of Japanese society and has formed the basis for Japanese hoarding of technology. In contrast, a Buddhist approach appeals to those attracted to the notion of sharing technologies. The Japanese language has developed to reflect the importance of hierarchy in interpersonal relations. The outcome of these values is the internal ubiquity and teamwork of business firms. The hierarchy of the firm is accepted, and senior management commands respect. In turn, management accepts its obligation to develop and support the employees. The culture's emphasis on relationships helps break down interdepartmental rivalry and foster strong mutual interdependence between suppliers and customers. Competitors at all levels in the manufacturing chain must continually supply new products to stay ahead of rivals. Confucian ethics also stress policies for the good of the nation. Japanese firms are able to overcome traditional merchant rivalry and work together on problems which can call on their loyalty to the state. Research projects jointly funded by government or industry are the outcome. The same collective spirit enables competitors to share confidential data on production and sales, thus enabling each to measure its progress minutely in the competitive struggle.

The family is the basic unit of social structure and revolves around the household and hierarchical relations, obedience, filial piety, solidarity between family members, and a deep sense of importance in carrying on the family line. This is reflected in respect for one's parents, taking good care of them, and acting according to their wishes; the obedience commensurate with being a young brother means adherence to the wishes of elder brothers and seniors. Harmony is also essential for the achievement of benevolence. This signifies people's being in accord with one another and preserving accord within society. Males rank higher than females, elders rank higher than juniors, the eldest son carries on the family line and succeeds as the family head. The president or owner of enterprise is like the head of a household, with new employees being new family members and the employer-employee relationship resembling that of a father-child.

In Confucian ethics, the parent-child relationship becomes the model for all other relationships. The state is thought of as an enlarged family, as is the company. Management understands that the relationship between the company and its employees is not merely an economic function of convenience. *Kaisha* (my company) symbolizes expression of group consciousness; it the community to which one belongs primarily and which is all important to one's life. It is of utmost importance for children to serve, support and obey parents and to honor ancestors. The major cause of the lack of a consumer movement in Japan's land of high prices and poor living conditions is the willingness of one to sacrifice for the good of the nation. Compared to Western firms, Japanese firms are better equipped to overcome rivalries and to work out problems.

The Confucian ideal of family and society considers hierarchy to be natural and unavoidable. Japanese culture legitimates differences. Acceptance and respect of hierarchy order is fundamental to the Confucian strategy for achieving harmony, and no goal is greater than harmony. If people do not observe propriety in all matters, anarchy and disorder will follow. The most important requirement for social order and harmony is for each individual to be continuously aware of his or her position in society and to act in strict accordance with what society demands of the position.

Every social encounter requires knowledge of the relative ranks of the parties to the encounter, from the proper form of greeting to the appropriateness of the content of the interaction. The Japanese language is full of connotations of differentiation, and the most strongest differentiator is age. Rank, respect, power, and privilege correlate closely with age in Japan. Sex differentiates; women are afforded a lower status than men. Education is the third major differentiation. The Japanese accept the necessity of differentiation and legitimize it. A Japanese person does not feel comfortable in any personal relationship that does not include recognition of the relationship between parties. Once a relationship is established, both parties tend to expect more from it than work itself and so involve themselves emotionally.

Other Religions

Shintoism, the state religion of Japan, emphasizes ancestor worship. It reflects the idea of family solidarity and respect due to age. Shinto (way of the gods) is a benign belief, demanding very little of the Japanese. In return for a few offerings, an attitude of reverence before its shrines, and regular attendance at festivals (which were anything but solemn), Shinto imbues the Japanese with a calm acceptance of the life and death cycle, an appreciation of the secrets and beauties of nature, and a deep concern with cleanliness and orderliness. When the emperor was returned to power in 1867, Shintoism became a state cult which not only proclaimed the emperor divine but also encouraged the Japanese to believe that it was their sacred duty to bring enlightenment to the rest of the world and attain their proper place among nations. This contributed to Japanese militarism. Most homes, especially in rural areas, have at least one Shinto god shelf near the entrance to protect the household against the entry of harmful spirits and other types of ill fortune.

The typical Japanese person has absorbed the surface tenets of Buddhism (impermanence of all things, futility of early ambitions, and a concept of life after death). Little exists in Buddhist tradition to encourage anyone in the pursuit of wealth for its own sake. Followers are rather inclined to accept their position in the world (thus being content with their salary and having no desire to set up a new business of their own). The tendency exists to encourage mediation and simplicity. As a result, the Japanese have had a rather austere style of living, searching for tranquility rather than ostentation. Buddhism urges its devotees to work relentlessly to achieve enlightenment. Effort is to be exerted in daily life. Many Japanese organizations commit considerable resources to the pursuit of spiritual development by their employees. The organizational philosophies of many Japanese companies rest on the premise that work should be performed with the correct spirit or attitude. Poor performance is often seen as a spiritual failure.

Homogeneity versus Heterogeneity: Ethnocentrism

One of the characteristics of Japan is that the sovereignty area of the Japanese state, the Japanese people, the Japanese language, and the Japanese culture are virtually identical: 98 percent of all residents of Japan are Japanese citizens, 97 percent are direct descendants of Meiji Japan, and 97 percent of all ethnic Japanese live in Japan. For a Japanese, leaving Japan and residing overseas often means ceasing to be Japanese. A Japanese person often cannot live outside the community of other Japanese. The Japanese culture is far more uniform than that of most any other country; on any one day, one can almost tell with absolute certainty what material is being taught to what grade level at any school in the entire country.

The more adapted people are to a foreign culture, the less Japanese they will become and the less capable they will be of fitting back into Japanese culture after their return home. Losing one's Japaneseness is generally a liability to be avoided. Internationalization and Japanization are contradictory goals. Once children with overseas experience return to Japan, problems await them. Their identity is questioned. In Japan, their foreign mannerism and their foreign ways of thinking and behaving draw the attention and criticism of other Japanese, who have little tolerance for cultural diversity. If they manifest some even mildly deviant behavior, this is immediately interpreted as an undesirable consequence of foreign experience. Returnees, therefore, must be de-internationalized. Feelings of uniqueness mean that Japanese who have spent time abroad and picked up foreign thoughts are treated as outcasts in their own society upon their return.

Gaijin (literally "outside people") denotes people of all foreign countries and in a popular sense means "whites." Foreigners are foreigners in Japan no matter how well they speak the language, how well they have adapted to Japanese culture, or how many generations they have lived in Japan. Separation between themselves and others allows the Japanese to import and incorporate foreign cultural elements at will. This absolute exclusion of foreigners is rooted in the Japanese definition of themselves as one race and one culture. *Gaijin* are often not admitted to certain areas on weekends, and many Japanese want them to stay within their own enclaves (Frost, 1987). Foreigners must carry ID cards (alien registration cards). Due to its distinctive ways and emphasis on homogeneity, the Japanese do not suffer *gaijin*, or foreigners, gladly. Their distinctive ways are a source of pride and a font of national strength and form a wall of exclusivity and segregation. Hegemony is vital to holding the center firm. For instance, interracial marriages are frowned on and are rare (Morgan and Morgan, 1991). Westernization is not seen as a positive trend; it is a threat to the age-old fibers that bind the society. This is not to say that Japan today is not involved in Western ways. It is, but outside ideas are processed and amended by Japanese society to work within the existing boundaries.

Over 700,000 Koreans live in Japan, most of whom are third-generation descendants of laborers (grandparents or even great-grand-parents) shipped over from then-colonized Korea to do dirty jobs for the Japanese before and during the Second World War. Almost all were born in Japan, raised in Japan, speak Japanese fluently, and know no other home but Japan. Yet they have never been accepted as members of Japanese society. They cannot vote or join the civil service. They have to reapply for entry every time they leave Japan. Few, if any, are ever granted Japanese citizenship. To simply be in Japan is not a substitute for being Japanese. Japanese is not just a language, an ethnic group, but a total way of life.

This national pride in a pure, self-perceived superior race is in obvious conflict with the American melting pot. Japan's striving for purity is at the opposite pole from the American idea of open doors and diversity as strength. To this day, Japan remains relatively closed to immigration from outside countries. And although it is possible for an immigrant to become a citizen, why would anyone want to. As the saying goes, you can gain Japanese citizenship, but you can never become Japanese. The underlying feeling that you as a foreigner can never become "one of us" and therefore trusted and loyal has a negative impact on the ability of foreigners to build strong business and personal relations with the Japanese. Paradoxically, the Japanese have an inferiority complex. This is probably because the Japanese know that their economic house is forever on shaky ground. Japan is eternally at nature's mercy, vulnerable to the sea that surrounds it, to earthquakes of the soil beneath it, and to a real shortage of raw materials (particularly food and fuel).

Many major Japanese companies do not hire non-Japanese employees within Japan. Non-Japanese do not and cannot fit into the Japanese system because they are not Japanese. As another example, the Japanese justified import barriers against foreign-made ski equipment by claiming that snow in Japan is different from snow in other countries while simultaneously exporting Japanese-made skis. Although hypocritical, this statement is logical from the Japanese perspective.

Long-Term versus Short-Term Perspectives

Japanese employees are urged and motivated to upgrade skills continually and be quick to enter new markets: The existence of a state of constant change is recognized and accepted. The employer is responsible for the survival of the work force. Management at all levels is involved in innovation decisions. The Japanese understand and appreciate the risks involved in innovation (process and evolutionary innovations, that is), especially the necessity of a long-term view. Secure in their employment, people will allow themselves to be redeployed in jobs according to the needs of the firm, and if this means a geographical relocation, they will subordinate the short-term interests of the family or individual to those of the firm. In the long term, the interests of both converge: The psychological contract between a company and its employees is long term (Boisot, 1983). Generations, not quarters, is the firm's outlook. While American companies prepare 5-year plans, their Japanese counterparts prepare 100-year plans.

Industry acceptance of its responsibility for the survival of the complete work force, or clan, includes the responsibility for a larger than usual burden for the social health and welfare of the work force. This attitude forces Japanese companies to be adaptable and to respond quickly: They are tough and durable in adversity, are prepared to invest heavily in in-house education, and are long range in their vision (MacDowall, 1984). Japanese culture urges continuity. The Japanese understand time as cyclical—the ebb and flow of seasons, rather than the inexorable and linear march of time. In time, the disturbance will fade and things will return to their original alignment. The continuity of the family's good name is mandated. The Japanese individual is reluctant to deviate radically from the path laid out by his or her ancestors. Long-term commitment can be seen in the fact that the Japanese have buried a time capsule which they don't plan to open for another 5,000 years.

Once long-term planning is desired, it is conducive to the generation of interpersonal relationships that foster mutual understanding and implicit goals. The timeframe of all plans tends to lengthen and immediate pressures tend to diminish. Deliberate planning and communication exhibit themselves in orderliness and diligence of production operation implementation. Time exists to produce customized in-house process equipment and to select employees whose skills match the equipment or to train those that do not. A supportive stable environment is thus produced for industries. Long-term efforts in training and development are reflected in rotational training programs, acceptance of changes in work methods, and technology that enhances productivity. Heavy emphasis is accorded to the socialization factors the fit of the employee to the organization, the philosophy, the peer groups, the management style. Hiring is often based more on social factors than on entry skills. Intensive socialization is achieved through ritualistic practices such as calisthenics, the company song, after-hours socializing with coworkers, and company-sponsored vacations. This promotes trust and support of organizational leadership, accommodation and unity of interest, and company identity.

Information Flow and Context

Japan is considered a high context culture; for most normal transactions in daily life, the Japanese do not require, nor do they expect, much in-depth background information. This is because it is in their nature to keep themselves informed about everything concerning the people who are important in their lives (Hall and Hall, 1987). In high-context cultures, information flows freely. The emphasis is on stored rather than transmitted information. Schedules and screening (as in the use of private offices) are avoided because they interfere with the vital function of interpersonal contact. In a high-context culture, being out of touch means that essentially one ceases to exist. The day starts with the use of honorifics (formal forms of address attached to the name). If things are going well, the honorifics are dropped as the day progresses.

In Japanese meetings, the information flow is high, and everyone is expected to read other people's thoughts, to know the state of their business, and to know what government regulations are in the offings. Most, if not all, of those present have a good idea of what will be discussed beforehand. The purpose of the meeting is to create consensus, to open the information channels and determine whether the group can work together, and to appraise the chances of coming to an agreement in the future. The committee is neither a debating forum nor a rubber stamp; it exists to exchange different views and to achieve harmony in the process. To the Japanese, the law is not a norm but a framework for discussion. The good Japanese judge is a man who can arrange and settle the most compromises out of court. When a Japanese person calls a lawyer, he or she is admitting that the social system, a system of personal commitments, has failed.

In Japan, the underlying intent of a regulation or agreement is considered to be the real contract, and that intent must be implemented in keeping with the changing situation; little weight is given to actual written words; provisions can be disregarded when situations change and actual problems arise. The Western understanding of the word *fair* is "an action carried out on the basis of certain rules or principles which is defined by religion, morality, or ethics." Right and wrong are relative values. The Japanese word for *fair*, *kohei*, has a different connotation. It can suggest an action carried out on the basis of the balance of power. A rich person meeting a poor person in the Western world might give the poor person some money. In Japan, if a rich person were to meet a poor person, no such compulsion would exist; the poor person's absence of wealth would be taken as a sign that he or she had failed as person and therefore should be despised. If the rich person chooses to spurn or exploit the poor, it would be considered fair because the poor person had no power, no standing. If an American says that he or she wants better "understanding" with the Japanese, the Japanese would take it as meaning that the American accepts the Japanese power or agrees with their position. "Better relations" to a Japanese means that one would stop carping against Japanese interest. The Japanese word for internationalization is *kokusaika,* "country-borders-meet." The meaning of this to a Japanese person is that Japan expands its borders and its relations with the outside world on Japanese terms (Holstein, 1991).

THE RELATIONSHIP BETWEEN JAPANESE CULTURE AND INNOVATION STYLES

Traditional Japanese characteristics include submission to authority, fear and avoidance responsibility, a view of consumption above and beyond basic needs as a social evil, an inordinate pride about all things Japanese, and a view of the world at large that is emotional and subjective by valuing beauty and harmony above function and ethics. These characteristics still exist within the Japanese society and culture, but many Japanese do not personally follow them. Old traits that remain more or less intact include extraordinary diligence, ambition, perseverance, and a capacity to endure hardships without becoming cynical and mean.

Japan possesses many strengths: a highly educated work force, a long-term commitment to developing key industries, easily available capital at low interest rates, high levels of R&D investment, masses of engineers, and a dedication to top-quality design and efficient production. Cutthroat competition among Japan's automobile and electrical industries drove them to invest in new machines to increase productivity; a government-encouraged leasing company (JAROL) offered advice and machines at a low cost, and robots were carefully integrated into the factory culture.

Japanese willingness to pool and share information has its roots in rural village life, in which the planting, irrigation, and harvesting of rice are activities which must be shared. Pressure for innovation comes from the Japanese consumer's love of new things, almost to the point of being fanatical about innovative products. Customers' loyalty to suppliers helps make innovations the basis of competition. Relationships with suppliers are normally stable and long lasting, and this increases innovation. When buyer and supplier have a close relationship, frank and open exchanges of technical information usually take place. And because buyer and supplier are closely linked, a new supplier can only break in by offering something significantly different. The existing or in-supplier is usually working hard with the customer to develop new and improved ways of doing things, whereas the out-supplier must work even harder to gain a foothold. The Japanese generally will not do business of any kind with anyone whom they have not met face to face and with whom they have established a fairly close relationship. Making an initial contact by phone (to get an introductory appointment and begin the process of establishing the necessary relationship) is accepted but requires considerable skills in using polite forms of the language, and in explaining where and how you got the other party's name and why you are calling in the first place.

The lack of departmental barriers also facilitates innovation. Many Japanese companies prefer generalists to specialists. Japanese companies do not like scientists to be isolated. Regular job rotation is the norm. *Keiten aijin* means fostering the spirit of participation. The humanistic firm encourages innovation. The enterprise union supports and actively participates in the firm's innovative efforts; its members know that if the firm's technology stands still, it is only a matter of time before the firm will start to slip behind. Such members also understand that the introduction of new technology is designed to enhance the firm's productivity and competitiveness and not to replace labor (Ozaki, 1991). Top managers of Japanese industries are constantly concerned about the welfare of their employees. Profit for many is secondary to the maintenance of harmony and job security for employees. New technology offers a promise of increased efficiency and personnel adjustments. Layoffs are not considered except in cases of dire financial difficulties or imminent bankruptcy.

LIFETIME EMPLOYMENT

In the West, the church and the state have historically played an important role in the social and moral welfare of the population; This has traditionally not been the case in Japan. Consequently, the gap was filled by companies who came to regard themselves as responsible for all aspects of their employees' lives (Campbell, 1985). Lifetime employment is commonplace, and changing jobs is infrequent. When workers buy homes or cars, they arrange loans with their companies, and they invest part of their salary in company savings and insurance plans. Companies assure their workers security. In return, companies can expect good productivity and loyalty from employees. Honor and discipline in Japanese life are based on highly personal loyalties—in the past to the feudal lord, always to the honor of the family, and today to the corporation. The lifetime employment system makes job transfers in Japan disadvantageous; it is difficult to find a new job with good conditions, and salary and rank fall drastically upon entering a new company. The lifetime employment system therefore links the fate of each of the employees to the company as a whole.

It is rare for a university graduate to gain employment at any other time than April. Interviews start the previous August. The system creates competition among firms to secure the best students as soon as possible, and all firms have their own selection day on October 1. This gives the student only one chance to apply to a big firm. Applicants do not seek a specific job but apply to the firm itself. New graduates are considered a sheet of clean paper. The company then trains the graduate in its mode. The system of management development and training in Japan is geared to producing general managers rather than functional specialists. The effectiveness of the organization is the group, not the sum of individuals. This system has its merits. It is almost perfectly controlled within the company because of the lack of mobility, and it can be planned on a long-term basis due to lifetime employment. Each company has its own climate, and those who enter stay, and are developed there for that special climate, losing their availability to other companies. These managerial resources, in a sense, have become the sole possession of the company. The widespread use of part- time and temporary workers provides an escape valve in times of flexible needs and protects the job security of regular employees. Loose job specifications and acceptance of frequent job rotation add flexibility, which contributes to employment continuity. The extensive use of subcontractors tends to shift risk from the parent company and allows it to offer stable employment to its own employees. Japan's lifetime employment and seniority systems have lacked horizontal mobility (i.e., movement of labor between firms). Entry into large enterprises or public institutions is quite strongly biased in favor of graduates of top-ranked universities.

Japanese loyalty to their companies is a form of submission to a highly controlled environment. Lifetime employment becomes a tool to give managers power over workers rather than a motivating device. Decisions are usually top to bottom, although lengthy discussions are held to make sure that everyone understands what is happening. Slow but automatic promotions create resentment in able employees and lassitude in poor workers. The development of general rather than specialized management skills does force people to talk to each other, but the loss of expertise is a costly trade-off. The Japanese workplace is characterized by order, stability, predictability, and cohesion, which emerge from the subtle and not-so-subtle controls devised by power managers. What comes first is getting the job done, not the employee's well-being. Changes will be implemented gradually so as not to disrupt existing power relationships and proposed radical innovations, no matter how worthwhile, will be studied until they die a quiet death. As long as workers do what is required of them and avoid complaining, they will be well taken care of. Sincerity, defined as an implicit acceptance of the existing order, almost always results in positive action.

The benefit of lifetime employment is loyalty. This increases employee commitment to the organization's goals because the employee's long-term career with the company will ensure that its interests and the worker's interests will coalesce. This mutuality of outlook inspires a communal environment filled with harmony, sincerity, and trust. Another benefit is high-quality economic performance. Firms with employees who are not expected to quit can invest heavily in their training, with a resulting improvement in productivity and output. The absence of an external labor market gives firms a chance to develop highly efficient internal markets through which workers and jobs are well matched. Another benefit is motivation. With security and regular pay increase, employees become highly motivated to work hard. The final benefit is control. Managers have almost unlimited power over job assignments, overtime, training, and geographical location. Employees who are not satisfied cannot quit because they cannot get tenure elsewhere. An unsatisfied worker will be reassigned or offered more training.

The Japanese have traditionally viewed employment as a social contract; leaving an employer is difficult. The emphasis on personal feelings and human relationships makes job hopping extremely tough for the Japanese, who value face and family honor above career prospects and salary. For example, in 1991, it was believed that true unemployment within the private sector averaged over 10 percent. In other words, private companies were carrying 10 percent more employees than they required to function. At the same time, national unemployment figures were quoted at about 2 percent. It is not considered acceptable for companies to unload their labor onto the rest of society. Private companies are therefore forced to keep their employees occupied and to be flexible and curious about new technology and new markets.

In Japan, both for the company and for the individual, employment is a lifetime commitment similar to marriage. When a company assesses an individual's suitability for employment, the person's character, sense of loyalty and potential ability to contribute to the company over the long run are regarded as more important than the individual's immediate labor productivity and skills. A company is paternalistic—one large family. One of the best ways to win advancement in a company is to get one's superior to take an active role in one's private life; if your boss finds a wife for you, he is naturally going to be more interested in your welfare, especially if he arranges for you to marry a close relative of his.

The system requires of the worker not merely the stipulated work but also that the worker devote all waking hours to the company. Attendance at company events during the weekend may be voluntary, but it also represents that the worker is loyal and cares for the company. In this way, an employee's life becomes tied to the company, even outside working hours. A worker must continually strive to demonstrate loyalty to the company. The extent of that loyalty is measured in terms of the degree to which the worker is prepared to sacrifice self. The company values the worker's loyal service, loyal employees are given good posts in the future. In Japan's Confucian capitalist society, devoted service is the most important virtue in both ethical and materialistic terms. In this society, the freedom of the individual is often regarded as a challenge to society (the majority, the company), and anyone who dares to assert freedom will in all likelihood become completely isolated.

The labor market, therefore, is considerably different in Japan. The offer of lifetime employment is made only once to an individual, immediately after graduation from college. His or her whole life will revolve around that one decision made at such a young age: the hobby club he or she will belong to will be the one organized by the company; the housing he or she gets will be subsidized by the company, etc. The company is not just a profit-making organization, it is a complete society in itself and frequently so all embracing that all the activities of the daily lives of the company's employees can take place within the company framework. The salaryman has no life and no identity of his own, only that of his company. Private life and business life are not separate, they are merged. If for any reason this commitment ends in disaster, the individual has no alternative but to look for a new employer on the second, mercenary market—a market with wages appreciably lower than of the larger enterprises in the first lifetime market. The employer must keep the employee, even if incompetent or marginal. The larger companies have virtually no mercenary workers among their employees. Not only does a considerable wage difference exists, but there is a large difference in social status between large and second-tier enterprises.

SUMMARY

The ranking of factors of innovation in an Arthur D. Little Inc. survey conducted in 1988 among executives in the United States, Japan, and Europe indicates clearly the cultural differences in the importance of certain facets of innovation. Japanese managers devoted more of their effort to product innovation than either American or European managers. Japanese companies were more concerned about product appeal (90 percent) than other aspects, which was significantly higher than either European or American managers. For Japanese companies, the greatest barriers to product innovation were "poorly communicated vision and objectives for new products" (91 percent), "insufficient attention to product specification to meet customer requirements" (90 percent), and "lack of systems and guidelines" (87 percent). The American and European companies rated "lack of skilled leaders" as their greatest barrier to product innovation. Japanese companies focused on improving the process, whereas American and European companies appeared more concerned with people and resource issues. In measuring product innovation results, Japanese companies emphasized sales volume (75 percent) and profitability (68 percent), whereas American companies emphasized product cost and profitability and European companies emphasized lead times and profitability.

The top three concerns for Japanese executives in their approach to product innovation were "to improve appeal" (90 percent), "to be on time" (75 percent), and "to move faster" (67 percent). The three top concerns for the American executives in their approach to product innovation were "to be on time" (71 percent), " to improve appeal" (69 percent), and " to make easier to use" (68 percent). The three top concerns for European executives in their approach to product innovation were "to be on time" (78 percent), "to move faster" (74 percent), and " to improve appeal" (72 percent).

Japan has demonstrated great abilities in the area of process technology whereas the West, particularly the United States, has been more capable in product development; when research targets are clearly defined and fixed, Japan excels; Americans do better when targets are vague, allowing for more personal freedom and individual creativity. The Japanese culture does not encourage breaking way and does not promote individuality. Japanese management styles work in Japan because its culture, values, goals, and ideology all merge and act as an extended family that emphasizes commitment, loyalty, and identification to firm and to nation. The Japanese culture places a premium on dependability, quality, cooperative behavior, and respect for authority. It pays particular attention to the overall flow of things, the process (Harper, 1988). The Japanese emphasize learning, patience, adaption throughout one's personal career life, and a long-term horizon. The Japanese avoid risk due to the high degree of collectivism and homogeneity in their culture.

Chapter 7

A Comparative Analysis of the U.S. and Japanese Innovative Sourcing Capabilities

INNOVATIVE STRENGTHS AND WEAKNESSES: JAPAN VERSUS THE UNITED STATES

Most of the relative innovative strengths and weaknesses for both the United States and Japan have been discussed in detail earlier in this book, particularly in chapter 3. The differences in innovation styles seen between Japan and the United States can be summarized as follow:

1. Although Japanese companies dominate in the number of patents issued in the United States and in the total numbers of patents issued throughout most of the world, the extreme differences in patenting style between the two countries make patent statistics unusable in reaching conclusions. The larger number of Japanese patents can be attributed to the relatively small advances reflected in each patent.

2. The United States has absolute advantage in terms of R&D dollars spent but Japan spends more on a percentage of GDP basis. Differences abound, though, in the composition of this spending, with Japan almost exclusively spending on commercial R&D whereas the United States splits its R&D monies between defense and commercial.

3. The United States still graduates more engineers and scientists than any other country, but Japan has a greater per capita average. Yet the United States has an overwhelming lead (in both numbers and per capita) in postgraduate instruction (Masters and Ph.D.s) in engineering and the sciences.

4. A dramatic difference does exists between Japanese and American firms in their allocation of R&D resources between process and basic research. American firms devote about two thirds of their R&D expenditure to improved product technology (new products and product changes) and about one-third to improved process technology (new processes and process changes). Among the

Japanese firms, the proportions are reversed, two-thirds are spent for improved process technology and one-third goes for improved product technology with a bare minimum of expenditures—2.3 percent—spent on basic research (Mansfield, 1988b).

5. The Japanese devote a much larger percent of their R&D dollar to tooling and manufacturing facilities and equipment—applied R&D—almost double proportionally than is spent in the U.S.

6. Without a doubt, the leader in radical innovations over the past fifty years has been the United States. Japan hardly qualifies as an also-ran in this innovation segment.

7. American scientists lead the world in Nobel Prizes; Japan has had as many Nobel winners as has Denmark. Most of the Japanese winners had studied and worked overseas when they did their prize-winning work.

8. The United States has been both giving and receiving technology while Japan has been primarily a recipient of technology. Technology transfer from America to Japan is on the order of three to almost four times greater than the reverse flow.

9. The Japanese have great advantages based on external technology, but very little comparative advantage in carrying out innovations based upon internal technologies (Mansfield, 1988a). Most innovations based upon external technology are imitative in nature and can be adapted and improved at a relatively low cost. Japan's greatest technological strength is the speed at which they develop products and processes, and improve and cost-reduce them. However, these advantages of time and cost seem to be confined to innovations based on external technology (25 percent less time and 50 percent less money). Among innovations based on internal technology, there seems to be no significant difference in average cost or time between Japan and the United States (Mansfield, 1988a).

10. Japan excels at evolutionary and (especially) at process innovations but not at radical innovations or basic science. The United States appears to excel at the radical innovation and invention but does poorly (comparatively) at evolutionary and process innovations. In the United States, the most important thing is the frontier spirit (Hooper and Schlesinger, 1990).

Therefore, the conclusion is that the United States excels in radical innovations, inventions, and basic science. The Japanese excel at evolutionary and process innovations but fail to even contend in radical innovations or major inventions and basis science. Can we relate specific cultural attributes which are logically related to the requirements for radical innovations or inventions which exist for the United States but not so for Japan? Conversely, can we establish a set of cultural attributes which are related to process or evolutionary innovations which exist for Japan but not for the United States? Can we explain the Japanese superiority in process innovation and their relative inferiority in radical innovation by an examination of basic cultural attributes?

CULTURAL EXPLANATIONS

Hofstede's (1984) dimensions have been widely used not only because they are robust and manageable in number but because they have been quantified to allow relative differences in cultural attributes to be objective and not subjective. The table below shows the Hofstede dimensions and the values for both the United States and Japan. The range of scores is from 0 (lowest) to 100 (maximum); the scores are relative and not ratio based. The scores were computed by scaling each country's mean score from a factor analysis of the Hofstede IBM international managerial survey.

	Japan	United States
Individualism	46	90
Power	54	40
Uncertainty Avoidance	92	46
Masculinity / Femininity	95	62
Confucian Dynamics	80	29

As can be seen, substantial differences exist in four of the five categories. The differences between the two cultures for each attribute will be discussed in turn as well as their likely implications for innovative sourcing differences. In addition, homogeneity and time orientation (long-term versus short-term) of the culture will also be reviewed.

Individualism versus Collectivism

Clans or groups are common to all societies. In an individualist society, one can have membership in many groups and membership is flexible, nonpermanent, and usually noncommittal. In a collectivist society, there are a few groups with lifelong formal commitments. In this definition, the Japanese rank as one of the most collectivist societies in the world. Japanese groups are determined largely by school and college affiliations, year of graduation, place of employment, and date of entry into the hiring institution. Other Japanese groups include families, companies, government departments, and even clubs and organizations. In Japan the group can be exclusionary; the Japanese are "group-centric" in that their groups exclude everyone, including other Japanese, from the in-group. Nonmembers, be they Japanese or foreign, are viewed with suspicion. A newcomer without proper introduction is not fully accepted as a fellow human being (Frost, 1987).

The two major aspects in defining Japanese collectivism are *amae* and *wa*. *Amae* is defined as "indulgence or dependence on other," and it denotes the connectedness, and the complex hierarchical, collective interrelationships which exist in Japan. It is the attitude that nothing of consequence occurs as a result of individual effort, that individuality is expressed only within the context of the group.

Wa is the Japanese context which stresses group harmony (loyalty), trust, sensitivity, and social cohesion; it translates as the search for mutual cooperation so a group's members can devote their total energies to attaining group goals while submerging their individual (selfish) goals in favor of the group's goals. The Japanese are taught from an early age to adjust their own desires to the demands of the group. Gifted individuals are supposed to let the rewards of talent flow back through them anonymously for the benefit of their group. Even speaking about one's self let alone of one's achievements is considered inappropriate (Frost, 1987).

This groupism is reflected in the Japanese definition of the word *individualism*. The original term in the Japanese language has always been in ill repute in Japan, denoting selfishness rather than personal responsibility, isolation from others, and that a person is concerned with his or her own advantage as against being willing to work for the welfare of others. To be individualistic means that the person gains by weakening the group or in spite of the group. On the other hand, everyone gains when each member seeks to make the group more efficient, or when the individual works to help the group as a whole, whether a team or a company. This is the other side of group loyalty. Nonmembers are outsiders whose concerns are less important than the group's. *Wa* is so predominant that business relationships and dealings take place between friends: Japan is the ultimate who-you-know-society. The Japanese do not like to deal with strangers.

A Japanese worker seldom interacts as an individual but as a member or representative of one group or another. Unlike the United States, the worker's specific talent (e.g., accountant or salesman) is typically less important than his or her group membership (Toyota or Honda). Within a Japanese organization, an individual's rank is normally more important than one's own name and the manager might even introduce himself merely by job title. A job in Japan is not merely a contractual arrangement for pay but means identification with a larger entity—a satisfying sense of being part of something big and significant, of bringing a sense of security, pride, and loyalty to the firm, of status to be shared with one's family. Employees regard themselves first and foremost as members of the clan rather than as individuals who have a certain skill and are only connected to the company by a contractual link, and thus are narrowly constrained to a particular set of functions. Japanese employees can and will do any task necessary for clan survival. Japanese staff are therefore ready for any efforts to ensure company viability rather than willing to meet only personal and professional goals.These values of obedience, loyalty, commitment, and harmony derive from Confucian traditions. The outcome of these values is the internal unity and teamwork seen in Japanese firms.

In the West, the church and the state have historically played an important role in the social and moral welfare of the population, but this was not the case in Japan. Consequently, in Japan after World War II, with the humanization of the emperor and the defeat of the military state, the gap was filled by companies that came to regard themselves as responsible for all aspects of their employees' lives (Campbell, 1985). Lifetime employment is commonplace, and changing jobs is infrequent. Companies assure their workers' security. In return, companies can expect a good work record and loyalty from employees. Japan is a honor-driven society, in which individuals are deeply bound by obligations of gratitude, loyalty, and deference. The honor and discipline of Japanese life are based on highly personal loyalties—to the feudal lord, to the honor of the family, and in these days to the corporation. A "stick" aspect of loyalty exists among the Japanese: People are loyal to their companies throughout their careers at least partly because no one else will hire them if they resign. Although lifetime employment is only prevalent at the top-tier companies (comprising about one third of the employment) and the emphasis has been moving away from it, lifetime employment influences employment practices throughout the country.

Corporate success and company goals are achieved through group effort and not through the exceptional activities of individuals. Ideally, there are no production heroes in a large company. Instead, there are persons whose work groups, teams, or departments have improved their productivity and gone beyond quotas. This emphasis on the group is the most important difference between American and Japanese work philosophies (Rosenberg, 1986). Sacrificing one's personal life for the good of the company is expected; this can result in giving up accrued vacation time or controlling one's inclination to confront others for the sake of maintaining harmony. This can also mean the ultimate sacrifice, to die for one's company while working (*karoshi*). This loyalty to the group leads naturally to policies favoring security of employment and against individual job moves and headhunting.

The concept of *w a* also requires consensus of the group. Members of a group must cooperate with and trust each other. One must sometimes subordinate the truth to maintain group harmony. Sincerity means support, not honesty. The group's survival is keyed to long-term behavior, and hence once accepted it is for life. Promotion of group harmony means that one's individuality and originality must be subdued. This extreme pressure to conform results in an intolerance of mavericks and original thinkers. Major groups include families, schools and universities, companies, government departments, and even clubs and organizations. In Japan the group can be exclusionary; the Japanese are "group-centric"—their groups exclude everyone, including other Japanese, from the in-group. Without a group, one is literally lost. How can workers step out of rank under these circumstances? As soon as an individual is rejected by a group, he or she loses social identity.

Another Japanese trait, insistence on harmony above all else, can often get in the way of results and efficiency. An American engineer who worked with Japan's space program observed that: "when harmony supplants physics, chaos results." Japanese space engineers installed a stress meter on a communications satellite incorrectly and ruined the $50,000 device when they tried to coax it to yield data. Asked why they had not changed their approach after it became clear that the instrument was not working, the engineers replied that they could not alter the original consensus decision about how to install the meter (Bylinsky, 1987). The Japanese promote social harmony, which is secured by insisting on conformism and deference to the point of repression. Instead of encouraging creativity, the entire Japanese educational experience is based on memorization of facts and group think—features which reappear in factory and business organizations, in which an unquestioned harmony is supposed to prevail. The system is rigid and hierarchical (the more important the boss, the deeper one's bow), and it accords enormous privileges to a male elite. Women are meant to take care of the home, manage the savings, and ensure the children's after-school education. Because of the consensus approach to management, the decision process in Japanese organizations (government or private) is a long one that takes weeks and months before a final decision is reached. However, such decisions allow fast and smooth implementation. Innovation, however, is considered to be one area in which the consensus approach may not work and in which thinking and decision by individual scientists and engineers would count more than their collective group-think. Thus a major difference between the two cultures as concerns the sociological unit: In Japan, the group is more important and dependence totally on the group.

Contrast this collectivist behavior to the intense individualism seen in the United States, which is indisputably the most individualistic society in the world (with the highest rating of any country in Hofstede's analysis); in America, the individual reigns supreme, with individual rights and a focus on individual success. Group cohesiveness, discipline, and consensus have helped Japan excel in applications—allowing process innovations and step-by-step innovations (evolutionary innovation) to flourish. This cultural tendency toward group working and group solidarity has contributed to the Japanese emphasis on mass production and total quality control, but these same factors have inhibited entrepreneurship and individual creativity. The Japanese are typically unwilling to differentiate themselves by stating new ideas or using different methods (Rosenberg, 1986). Hence, the acceptance of misfits, geniuses, entrepreneurs, and in general the ability to be different, which is a catalyst to the pursuit of inventions and radical innovations, is lacking in Japan but is readily apparent and available in the United States.

Power: Status, Hierarchy, and Authority versus Egalitarianism and Equality

The Japanese have been conditioned to accept authority unquestioningly in nearly every aspect of their lives. In Japan, there is a reluctance to take individual action against what is, for the moment, the established power. The average Japanese people are not mindless followers but, like Catholic priests and members of the Marine Corps, they live in a culture that honors authority and especially authority in the guise of seniority (Campbell, 1985). This is symbolized by their ritualized but ineffectual protest movements, their historical virtual one-party political rule, and the infrequency of lawsuits. The hierarchy of the firm is accepted, and senior management commands respect. In turn, management accepts it obligation to develop and help the employees. This reflects the Confucian ideal that a person always owes a debt of gratitude to parents and leaders. This debt can never be completely redeemed, and the group forever has a hold on the individual. This debt continues no matter how long the relationship lasts. An emphasis on titles establishes an individual's rank within the organization, thus reinforcing the hierarchy and group identity. The importance of hierarchy is the reason for constant exchanging of business cards in Japan. The main significance of the exchange is to make clear a manager's specific position and group affiliation.

Seniority is also measured in minute and seemingly rigid ways. An age difference of merely a year will identify who is senior and who is junior for the rest of their lives. Many relationships may be described in familial terms, and a boss is expected to act as a father figure to subordinates (Frost, 1987). Corporate workers are paid partly on the basis of seniority, not on individual productivity. Promotion is also based on seniority. These policies decrease the likelihood of individual jealously and competition. Hierarchies appear most everywhere: There is a well-understood if not formally acknowledged hierarchy of colleges in Japan, with Todai (Tokyo University) being foremost, Kyoto second, and so on.

The Japanese drive to excel has produced superior results in tests of achievement in math and science, on which many Japanese students score near the top. The Japanese educational system has created a highly literate, highly disciplined work force that is rightfully the envy of the world. But graduates end up being risk averse with lifetime jobs. The education system provides intense pressure to conform and not be different. There is a right way to do everything instead of different ways to solve a problem. Listening skills and obedience, rather than debating skills, are rewarded in Japan's educational system.

This system tends to favor the use of memory to an excessive degree, to the detriment of learning to use and develop a deductive form of reasoning. This is understandable when one considers that sheer memory is the only way to master the thousands of characters in the Japanese language. However, dependence on rote learning and conformity has severe disadvantages; it discards many strong personalities and potentially creative persons. The pressure to conform results in an intolerance of mavericks and original thinkers. The purpose of a Japanese education is not so much to develop the self but to enable the person to conform to the Japanese society (Murray and Lehner, 1990).

The education system values the effort that goes into activity as much as, if not more than, the output. The Japanese standardized tests—exam hell—are primarily tests of straightforward memorized information; they are measures of determination and effort, pure and simple. The pointlessness of their content actually enhances their value as tests of will. Colleges and businesses often admit and hire strictly on basis of test scores (Fallows, 1989a). The Japanese school system teaches students not to ask questions but to conform. Japanese education tends to place a limited value on conceptual thinking, which is essential for pure science (Bylinsky, 1987). This makes Japanese researchers reluctant to stand out or even ask questions after a lecture.

Japan's regimented society may be the secret to industrial triumph, but it spells disaster in the lab. In the Japanese laboratory or scientific organization, seniority is idolized, individuality denied, and debate stifled. Young scientists are expected to seek life-long employment. During a scientist's most productive years—the thirties—the scientist is at the mercy of the boss with little freedom to think or travel. Professors and lab managers in their late forties and fifties hold absolute power, whereas their underlings wait patiently, building seniority. Only time (not ability) in Japan counts toward advancement. Scientists are forced to work under more senior professors, and only seniority brings with it a chance to do independent work. The youngest, brightest, and most motivated often are treated like field hands at the mercy of their bosses, expected to keep their ideas to themselves and do their bosses' projects. Many Japanese labs are full of deadwood who have retired on the job (Yoder, 1988). A scientist can't job hop in Japan; it is not considered professionally acceptable. This weakness is now recognized and the seniority system within academia is weakening rapidly, but its effects will take decades to overcome and correct.

Japanese graduate students in the basic sciences are encouraged to look to Western journals rather than to try something new. The prevailing attitude is: "Don't rock the boat; if you're different, you're a minus." Even dissent is not approved since it could cause seniors to lose face: "Too many times in a typical lab, younger researchers have good ideas but hesitate to bring them up in front of a senior, either out of fear of having their ideas critiqued, or sometimes fearing that it would be an embarrassment to the older researcher" (Berger, 1987). Since grants are predominantly government provided, there are powerful incentives to play by rules: If one doesn't, one's applications for grants could end up rejected. Grants are not given on the basis of track record but to position and title. Peer review is unknown. Doing what everyone else is doing is the preferred way to get along, win tenure, gain recognition, and obtain grant money. The attitude is: "Why do an experiment no one else is doing? You should be doing what everybody else in the world is doing." The Japanese think of science as something you study, not invent. Japanese culture views the future as something that already exists and is waiting to be discovered. The proactive Western tradition views the future as something to be created (Yoder, 1988).

For all the press about Johnny not being able to read in the United States, the United States' education system continues to excel at the graduate level, with foreigners flocking to study in American colleges (including tens of thousands of Japanese students of engineering and basic sciences). The superior research environment, relative openness, tolerance, heterogeneity, and open nature of this melting pot has induced many foreigners to stay. The United States grants five times as many Ph.D.s per capita in science and engineering as Japan. The scientists and engineers who populate American universities and laboratories think of themselves as members of a global community of researchers who work jointly on papers, meet periodically in international conferences, exchange papers, and publish their findings worldwide. American graduate students come from every nation on earth (more foreign students receive Ph.D.s in engineering from American universities than American students), and most return to their home countries (Reich, 1987). Japan, which is closed, conformist, homogeneous, and intolerant to any non-Japanese, attracts few immigrants and even fewer students.

Contrast the Japanese status consciousness to the American egalitarian philosophy. In a status-conscious society, there is considerable risk avoidance (which is the case in Japan), and the fear of being different from one's in-group. The greater the power-distance rating of a society, the less radical innovation and inventions. On the other hand, the less status consciousness within a society, the more basic science and radical innovations.

Uncertainty Avoidance: Acceptance or Avoidance of Risk

The Japanese culture does not encourage breaking way and does not promote the rugged individuality that is usually an integral part of any entrepreneurial activity (Harper, 1988). Japanese management styles work in Japan because its culture, values, goals, and ideology all merge, act as an extended family, and emphasize commitment, loyalty, and identification to firm and to nation. The Japanese culture places a premium on dependability, quality, cooperative behavior, and respect for authority. The Japanese culture pays particular attention to the overall flow of things , the process. The Japanese avoid risk due to the high degree of collectivism, group think, and homogeneity within their culture.

Japanese firms manage risk differently than American firms: They tend to share the unanticipated costs of economic change. The primary subcontractors of large Japanese corporations often receive a great deal of financial and technical support from the core firm. This encourages small companies to experiment and innovate because they know that the penalties for failure seldom include outright termination of the relationship. Likewise, if a risky R&D project undertaken by a subcontractor does produce a breakthrough, the gains are shared throughout the production system, and are not appropriated entirely by the large firm. This holds true even if, as is common, the core firm has financed much of the cost of doing the research in the first place.

One of the necessary ingredients for innovation is the entrepreneur. However, the presence of entrepreneurs does not guarantee innovation. It is the entrepreneur's willingness to venture out, be nonconformist, and look for new solutions (which larger companies cannot or will not do) that allows innovation to flourish. In Japan, it is unusual for an individual alone or as part of an entrepreneurial team to set out on his or her own, raise venture capital, and establish a new company. An individual who would leave an established company to start a new company would be considered an eccentric and a social outcast in Japan, not a hero as he or she would often be in America. In the Japanese culture, no role model equivalent to Horatio Alger exists. The occasional Japanese entrepreneur succeeds not because of the system but despite it. Soichiro Honda built his successful automotive company despite the extreme pressure put on him by the government-business establishment to stick to motorcycles (Ramo, 1988). The risk-taking entrepreneur in Japan has social pressures as well as financial obstacles in the way of success. It is risky to leave one's group, to dare to be different. Clearly, entrepreneurism is stronger and has a longer heritage in the United States than in Japan. As we would also expect, the role of the independent inventor differs considerably: An estimated 20 percent of inventions in the United States versus only 4 percent in Japan are derived from independent inventors.

Contrast this risk avoidance tendency for Japan (extremely high, as the Hofstede scores indicate) to the United States, where risk taking may not always be enjoyed or sought after, but risk is accepted as part of life and Americans are more likely to seek risk or accept those who do. Americans who do seek risk (entrepreneurs) are often admired and their actions are imitated. The penalties to go out on one's own, to go try and make it alone, are minimal in the United States but often prohibitive in Japan. In Silicon Valley, failure does not condemn the individual but actually enhances his or her value, as it indicates lessons have been learned. This is not the case in Japan.

One would expect that avoidance of risk inhibits radical innovation and invention, whereas a more accepting societal attitude toward risk would tend to be positively correlated to the generation of radical innovation and inventions.

Masculinity versus Femininity: Aggression and Competitiveness

The great pressures of preserving honor and face drive the Japanese need to achieve, to succeed. Often, unrealistically ambitious personal success drives them. The dependent child may be compulsively driven by his mother's expectations of him. Japanese children are socialized by their families to value achievement as well as to need to be part of a group.

Japan has a national industrial ideology that is oriented toward self-improvement (i.e. greater quality and efficiency), toward a world view in which exports are emphasized, and toward evaluation of performance on the basis of long-term rather than short-term results (Alston, 1986). The drive to excel, to be number one in everything, rules the Japanese mentality. The debacle over the FSX during the late 1980s was a prime example of this. The Japanese can buy fighter planes from the United States at one third the cost of making them in Japan, and with their low defense posturing there is no great need for the capacity to build them. So why go to all the effort? A Japanese planner said that "this is another industry we must participate in and try to dominate." Part of this achievement drive can be seen in the Japanese acceptance of change. Japan exists as a series of volcanic islands, and the Japanese have always lived with geological change and therefore have adapted to the constant dynamics of their land as a way of life. Change is treated as a positive force and one that will always exist.

Another reflection of the traditionally masculine drive of Japanese society is its attitude towards women; in this, the Japanese must rate as nearly the most chauvinistic of any society in the world. Women seem shamefully exploited in Japanese society. The old Confucian adage that a woman should in her youth obey her father, in maturity her husband, and in old age her son still has many hard-line followers in Japan. Likewise, the double sexual standard is still expected and accepted standard for many in Japan. Women are subordinated to men. Married women often have virtually no social life outside of the family. In the home, however, the female traditionally ruled supreme, making most of the decisions and spending all the money. Most older Japanese men in Japan have no money except that which is company money and that which their wife gives them as a daily allowance. Japan is still a man's world, with women confined to a secondary position; this is changing but is still prevalent.

Thus, one is likely to find that the more masculine the society, the greater the drive for achievement (within the established social structure) and the higher the process and evolutionary innovations will tend to be.

Confucian Dynamics

The "Confucian Dynamism" dimension has the relative importance of: persistence (perseverance), ordering relationships by status and observing this order, thrift, having a sense of shame, protecting your face, respect for tradition, and reciprocation of greeting, favors, and gifts. A sense of shame supports interrelatedness through sensitivity to social contacts. Thrift leads to savings, which means availability of capital for reinvestment (an obvious asset to economic growth). Persistence or perseverance suggests a general tenacity in the pursuit of whatever goals a person selects, including economic goals.

Confucian societies uniformly promote education, a desire for accomplishment in various skills (particularly academic and cultural), and seriousness about tasks, job, family, and obligations. A properly trained member of a Confucian culture will be hard working, responsible, skillful, and (within the assigned or understood limits) ambitious and creative in helping the group (extended family, community, or company). There is much less emphasis on advancing individual (selfish) interests (Kahn, 1979). Thus, societies with high Confucian characteristics have patience, a long-term viewpoint (decades, not quarters), and a family philosophy which is conducive to evolutionary or process innovations.

Homogeneity versus Heterogeneity: Ethnocentrism

Japan is a highly homogeneous population, has been resistant to invasion and immigration for thousands of years, and has cultivated a society that, with only slight variation, shares the same values, norms, language, and aesthetics. A strong sense of national identification exists, and a somewhat greater ease of communication may result from this shared tradition. Japan's cultural premises have been shaped not by a single religious faith but by three: Confucianism, Shintoism, Buddhism. Yet all have a form and context that are uniquely Japanese, and they converge more than they diverge. Out of Confucianism has come a vertical society, a hierarchical ordering of society based on status differences with regard to age, tenure, sex, and ability. Out of the Shintoist tradition has arisen an empathy with nature and search for harmony. The family not only dominates; it is the prototype model for the entire society. Buddhism brought with it the love of nature seen in Japan.

The Japanese today are the most thoroughly unified and culturally homogeneous people in the world. Isolated by an accident of geography and equally by deliberate policies of exclusion, Japan has had no significant immigration by outsiders throughout its history. The nation has little ethnic diversity. Despite a population half that of the United States and the seventh largest in the world, outsiders constitute less than 1 percent of the population and are not tolerated or assimilated in society. Few, if any, Japanese venture outside of their own country (less than 5 percent in any one year, substantially less than in the United States or Europe), and even those that do travel in tour groups, which by their very nature limit or avoid contact with the local population. Members of a tight-knit Japanese work group or neighborhood will spontaneously sacrifice more for one another than their counterparts in the United States, will but they are a lot less likely to sacrifice for someone outside the group. Volunteer work and charitable organizations, like the United Way and Community Chest, are virtually unknown in Japan, and there is little instinctive concern about starving children in Ethiopia, earthquake victims in Armenia, or refugees from Indochina.

Few, if any, truly sharp differences divide the population or culturally alienate one group from another. Writers often refer to Japan as resembling an extended family more than a corporate state. As is the case with families, it is thought that less needs to be communicated through words: Thoughts and feelings can be more cryptically conveyed through subtle physical cues understandable by members of the clan but not by those outside the group. Many Japanese do not know how to function comfortably with a non-Japanese in their midst: How is one supposed to deal with a *gaijin* who does not know the instinctive rules of conduct?

Japan may be a country open to new ideas, but it is hardly open to foreigners. The Japanese themselves are often xenophobic and considerably ethnocentric. Former Prime Minister Nakasone, who was considered to be one of the Japanese leaders most open to the outside world, declared on September 22, 1986 that "the intellectual level of the United States is much lower than that of Japan, because of the presence of Blacks, Puerto Ricans, and Mexicans." The Japanese view themselves as culturally superior to the rest of the world; some of them assert seriously that the Japanese are physically different from the rest of the world. Many Japanese presume that non-Japanese are physically, culturally, and mentally incapable of speaking Japanese. They have avoided for years accepting any refugees and even today accept only minimal token numbers; they would rather pay for refugee camps somewhere else. Although Japanese foreign aid now exceeds that from the United States, it usually has lots of strings attached, which lead to only Japanese companies benefiting. Third-generation Koreans, born and raised in Japan, carry Korean passports and are unable to obtain Japanese citizenship (Fallows, 1989a). Even with a looming labor shortage, Japan is opposed to bringing in workers from other countries. The government argues that the country's precious homogeneity must be protected.

Japanese ethnocentrism can easily be seen around the world. American and European multinationals tend to have locals run important divisions and most certainly the local operations; contrast this to the Japanese policy of Japanese citizens running virtually all important divisions and almost all overseas offices of major Japanese firms. Japanese firms select few, if any, non-Japanese for local management jobs, let alone home office corporate responsibilities: "Westerners do have to think about one day being the noncommissioned officers in Japan's economic army" (Fallows, 1989b). The Japanese do not believe that foreigners are able to practice business or make decisions. Even today, consciousness of foreigners is still pervasive.

Contrast this ethnocentrism to one of the foundations of the United States, which Americans believe enabled them to climb to the top of the world system—the concept of the melting pot, the bringing together of the banished and the disinherited of this world in a society with equal rights and freedom for all. One of America's major strengths is the ability to absorb and assimilate all nationalities, not rejecting them for their differences but accepting those differences and integrating cultures into the American mainstream. This could never be possible in Japan. Homogeneity suggests a fear of being different and thus doing what everyone else is doing. Homogeneity tolerates little diversity; people are rejected if they are different. In a heterogeneous society like America, people can afford to be individualistic. Individualism allows tolerance for others, for misfits and nonconformists, and for the views of others, no matter how deviant or off-the-wall they may be. Tolerance is a necessary trait for the sourcing of radical innovation.

One would expect that homogeneous societies would inhibit radical innovations or inventions but would tend to propagate process or evolutionary innovations. On the other hand, heterogeneous societies would tend to have more flexible attitudes and allow differences, which would be more conducive to the generation of radical innovations and inventions.

Long-Term versus Short-Term Perspectives

Unlike U.S. business executives, Japan's attitude is more long term and gives less weight to the short term (Fallows, 1989b). The Japanese decision-making consensus does not allow the Japanese to respond quickly. They may not be the first to market, but they are excellent followers. They will sacrifice short-term profits for long-term market share. The Japanese appear to operate with a hit-a-single mentality. If you get on base every time you go to bat, in the long run you will score many runs and never be shut out. The Japanese hire people for their potential to learn, grow, and change as their company changes. Performance reviews and promotions are sometimes postponed for years so people have a chance to show their true value. Japanese firms are not victim to Wall Street's preoccupation with quarterly financial results; they are financed primarily with long-term debt by banks, which also tend to be major stockholders and therefore have an investment in their long-term survival.

There may also be something to the idea that short-term pressures for ever-rising quarterly profits are more intense in the United States than elsewhere. R&D spending in the United States is, for example, cyclical—falling in recessions and rising in booms. This pattern is not observed abroad, and it does not make economic sense. If a project is bad, it should have been killed before the recession began; if a project is good, it should not be killed simply because of a few months of negative sales. Cutting R&D is the easy way to make those quarterly profits rise while sales are falling, since doing so has no short-run negative effects on sales. During recessions, plant expansion is also cut back more radically in the United States than abroad. Often, as was the case in the semiconductor industry, this has given foreign competitors a chance to grab market share when demand expands at the end of recessions, since their American competitors do not have the immediate capacity to service expanding demand and have fallen behind on developing new products or processes. The Japanese thought that the long-run payoffs from higher quality cars were so great that in the short run they were willing to make noneconomic investments that did not meet their own rate of return criteria. American firms were not willing to pay a premium for quality and usually waited for those rates of return on investment to reach the right economic levels before they invested in robots (Thurow, 1987).

Thus, long-term perspectives appear to be conducive in evolutionary and process innovations, whereas short-term perspectives inhibit the ability to derive or adopt them.

PROPOSITIONS

The following propositions would appear to be reasonable (Herbig and Miller, 1991):

Proposition 1: The higher the individualism for any given society, the greater the tendency to generate radical innovations and inventions.

Proposition 2: The greater the collectivist nature of a society, the greater the tendency to generate evolutionary and process innovations. The greater the collectivist nature of a society, the fewer radical innovations and inventions that are generated.

Proposition 3: The higher the power structure in a society, the less the ability to generate radical innovations and inventions. The higher the power structure in a society, the greater the tendency to concentrate and excel at process and evolutionary innovations. The lower the power structure in a society, the greater the ability to generate radical innovations and inventions.

Proposition 4: The higher the uncertainty avoidance (risk avoidance) in a society, the greater the tendency to generate process and evolutionary innovations and the less the ability to excel at radical innovations and inventions. The lower the uncertainty avoidance (risk taking) in a society, the greater the means to generate radical innovations and inventions.

Proposition 5: The higher the masculinity and, the more sexist a society, the less the society is willing to utilize the talents of its female members; hence, its relative contribution of radical innovations and inventions should be lower.

Proposition 6: The higher a society's tendency toward Confucian characteristics, the more the emphasis on evolutionary innovations.

Proposition 7: The more homogeneous a society is, the greater the tendency toward process and evolutionary innovations and avoidance of radical innovations and inventiveness. The more heterogeneous a society is, the more capability it has to generate radical innovations and inventions.

Proposition 8: The longer term horizon a society has, the more impetus is provided to produce process and evolutionary innovations. The shorter term horizon a society has, the more process and evolutionary innovations are inhibited.

Proposition 9: Individualism, risk taking, heterogeneity, and entrepreneurism are a cultural cluster that tend to reinforce each other's presence. The presence of this cluster in the United States acts to create a climate favorable for radical innovations.

Proposition 10: A collectivist orientation, status, masculinity, homogeneity, and long-term horizons in Japan tend to encourage process innovations and evolutionary innovative capabilities.

Table 7.1 provides a single matrix comparing the types of innovation and the dimensions of culture and their proposed effects.

Table 7.1
Culture-Innovation Impacts

		INVENTION	RADICAL	EVOLU-TIONARY	PROCESS
I-C	INDIVIDUALISM	+	+	-	-
	COLLECTIVIST	-	-	+	+
POWER	STATUS/HIERARCHY	-	-	+	+
	EGALITARIAN	+	+	o	o
RISK	AVOIDANCE	-	-	+	+
	TAKERS	+	+	o	o
M-F	ACHIEVEMENT/ COMPETITIVE	u	u	+	+
	LAISSEZ FAIRE	u	u	o	o
COMPO-SITION	HOMOGENEOUS	-	-	+	+
	HETEROGENEOUS	+	+	o	o
TERM	SHORT TERM	u	u	-	-
	LONG TERM	u	u	+	+

KEY:
+ Positive Impact
– Negative Impact
o No Conjectual Impact
u Unknown Impact

Source: P. Herbig and J. Miller. (1991). "The Effect of Culture Upon Innovativeness: A Comparison of United States and Japanese Sourcing Capabilities." *Journal of International Consumer Marketing* 3/3: 48. Reprinted by permission of Haworth Press, Inc.

SUMMARY

What provides the Japanese with their strengths in process and evolutionary innovation are exactly those elements that cause their weaknesses in radical innovations and inventions. American cultural strengths of individualism, entrepreneurism, risk taking, and openness tend to explain the propensity to seek newness and apply creativity through radical innovation and invention but may work against the teamwork and patience, which are necessary for process innovations. The Japanese cultural strengths of group cohesiveness, loyalty, homogeneity, and long-term outlook tend to explain their strengths in process and evolutionary innovations but at the same time act as a barrier to the factors necessary for invention and radical innovation.

It would be simplistic to expect cultural attributes to be the only determinants of innovative capabilities in a society. However, there appear to be significant and substantial relationships in this respect for Japan and the United States.

DISCUSSION

Can the Japanese culture generate creativity based on the special characteristics of the Japanese people? If Japan wants to develop more basic science and radical innovations, it must restructure its educational institutions and social institutions, with more emphasis on individualism and less on deference to superiors and group opinions (Christopher, 1983). The highly authority-respecting, status-conscious aspects of the culture must change if its natural creativity is to appear. The Japanese people themselves agree that changes are necessary. If the society is not willing or able to change, then the Japanese must either overcome their greatest challenge ever—creativity without an environment conducive to it (a typical Japanese solution would be to integrate creativity in their society)—or be forever cast as the supreme imitators.

Japan has prospered by borrowing licensed Western technology and improving on it. Need Japan innovate at all? Perhaps manufacturing efficiency and getting products out the door quickly and in high quality may be what Japan does best and should continue to do. Until now, the Japanese have seen no reason to go to the trouble of innovating; they've been able to acquire all the innovations by the simple expedient of buying them; in the past thirty years, they have spent more than $10 billion on purchases of foreign technology and in the process has saved a great deal of time and wasted motion (Christopher, 1983). As long as Japan retains the ability to make more effective practical use of Western scientific innovation than the West itself does, borrowing technology may be a valid strategy for the Japanese. The potential inherent in developing already known technology is so enormous that it will provide room for growth for the next half-century. And as long as others are impelled to provide the creativity, development will always be a better financial bet (Berger, 1987).

The Japanese will gladly give to the Americans all the Nobel prizes; they're not worth anything practically unless converted into products—and this is where the Japanese excel. Unless something changes, the more inventive ideas the United States dreams up, the farther it will fall behind. Each one will be just another opportunity for a foreign rival to out-innovate a U.S. company in producing it. Product innovation is like a ladder: Climb and you acquire new knowledge that confers a competitive advantage, but only until your competitors join you; then you have to climb some more. The more productive route is process innovation: unveiling not entirely new products that keep getting better, more reliable, and cheaper. The cumulation of a large number of small improvements is the surest path in most industries to increasing competitive advantage: This is where the Japanese excel. Japanese innovation is the result of tiny improvements in a thousand places.

Americans will always lead the world in the creation of new ideas. They are pioneers, rebels, and tinkerers. In the new technology fields of cold fusion, superconductors, optical computers, organic computers, and quantum transistors the United States is still in the forefront of technology (*Business Week,* 1989 special edition on innovation). The United States' comparative advantage is still in advanced technology. However, information about technology now flows quickly around the world. In the past, a U.S. industry with a superior technology could count on maintaining a worldwide advantage for several years, but this is no longer true. New products often come from overseas and further erode returns to U.S. investors. The short half-life of a technological edge leads to underinvestment in R&D.

If America is to prosper and maintain its leadership in the world, it must become more long-term focused and more customer oriented. R&D, instead of being the first item cut in troubled times, must be increased drastically. The United States can then continue to excel at inventions and remain the idea generator of the world. But since the money seems to be in the production end, unless America is to become the consumer of the world, productivity and process improvements must be given equal, if not higher, weights than basic research. It does the U.S. little good to design state-of-the-art products, if within a short time its foreign competitors can manufacture them more cheaply. This entails reprioritizing funds, prestige, and status to the manufacturing floor as well as lengthening the business outlook of the American corporate manager from a quarterly perspective to many years. Only then will the United States be competitive internationally.

Only by capturing the "rent" on an innovation through volume sales of a product can a company amortize its R&D costs and invest in R&D for the next-generation product. If a firm simply tries to sell a lab product to someone else to produce, the value of the design is lower than that of a prototype; prototypes are valued lower than products that have established markets; and each step toward the market decreases uncertainty and increases value added. A producer with a strong market position often can buy a portfolio of technologies at a low price and capture the technology rents through volume sales. For the firm, production matters.

The economic value of first-mover advantages is overrated because innovations are often poorly designed in their earliest stages and in numerous ways ill adapted to their ultimate applications. Copycat producers can always undercut prices because they do not have hefty development costs to recover. The incremental improvements underlying development play a critical role in the eventual capture of returns from innovation (Rosenberg and Steinmueller, 1988).

Even America's advantage in basic science is at risk. The United States is in jeopardy of becoming a technology colony of Japan. Just as oil is a raw material shipped from Indonesia or the Middle East to Japan to be returned in the form of manufactured goods; so might be the case for technology and the United States. The Japanese are finding that they can buy raw technology from the United States cheaply, in the form of ownership of high-technology firms or interests in lab projects. America is selling its birthright for virtually pennies. Often a new venture or an institute attempting to find corporate backers for a project will find few domestic takers but hoards of Japanese firms wanting to participate. The Japanese companies are outdoing their U.S. counterparts in tapping America's reservoir of budding technologies. On many campuses, Japanese delegations are more common than U.S. visitors. Foreign companies are setting up research laboratories in the United States and staffing them with American scientists and engineers. In 1986, Japanese companies placed more than $250 million in American venture capital funds. The Japanese want licensing, marketing, and joint venture agreements with the companies they back. Faced with extensive Japanese competition, even the largest and most endowed American firms have concluded that joining them is the wiser strategy than trying to beat them. Motorola linked up with Toshiba to build a new chip making facility in Japan. AT&T and Fujitsu will share their technology (Reich, 1987). Even acquisitions are not unusual; Fairchild was almost acquired during the 1980s until the cries of the U.S. defense establishment forced the Japanese partner to withdraw from the deal.

One alternative is a United States (and Western) embargo of technology, of basic science, toward Japan. This is not viable or realistic. You can't put the genie back into the bottle. In today's world of global communications, scientific exchanges, technology transfer, and the increasing blurring of national entities (is IBM American?; is Honda Japanese?), information is fluid and almost impossible to contain. Such an action, even if possible, could be analogous to the embargo of 1940, with high technology (basic science) replacing the scrap iron, oil, and rubber (basic raw materials) of the prior era. The result could be the economic equivalent of Pearl Harbor and a worldwide trade war.

The only true alternative is twofold: (1) For the United States to encourage adoption and an emphasis on process innovation; reestablish onshore manufacturing; and increase the emphasis on its own source of venture capital, entrepreneurs, and R&D funding; and (2) For Japan to accept free trade; open its economy to both foreign manufactured goods; make its distribution system more equitable and efficient; concentrate more on its consumers and its poor infrastructure; make itself more hospitable and open to outsiders and make the necessary changes to its societal and educational structure that will enhance individualism and egalitarianism and openness to its society. The future will be one of continuous change and incomplete information. To be successful, risk, entrepreneurs, and a willingness to explore uncharted terrain must be available. It appears highly probable that Americans will be the pioneers and entrepreneurs in creating the next set of new technological innovations. But who will be the managers: American owners or Japanese expatriates?

Chapter 8

The Future of Japanese Innovation: Leader or Follower?

REVOLUTIONARY INNOVATION AND CREATIVITY

The Japanese government and corporations are engaged in a serious bid to eliminate their poor basic innovation record. Six of the strategies being pursued by Japanese corporations to instill creativity include new research centers (technopolises), aggressive recruiting, liberalized R&D management policies, corporate spinouts and buyouts, strategic alliances, and donations to foreign universities. Suggestions for improving research in Japan (Makino, 1987) include the following: (1) Introduce performance rating in national research institutions and university research departments, which will allow for firing of personnel or disbanding of organizations that fail; (2) give government funds to private research institutions; and (3) replace government research personnel with more aggressive researchers from private organizations. To obtain immediate returns on R&D investment, the largest proportion of Japan's R&D activity has continuously gone to development research. The Japanese corporations must strengthen R&D activities by increasing R&D expenditures and staff and reorganizing corporate organizational structures in favor of larger, more independent, and more powerful R&D departments, divisions, labs, institutes or corporations.

Government policy incentives for promoting radical innovation in the private sector include (1) the provision and improvement of economic and social infrastructures for promoting R&D activity and technological innovation, including expanding scientific and technical education and engineering training institutions, streamlining technical evaluation procedures, and improving government research labs; (2)

the adoption of fiscal and financial measures, such as accelerated depreciation allowances for plant, machinery, and equipment utilized for R&D activities; allowing contributions to designated institutions to be deducted from income tax; by providing low-interest loans by government; and encouraging growth of small R&D venture businesses by guaranteeing their loans and insurance coverage; and (3) by the development of additional private sector institutions for technological innovations. Since Japan and the West appear to have complementary strengths, both stand to gain from cooperative research. The Japanese bring a new way of viewing and using ideas that have been generated in the West. Japanese approaches offer Westerners prospects for new creative breakthroughs. But technologies must be shared to enable this to work.

Technopolises

In 1980, MITI announced the Technopolis Concept, a plan to build a network of nineteen high-tech cities throughout Japan. These cities were planned to be the engines for Japan's economic growth in the twenty-first century. They would be located in unspoiled rural areas and offer ample housing, shopping malls, schools, recreational areas, lifelong learning centers, and a relaxed lifestyle more typically found in the West. Telecommunications networks and online databases would link researchers to the latest developments around the world During the twenty-first century, MITI expects these technopolises to become the greenhouse for creative new researchers and technologies. They will be the focal point for advanced research in sunrise industries such as biotechnology, electronics, new materials, robotics, mechatronics, computers, and software. Companies relocating to these technopolises will be eligible to receive tax incentives and Japan Development Bank loans. Special retraining programs will be available for people returning from larger cities. Figure 8.1 shows the projected technopolises.

One example of a technopolis is the science city at Tsukuba. Tsukuba (thirty miles north of Tokyo) is an hour's drive from Tokyo, far enough away to provide large, uncluttered laboratories in a green environment, yet close enough to escape to easily. It has over 13,000 researchers and is home to over 200 companies. It has two universities, fifty-two research institutes, a medical center, and residential housing and has become the focus of industry/government laboratory R&D coordination. Tsukuba is home to half the public sector research institutes in Japan,

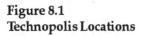

Figure 8.1
Technopolis Locations

Hokkaido

Aomoi

Akita

Yamagata

Nagaoka

Nagano

Toyama

Motioka

Sendai

Fukushima

Utsunomiya

Kolu

Hamamatsu

Nishiharima

Okayama

Hiroshima

Ubo

Kagawa

Ehima

Kuruma-Tosu

Nagasaki

Kumamoto

Kagoshima

Oila

Miyazaki

Source: MITI

measured by personnel and budget. Fifteen billion dollars in government money has been spent in this technopolis. Most large corporations maintain some liaison or coordinating presence at Tsukuba with the expectation of enjoying the benefits of those government laboratories. The Japanese government has relocated older government research institutes from other parts of Japan to this central site and has equipped them with the latest apparatus.

Other such technopolises are being created throughout Japan, which has a thirty-year plan to create nineteen Japanese versions of Silicon Valley. On the island of Kyushu, the Kumamotot technopolis will cost an estimated $300 million to develop and will have up to 1,000 scientists working at the technology headquarters and new start-up companies nearby. This technopolis will specialize in automation, biotechnology, computers and data processing. The technopolis in the vicinity of Okayama will focus on biotechnology. The technopolis at Hiroshima is mainly concerned with electronics, mechatronics (the combination of mechanical and electronic engineering), new materials, biotechnology, and new energy sources. Sendai City plans to combine private firms, government, and academic institutions into megaresearch programs such as the New Material Development Consortium (space equipment materials) and the International Research Institute of New Earth Creation (ocean, weather, and atmosphere research). Major highway and bullet train corridors will connect cities on the Sea of Japan and the Pacific Ocean, and a major new international airport will be built. The aim is to create new, internationally focused cities in which technology and human elements can coexist. Two dozen new research institutes have been built throughout Japan as part of the technopolis concept.

The world technopolis symbolizes the merging of two key ideas that drove Japan's industrial strategies during the 1980s and are expected to drive Japan during the 1990s. The first idea (technology) calls for modernizing Japan's sunset industries with an injection of creative grassroots technologies (i.e., doing what the Japanese do best, evolutionary innovation, updating mature markets with new products and new technologies). The second idea (polis) comes from the ancient Greek city-states, which emphasized a balance between private industry and the public sharing of ideas and responsibilities. The technopolis concept is based on the idea of forging a working partnership among businesses (*san*), universities (*gaku*), and local governments (*kan*). Coordinated through the technopolis process, MITI has encouraged heated competition among the prefectures for new programs and policies.

MITI is not trying to re-create Silicon Valley but to adapt the best features of American high-tech regions to a uniquely Japanese model of high-tech development. MITI's idea of *ikusei,* or nurturing of people and industry, is the key. This term refers to MITI's method of systematically nurturing infant industries through careful guidance and financial backing. In the past, *ikusei* referred to the transfer of technology and manufacturing techniques. In this regard, it is aimed at stimulating the process of innovation by cultivating people and high-tech cities. The key difference between the technopolis concept and Silicon Valley is that whereas the latter developed spontaneously and chaotically, the technopolises are being systematically planned and cultivated by local governments.

Risk taking and entrepreneurialism have long been ignored and forgotten stepchildren in Japan's cautious, follow-the-leader business environment. Worried about security and prestige, Japanese youth typically compete fiercely for limited positions in major corporations. Small businesses have been viewed as secondary players in Japan's economic recovery, a trend reinforced by MITI policies which gave short shrift to small businesses. Many obstacles block the development of a thriving venture capital market and venture businesses in Japan. The biggest roadblock is Japan's highly group-oriented society, which discourages individual actions. If one wants to be an aspiring entrepreneur, one's parents, family, friends, and colleagues will often work together to discourage the individual. Entrepreneurs are called *datsusara,* meaning "salarymen who have broken loose," which suggests that they are rebels who cannot work well with other people rather than ground-breaking pioneers. Start-up ventures have had an extremely difficult time finding qualified scientists, researchers, and other technical staff.

Other legal and organizational roadblocks exist. Japan's Federal Trade Commission prevents venture capital firms from placing their employees on venture business staffs and prohibits venture capitalists from owning more than 49 percent of new ventures. These rules enforce an arms-length relationship. Most Japanese venture capital companies act like finance companies, pursuing low-risk, low-return strategies due to their *keiretsu* connections with major banks. Thus, for most entrepreneurs, family and friends are the major source of funds. But this family operation style has its own problems. Once they have established a company, entrepreneurs are often reluctant to sell out because of family pressures. Yet in order to succeed, these start-ups usually need a vigorous shot of funding and marketing expertise, which most entrepreneur scientists are unable to provide. Thus, entrepreneurs have good ideas but no money and nowhere to go, and their mortality rate is high. What is lacking in Japan in comparison to the Western experience and is not likely to appear in the near future is the small firm set up by university scientists to commercialize new scientific inventions. This may be partly attributable to the Japanese regulation that prohibits national university professors from engaging in private business.

The sponsors of technopolises admire Silicon Valley's dynamism, pleasant climate, talented engineers, high educational levels, and recreational and cultural activities but are highly critical of its exorbitant housing costs, traffic jams, pollution, lack of planning, and worsening living conditions. The Technopolis '90 committee identified the key factors that led to the valley's success—its research universities, industrial parks, large pool of talented engineers, venture capital market, investment banking, management consulting firms, support services, and informal networks. The strengths of Japan's major high-tech cities are in their massive concentration of universities and corporate labs, easy access to technology and market information, highly qualified labor, airports, highways, telecommunications systems, management networks, and personal ties. These two models of high-tech developed were merged into the technopolis concept. This is a synthesis of three streams of thought: MITI high-tech research strategy, Japan's regional development programs, and Silicon Valley's process of innovation.

FOREIGN RESEARCH AVAILABILITY

The internationalization of the technology development function of large Japanese firms has been somewhat more complex and involves five stages. The first stage, technology scanning, is associated with the first stage of internationalization, in which Japanese companies manufacture products in Japan for sale abroad. In this stage, the company focuses on developing organizational systems to collect scientific and technical information and product information for use in the product development organization back in Japan. Some companies have relied heavily on sending individual scouts on specific technology-gathering missions; others established separate offices in the United States and Europe that were explicitly charged with technology scanning. The companies relied primarily on their own nationals in staffing these offices. These offices are the forefront of the Japanese international technological effort.

The second stage involves the creation of an organizational system to support the transfer of technology to production facilities overseas. Most production transplants have set up a technology department, thus following the standard Japanese pattern, in which each major factory is supported by a technology department or laboratory capable of process technology development and some incremental product improvement. In some companies, these technologies evolved to suit local markets, although new product developments remained concentrated in Japan. These offshore technology departments were usually heavily staffed by Japanese, although of course local engineers were also recruited.

The formal establishment of R&D laboratories marks the beginning of the third stage. However, for many Japanese companies, the overseas laboratory, despite being called an R&D center, has done very little actual research or product development. Most of the real research or development is still done in Japan at this stage. Instead, the overseas laboratory has often been a base for performing a range of other activities: technical cooperation with suppliers, support for technology transfer into production facilities, cross-licensing support, and the supervision of contract research. The overseas research laboratories of several of the leading Japanese pharmaceutical companies exemplify this stage. Instead of carrying out research directly, they contract out research to independent laboratories and specialized drug testing companies, which supervise the clinical trials necessary to satisfy local regulatory requirements. In addition, they monitor technological trends and evaluate emerging technologies and new products.

In the fourth stage, overseas research laboratories embark on new product development, which becomes their central mission. These overseas laboratories epitomize what is generally defined as an internationalization of R&D. The fifth stage extends the strategic mandate to encompass basic research, wherein the laboratory participates in an advanced, global division of technology development within the company.

Japanese firms want to become true international companies, on the model of leading Western multinationals like IBM. This will be difficult in an isolationist society and homogeneous culture as is found in Japan. In addition, Japanese managers anticipate a growing shortage of scientists and engineers within Japan itself, as the aging of the Japanese population reduces the numbers of university graduates and as they must increasingly compete for those graduates with the financial services sector (which is hiring more and more scientific and technical graduates) and with foreign firms establishing R&D facilities in

Japan. A survey of 177 leading Japanese firms (*Nihon Keizai Shimbun*, September 13, 1988) found that over 80 percent of the respondents were either actively working to establish R&D bases abroad or were interested in doing so. Otsuka Pharmaceuticals Co. Ltd., for example, has set up research facilities in Maryland and Seattle in the United States and in Frankfurt, Germany; its mandates cover basic research as well as clinical development. NEC has established a basic research facility in Princeton, New Jersey. Ricoh established a center for research in artificial intelligence in Silicon Valley (Sakakibara and Westney, 1992). During the period from 1988 to 1993, Japanese corporate labs opened abroad at a rate of one per week. By the end of that period, 276 research centers existed overseas, half in America and a third in Western Europe. The mission of most research centers is merely to tailor Japanese products to local needs, not a prescription for true internationalization.

Only a handful of Japanese companies have established full-fledged research and production bases abroad. Most of Japan's overseas investment has been in assembly plants, with more sophisticated design and manufacturing work kept at home. Ricoh's copier plant in Irvine, California triggered European protests of quota violations when it began exporting to Europe because its copier's American content was so low. Honda designed its Accord Station Wagon from its California studio, and it will be engineered and built in Marysville, Ohio. However, the technology came from its research and development center in Tochigi. Its North American operations are still managed by a Japanese executive based in Tokyo.

Japanese management structure is still mainly home based. Even low-level decisions must come out of face-to-face meetings in Tokyo. U.S.-based managers make grueling 13-hour trips for one-day meetings, many times a year. This has made Japanese companies especially effective in carrying out decisions but as expansion overseas continues, this becomes self-defeating. U.S. executives at Japanese subsidiaries have quit by the dozen and many are suing their employers for failing to live up to agreements and offering too little responsibility and too few chances for promotion. To be truly localized, a Japanese company in Germany or America should be regarded as German or American. Language barriers and a deep seated preference for Japanese-style centralized planning are to blame for slowness to delegate responsibility. Japanese companies will continue to keep tight reins abroad by sending Japanese executives overseas for longer assignments and by relying on video conferencing and faxes. They are trying to go global without becoming local.

Japanese companies are quickly building up a foreign R&D presence: sixty-six centers were opened by fifty-eight companies by 1988, with half of that total coming during 1987–1988. The three key reasons to open R&D centers abroad include being close to customers, getting access to foreign technology, and hiring foreign R&D talent. These research labs tend to focus on leading edge technologies. NEC Research Institute Inc. in Princeton, New Jersey wants unfettered curiosity from its American scientists. One possible way for Japan to overcome its weakness in basic research is to tap the talents of U.S. scientists. Every major U.S. research university has at least one Japanese corporate research facility nearby.

Matsushita Electric has established numerous research labs, both in Silicon Valley and in New Jersey. However, the president of the corporate R&D continues to make his headquarters in Osaka, closer to the Japanese R&D center and to the corporate headquarters, where consensus and decision making originates. Matsushita's Applied Research Laboratory in New Jersey is engaged in R&D planning for Matsushita's North American business strategies, undertaking applied research in support of its U.S. subsidiaries. Sumitomo Chemical Company, a major Japanese chemical company, invested $1 million in December 1988 in Regeneron Pharmaceuticals, a venture business in the development of new therapeutic drugs, and in return received access to any developments; this gave Sumitomo top priority in obtaining an exclusive license in Japan for the development and marketing of the firm's technologies and products (Herbert, 1989).

These efforts are propelled by the Japanese acknowledgment of their poor creative skills as well as recognition of their poor performance in creating basic innovations. Technology transfer from the West is drying up or being strictly limited and controlled. One solution is to go to where the creative spirit is and bring back the results. Another possibility is to encourage more foreign researchers to come to Japan. Twenty times more Japanese researchers work in the United States than Americans in Japan. In 1989, 56,000 Japanese researchers went overseas, whereas only 3,633 American researchers went to Japan. Over 30,000 Japanese students annually visit to the United States to study, whereas only 1,180 Americans study at Japanese universities during any particular year. Japanese companies with deep pockets are taking advantage of America's open system of education and idea exchange: At the U.S. National Institutes of Health alone, there are over 400 Japanese scientists, with few American scientists at its Japanese counterpart. Western scientists complain that Japanese labs tend to offer too little space, much poorer equipment, have inadequate maintenance, and too few technicians. Evaluation of research results in Japan is nowhere near strict enough. This has not worked well in the past and is not likely to do so in future. Foreign researchers face numerous obstacles: language barriers, long working hours, endless meetings, and reliance on *nemawashi* (the time-consuming process of decision making by consensus). This can be frustrating for people accustomed to more independence, better working conditions, and privacy at work. Many foreigners burn out quickly and leave Japan because of stress, low pay, and lack of freedom.

Access to research laboratories is another possible problem area. Europe and the United States are closing many of their laboratories to Japanese researchers because of lack of access to Japanese labs. Gradually, the Japanese government is opening its labs to foreign researchers. However since most of the crucial research is conducted in corporate labs, openness is still an issue. The Japan Industrial Technology Association has been established is to nourish the transfer of technology both domestically and internationally and to facilitate the dissemination and exchange of technical information between research laboratories and foreign countries.

To strengthen basic research, a Japanese government-led strategy sends teams of researchers to the United States, establishes or sponsors research activities, and invites American technical experts to Japan. A growing number of Japanese firms are placing their R&D scientists in American university labs or are engaged in joint research projects with large and small American companies. Some are opening R&D labs in the United States, especially in Silicon Valley, to learn more about the U.S. system and to take advantage of the openness inherent in the American culture. Others are making investments in American venture capital funds to gain accelerated access to new breakthroughs achieved in the United States. A few are investing in American universities to endow professorships, to join industrial liaison programs, and to build new laboratories on American university campuses. Japanese biotechnology firms are quickly building overseas R&D facilities to exploit U.S. biotechnology expertise.

Increasingly, North American startups (particularly biotech start-ups) hungry for financing (and having been spurned by American companies and venture capital funds either for initial funds or for subsequent funding) are being acquired by the Japanese or find themselves going to Japan in pursuit of capital. More than ninety of the 100 venture-backed American high technology companies surveyed in 1989 by Venture Economics expressed an interest in selling a stake to a Japanese company. Kubota alone invested over $190 million in equity positions in five Silicon Valley high technology companies between

1986 and 1989 (Ardent—graphics supercomputers; MIPS—RISC microprocessors; Akashie—thin film media; Maxtor—erasable optical disk drives; and Rasna—analysis software). In addition,Exabyte, a Boulder, Colorado maker of computer tape drives, sold part of itself to Kubota. Hitachi Koki purchased Dataproducts (computer printers) for $160 million. Fujisawa Pharmaceutical purchased Lyphomed (a drug company) for $850 million. Japan's TDK Corporation paid $200 million for Silicon Systems Inc. Komag Inc., which makes thin-film high-capacity disks for computer disk drives, sold 11 percent of itself to Asahi Class Co., Japan's largest glass maker, for $23 million. Asahi is sharing its valuable manufacturing technology to lower Komag's production costs while, in return, getting Japanese marketing rights for Komag's products. Minority investments in U.S. companies grew from forty deals in 1988 worth $166 million to sixty deals in 1989 worth $435 million and over $400 million in 1990. NKK purchased 5 percent of Silicon Graphics (3D workstations) for $35 million, and NIKON bought 5 percent of Electro-Scan (electron microscopes) for $1 million. In November 1989, Chugai, a leading Japanese pharmaceutical manufacturer, paid $110 million for GenProbe. Chugai thus acquired an American base to sell its version of erythopoietin. Japanese firms are attempting to combine biotechnology with existing manufacturing skills. JETRO (The Japanese External Trade Organization) in 1988 indicated that over 100 organizations were engaged in R&D in the United States. Over 359 joint United States-Japanese developments were officially announced in the first half of 1988 versus almost 400 for all of 1986. Says Wilfred Corrigan, chairman of the Semiconductor Industry Association, "These transnational arrangements will have to be monitored more closely so you don't have the vampire effect: Japanese companies sucking the blood out of American companies."

Japanese corporate interests over the last decade have funneled more than $4.5 billion into U.S. scientific, educational, and economic policy institutions, mainly to gain access to cutting-edge technology. Hitachi Chemical has provided $12 million for a research facility at the University of California at Irvine, which will give it access to biotechnology research. At this new biotech lab, patents will be jointly held with the university for those experiments done with regular faculty; Hitachi Chemical will get sole patents, however, on research conducted by Irvine adjunct professors. Of 200 endowed chairs at MIT, twenty-one have been funded by Japanese companies; Fujitsu Limited gave a $1.5 million grant in July 1988 to MIT to establish the Fujitsu Professorship of Electrical Engineering and Computer Science. Kobe Steel opened a research center near Stanford University. NEC opened a $25 million artificial intelligence lab in Princeton, New Jersey.

Daiichi Pharmaceutical Company set up a basic research center at San Francisco State University to research anti-thrombus treatments and drugs for hardening of the arteries. Eisai Company established a laboratory at the University of London to research and develop nerve domain drugs using molecular biology methods. There is a continuing disproportionately Japanese presence in U.S. university-related R&D programs. Many prestigious Japanese firms support the great U.S. research universities because they vastly outweigh in scale and character university research in Japan. The formal, hierarchical structures of Japanese educational institutions are not conducive to research. Japanese universities prepare a standard product of graduates, who then require several years of in-company training before they are deemed truly useful.

For example, the Japanese presence at MIT far exceeds that of any other country: Nineteen of the fifty-five corporate-endowed chairs at MIT are from Japanese companies ($20 million, or 3 percent of MIT's annual research budget). Of the 300 member organizations in the MIT industrial Liaison Program, half of the hundred foreign corporate members are Japanese companies. The Industrial Liaison Program provides access to more than 3,000 research projects, 1,000 faculty members, a full-time research staff of 2,250, and nearly 10,000 elite students. MIT's Materials Processing Center is working on materials such as high-strength ceramics and composite metals that may someday replace steel and plastic. The center's research is open to any company willing to pay a $10,000 fee; half the companies are American, and most of the other half are Japanese. The Japanese tend to participate with an enthusiasm that outstrips the Americans (Murray and Lehner, 1990). MIT's Japan program trains students in Japanese and places them in yearlong internships with Japanese companies. MIT has over 500 Japanese alumni, and only a quarter of the formal visits from industry to MIT are not from Japan. Japanese financial support of MIT research programs has been rising steadily.

Japanese companies gain access to U.S. technology by a variety of means, including relationships with elite research universities, joint ventures with U.S. firms, licensing, contracted R&D projects, laboratory adjuncts to Japanese subsidiaries in the United States, reciprocal arrangements to exchange research personnel, and export of technical knowledge via databases. Support of research by leading academic institutions (Herbert, 1989) gives Japanese corporations access to scientific and technical knowledge via databases and transfer of knowledge and technology to the parent company. But in Japan, foreign companies have no such opportunities since Japan's best research is locked in the labs of private corporations, shielded from takeover by the *keiretsu* system. The David Sarnoff Research Center still gets $40 million of its $85 million budget from GE, but the Japanese make up most of difference. Japanese industry has over 200 R&D bases overseas, employing nearly 4,500 researchers.

Limitations exist to this drive overseas. If seen as just another way to transfer technology, it could become obsolete by fiat or custom. There is increasing reluctance on the part of U.S. and European firms and individuals to license technology to Japanese firms and a greater aggressiveness in pursuing legal redress for the perceived infringements on proprietary technology. In 1989, American companies took in $2.5 billion selling technology to the Japanese but spent only $500 million to buy technology from Japan. Japanese companies have traditionally been hesitant to sell their technology (Moffat, 1991) to anyone and especially hesitant to sell to foreign firms. Protectionism and restricted technology transfer could threaten technological development in the coming decades. If one can view databases as a technological transfer vehicle, the differences become apparent: Nearly 2,000 U.S. databases are accessible in Japan; however only eighty-three of Japan's domestic databases are available abroad, and only twenty are in science and technology. The Japanese tend toward generalities and redundant information, which makes it hard to narrow a search for new, specific, and usable data. Technological secrecy is maintained in Japan by buying pertinent information deep in a sea of generalities. Most Japanese scientists' papers are published in Japanese and are not accessible to foreign readers. Japanese companies pay for 98 percent of their own research from their own funds, whereas the U.S. government pays one third of total U.S. research. Eminent Western scientists, including DNA co-discoverer James Watson, are calling for the Japanese to be excluded from international scientific projects unless they are prepared to foot a bigger share of the bill. Japanese government spending on science is under 0.25 percent, compared to 1 percent in Germany and 1.2 percent in the United States. The Japanese government has reported double that amount, but its figure includes as research money the salary of academics.

The Japanese must work on the basic problems within their society: that of poor basic innovation and creativity. If they are to become more involved in analytical design and invention, two types of adjustment in the R&D process and organization will be necessary. One adjustment is to amplify the Japanese approach to R&D processes toward more radical innovation. This has been started by establishing many central research labs and allocating more funds to basic research. Another is to activate market feedback loops that perceive potential market needs and make them clear objectives of analytical design of radically new products. Few Japanese companies have effectively achieved either. The second type of adjustment is difficult. Such a task requires more basic entrepreneurial leadership than merely constituent-based management. How can the Japanese firm meet the challenge of organizing an increasingly important multidisciplinary development project that may be vital for its future survival but beyond the capability of its in-house staff? One option is to acquire or merge with another firm that possesses the needed stock of knowledge.

When R&D activity leans toward the development of techne (the improvement of existing or borrowed productive technology), managerial leadership in R&D may remain a modest one and may rely on its internal body of engineers for knowledge as the basis of R&D and on the established line of its own businesses for the commercialization of R&D outputs. However, as R&D activity becomes more involved with the development of new techne—necessitating closer interactions between episteme and techne as well as the feedback of market potential to the conception of new analytic design—managerial leadership may have to become more entrepreneurial. If multidisciplinary research is to be carried out effectively, management may have to take a unique leadership role.

THE FIFTH-GENERATION PROJECT AND INFORMATION TECHNOLOGY

MITI's well-publicized Fifth-Generation project was initiated in 1982. The October 1981 announcement of the fifth generation indicated that the Japanese government would spend, over the next decade, nearly $500 million, an amount that participating industries would double, if not triple. Still recoiling from the auto industry near catastrophe and the total takeover of the consumer electronics industry, leaders in the information industry were rightfully fearful and believed their industry was next on Japan's hit list. In April 1982, the Institute for New Generation Computer Technology (ICOT) was formed. The project was started with fifty researchers and increased to ninety researchers by 1989. Three phases of the project occurred: (1) a study of existing knowledge in the fields of logic processing and parallel computing and the development of prototype hardware and software systems (1982–1984); (2) construction of small-scale subsystems for logic processing and parallel computing (1985–1988); and (3) completion of a full scale prototype (1989–1991). Although launched with earthshaking resolution, the project has failed to make even a nominal impact.

In addition, the information industry has rapidly become dominated by software and not hardware. Software appears to have characteristics which are unlike conventional engineering or factory operations and hence difficult to introduce or automate: little product or process standardization to support economies of scale, wide variations in project contents and work flows, and cumbersome tasks that are difficult and sometimes counterproductive to divide, deskill, or automate. The Japanese are years behind the United States in software development, and it is doubtful that they will ever duplicate American achievements in a technology like software development, which is highly dependent on individual creativity. Competition in overseas markets requires fluency in local languages and business practices related to computer usage as well as a surplus of personnel able to service foreign customers. The major Japanese computer manufacturers are attempting to apply factory concepts to computer programming in order to bring this technology up to the standards of other engineering and manufacturing disciplines. Japanese firms in their approach to software factories launched long-term efforts to centralize and systematize software production and quality control. As is custom, the Japanese emphasized process improvement first.

Nevertheless, evidence exists that many Japanese firms do perform reasonably well in many areas related to the process of software development: productivity, quality, tool usage, discipline, teamwork, maintenance, project management, and reuse. On the negative side, Japanese firms appear to rely almost entirely on tools and techniques adopted from the West and tend to create reasonably unsophisticated and costly software products. Japan seems to trail American vendors in operating systems, office programs, and basic research as well as presence in overseas markets (Cusamano, 1991). The major Japanese objective is to emphasize product development in standardized sectors, adding enhancements, stressing quality, and offering competitive prices.

The information technology sector requires different talents than the Japanese have been used to, since it is different from the others in which they have succeeded. Most segments of the information processing industry do not exhibit the characteristics generally associated with the automobile, motorcycle, or consumer electronics industries, for example. The mainframe computer segment, which has long been viewed as the primary focus of Japanese activities, has traditionally exhibited high margins, low unit volume, low price sensitivity, low product standardization, and a lack of mass distribution channels. IBM prospered for forty years, dominating this field. However, the early 1990s showed that IBM's strength was also its weakness; Mainframes were rapidly becoming extinct. Therefore, the traditional Japanese industrial strategy concentrated in mainframes will obviously be less effective, accessible, and applicable elsewhere (Methe, 1991).

The information industry exhibits rapid and frequent technological change, which limits potential product standardization and capital intensity in manufacturing. The sales and distribution process in most market segments requires a direct sales force and field installation and service and maintenance abilities. A high level of language skills is needed for software development, documentation, and customer service. Users of information processing equipment have high switching costs because of fixed software and training expenses. The result is a high level of vendor loyalty. In contrast to the automobile industry, the computer industry has a long history of improvements in price, performance, and other dimensions of product quality and is extremely sensitive to user needs as well.

Japan is the only market outside the United States in which domestic suppliers control more than half of the market for information processing equipment. Six companies—Fujitsu, Hitachi, NEC, Mitsubishi, Toshiba, and Oki—together account for over 80 percent of the market. The high degree of concentration and vertical integration is the conscious result of thirty-five years of government policy. Beginning in 1957, the computer industry was a targeted sector with direct grants, low-cost loans, protection against imports, and major government purchases of equipment. Japan Electronic Computer Company was created in 1961 to purchase computers directly from the manufacturers and then sell or lease them to end users. IBM was forced to license its technology. From 1962 through 1980, MITI organized and funded four major national projects designed to raise Japanese computer technology to Western standards. As a result, Japan now has a viable IBM-compatible mainframe industry—the sector with the lowest growth and least margins of any information technological sector (Davidson, 1984). Japanese companies are comparable to U.S. firms in large-scale complex software, such as IBM-compatible operating systems, but not in international standards or state-of-art software technology. Japanese companies have tended not to develop standardized software packages.

Software sales in Japan are $13 billion annually, the second largest market in the world after the United States, and are projected to increase to $33 billion by the end of the decade. In Japan, basic software for computer operating systems is usually designed and developed by mainframe makers, whereas applications software is produced mainly by the users. The largest number of software engineers and programmers are employed by users and manufacturers, not third parties. Software houses in Japan are small, with the top 150 having, on average fewer than 100 employees and annual sales of less than $5 million. Thus, the production of packaged software has been minimal. There has been a shift in focus toward software quality control to improve personal and team capability and to build quality into all stages of the software development process.

MITI guidance and protection of the software industry has accelerated the growth and productivity of these firms. A growing shortage of Japanese programmers (estimated at 1 million by the year 2000) will continue to haunt Japanese efforts in fifth- generation design as well as software design. Massive amounts of subcontracting are being pursued to alleviate this shortage. Much of this subcontracting results in almost permanent temporaries (temporary workers who work for a firm on an almost permanent basis) and appears to be similar to the subcontracting process used by manufacturers in other industries in Japan. The Japanese tend to be weak in the low-end, packaged-software, mass-market segment. High-end application products are custom developed for individual customers. Japanese packaged software lags behind the experience curves of U.S. firms by five years. Other software weaknesses are due to the fact that most software (systems and applications) uses English language documentation; most Japanese programmers are weak at English. System software design is an art, not a science, and requires a high level of conceptualization, something the Japanese are not proficient at. Of the three general types of software—high end (for customized applications), middle end, and low end (mass designs)—the Japanese are targeting the middle end. These tend to have partly unique designs and are medium-priced products for medium to large-size systems. The strategy is to balance customer needs and functionality with production costs and quality; use skilled workers mainly in the design and standard development process; use organizational skills to build large systems; reuse parts, methods, tools, and people systematically; and seek efficiencies across multiple projects.

The Japanese software industry developed differently than the software industry in the United States. Japanese computer firms initially provided free or highly discounted customized software to purchasers of their hardware as a means to compete against IBM. They built their own captive, in-house software departments. An independent software industry has been late and slow to develop. The larger companies created software factories and used a strategic, integrated approach to the software industry similar to the approach in automobiles and electronics: strategic management and integration of activities of software production and achievement of planned economies of scale—cost reductions or productivity gains that come from developing a series of products within one facility than building each product from scratch in a separate project. This includes sharing of resources across different projects, such as product specifications and designs, executable code, tools, methods, documentation and manuals, test cases, and personnel experience. This is doable since as much as 90 percent of the programs developed in any given year, especially business applications, are similar to work done before. Common elements in the factory approach include strategic management and integration, planned economies of scale, commitment to process improvement, product process focus and segmentation, process quality analysis and control, tailored and centralized process R&D, skills standardization and leverage, dynamic standardization, systematic reusability, computer-aided tools and integration, and incremental product variety improvement. The software factory approach was created to produce large-scale mainframe programs for large customers in service and manufacturing industries. Typically, each program is customized for the customer. The factory approach provides a way to reuse parts or modules and yet provide the customer with a customized product. This is accomplished by organizing production on a large scale and combining and recombining standard bits of software code. This environment, however, often stifles the creativity of the software engineer and developer. Toshiba employs approximately 2,300 persons in its software factory. As per Japanese tradition, teams are the norm. The Japanese believe that teams members working together are collectively more effective than individuals alone. In problem solving, a team can find defects overlooked by individual members in their own work. Japanese software developers are concentrating on developing both tools and techniques to increase human productivity including careful design, reusability of source-code blocks, and automation of code generation and design.

The trends in the computer industry toward smaller and less expensive computers, open nonproprietary systems, and the increasing importance of software provide additional problems for Japanese firms. Due to free and customized software, many Japanese companies are virtual captives of their hardware vendors; the aforementioned trends could provide a means to escape that control. Small, more flexible entrepreneurs can now penetrate the Japanese marketplace with the advent of the PC. PC software also is difficult for larger Japanese firms to manage. Each major Japanese computer maker (Fujitsu, NEC, IBM Japan, Toshiba, and Hitachi) essentially developed an operating system for its own personal computer, which enabled it to work with the rest of its computer line. They also bundled software with the computer to preempt the market for independent software writers. Thus no standard comparable to MS-DOS or Windows developed in Japan. During the early 1990s, aggressive American personal computer companies such as Dell, Compaq, and Apple began to invade Japan and attack the Japanese market with a typical Japanese ploy of aggressive pricing to gain market share. Because NEC is the dominant PC manufacturer in Japan, but also one which does not subscribe to the MS-DOS standard, it is losing share rapidly. This is just another example of the Japanese inability to change with the times.

Japanese companies are also increasing their investments in and alliances with American software firms. In 1990, Hitachi software engineering Company Ltd. purchased a half interest in Information and Graphics Systems Inc. In 1990 and 1991, ASCII Corp., a leading Japanese software firm, took a 5 percent share in Informix, a supplier of UNIX relational databases, made a $5 million investment in NEx-GEn Microsystems, and set up Hyper Desk Corp. The main question is, Will the Japanese ever duplicate their achievements in an area of computer programming which is highly dependent on individual creativity and innovation and in which customers and producers have yet to define product or process standards? This is highly doubtful.

MITI TO THE RESCUE?

MITI's primary tool for spurring innovation is a list of technologies that qualify for special tax breaks; published every other year, the current list includes over 150 technologies. MITI vision for the 1990s includes new national goals, such as the creation of a more relaxed society for Japan's elderly and the promotion of eating space in Japanese homes and restaurants. The main industries to be targeted are domestic resorts, interior decorating, and fashion. A key word for MITI for the 1990s is *technoglobalism*—the worldwide sharing of research. This follows MITI's vision of the 1960s published in 1963, which called for concentration in high-growth heavy industries and chemicals. The MITI vision of 1971 called for a knowledge-intensive economy and a national attention to this. MITI's 1980s visions were based on technology-intensive fields such as artificial intelligence and new materials. The new missions are designed to polish Japan's image abroad. Nonetheless, MITI still targets commercial technologies in which Japan lags behind other countries. The mission statements strenuously resist American pressure on Japan to open up what the Japanese consider strategic markets. MITI's funding of R&D projects during the 1980s and 1990s can be seen in Table 8.1.

MITI has set these goals for the remainder of the twentieth century:

- shifting Japan's industrial structure from energy-intensive heavy manufacturing to knowledge-intensive high technology
- creating a stable and supportive business environment
- reaching state-of-the-art frontiers in high-technology R&D
- improving economic efficiency and productivity
- improving the quality of life
- ensuring economic security
- integrating Japan's industrial economy smoothly into the international economic system

Major goals set for the twenty-first century by MITI include

- fostering human resources
- promoting information technology development
- promoting the development of comprehensive software
- promoting installation and usage of databases
- developing an interoperable database system
- standardizing information-related technologies
- developing capability of providing complete information services

In 1993, MITI's R&D budget was $301 billion yen (approximately $225 million dollars), a 16 percent increase from 1992. The question is whether MITI can be as effective in the 1990s and the twenty-first century as it was during the 1950s and 1960s. Can a government agency intervene successfully in an international marketplace no longer manipulatable by Japan to the exclusion of foreign companies? Probably not—the world has changed too much for its influence. Even MITI appears to recognize this. In 1994, MITI wanted to leave the design and construction of a $750 billion national fiber-optic network to the private sector. MITI may be at long last loosening the strings of control over Japan's industrial might; to do not so and "we (Japan) will slowly lose our competitiveness " (Hamilton, 1994).

Table 8.1
MITI's Thrust into New Technologies

Japan's Ministry of International Trade & Industry currently funds scores of R&D projects in corporations, institutes, and universities. Here are some major MITI efforts in cutting-edge technology.

Project	Duration	Funding*
SYSTEMS FOR UNMANNED SPACE EXPERIMENTS	1886-93	$34
Goal is to build equipment for experiments in unmanned satellites.		
SUPERCONDUCTORS	1988-97	$34
Actually two separate projects, one for materials and devices, the other for electric-power generation.		
5th GENERATION PROJECT	1982-92	$45
Most ambitious of several next-generation computing projects. Goal is to develop a parallel-processing computer using natural language software.		
SOLAR ENERGY PROJECT	1974-	$47
Part of the "Sunshine Project." Goal is to raise performance and lower cost of solar cells.		
FUEL-CELL POWER GENERATION	1981-95	$20
Part of the so-called "Moonlight Project" for nonsolar energy research. Goal is to develop fuel-cell power generating devices with efficiency of 40% to 60%. Looking at methanol and natural gas as fuels		
ADVANCED MATERIAL PROCESSING AND MACHINING	1986-93	$18
Studying excimer laser and ion beam processing.		
FINE CHEMICALS FROM MARINE ORGANISMS	1988-96	$8
Production of pigments, moisturizers, and coating materials from underwater resources.		
SUPER/HYPERSONIC TRANSPORT PROPULSION	1989-96	$10
To develop combined-cycle engine, incorporating both "ramjet" and high-performance turbojet, for superfast plane that can fly from New York to Tokyo in three hours.		
HIGH PERFORMANCE MATERIALS FOR ENVIRONMENT	1989-96	$6
To develop carbon composites, intermetallic compounds, and fiber-reinforced intermetallic compounds for use in space planes.		
NONLINEAR PHOTONICS MATERIALS	1989-98	$3
In today's fiber-optic communications, light must be converted into electrical signals for amplifying and switching. Nonlinear materials offer a way around that, facilitating optical computers and remote optical communications.		

* In millions for fiscal year ending March 31, 1991

THE BUBBLE BURSTS

Risutora—restructuring—is becoming a well-understood, dreaded word in Japan. Japanese productivity by 1993 ranked in the bottom half of the industrialized nations, far below that of the United States and many European Community (EC) countries. The United States currently has a gross domestic product (GDP) per employed person 26 percent higher than Japan's. To reach the U.S. level of productivity, nearly 20 million workers or a third of Japan's work force must be laid off. The effects of nearly a half century of lifetime employment, with no layoffs and thus no losers, accumulated deadwood (Fuji Research Institute estimates that several million Japanese are the working unemployed or the window gazers, who are paid to do nothing), and the retention of marginal employees, as well as negative growth rates have finally brought this issue to the center of Japan's business and political elite.

Management consultant Proudfoot Ltd. estimated that Japan's large public corporations have 12 percent too many middle managers, and for some companies the figure is closer to 20 percent. The white-collar arena is the least productive (Thornton, 1993). In the past, Japanese companies routinely hired people first, and then thought about what job they could do. Between 1976 and 1990, the cost of sales administration at publicly traded companies in Japan rose from 12.3 percent of sales to 16.3 percent. In the first six months of 1986, thirty of Japan's technology-oriented venture businesses, representing $1 billion of venture capital, went bankrupt. Although engineers are tempted by venture businesses, the top management talent and the best of university graduates tend to go to the giant *keiretsu* firms.

Japanese businesses have recently begun what is certain to be the first in many rounds of cost cutting, such as curtailing overtime, reducing hiring, asking employees to limit travel, and entertaining clients less lavishly. Pay systems oriented toward merit are becoming popular; Fujitsu has begun a pay-for-performance system. Slower growth and overcapacity require plant closures. Other measures that Japanese businesses have begun in earnest include offering early retirement and hinting that nonproductive or nonessential personnel should leave the company (if hints don't work, titles are taken away). Often, senior employees are told to stay home. Unfortunately, layoffs overseas employees are typical and politically more acceptable than at home. Streamlining product lines is another possible measure, but then the question arises about what to do with workers for discontinued products.

The traditional Japanese management style of lifetime employment, consensus decision making, and seniority works only if you can count on a minimum annual growth of 5 percent; most economists believe that the 5 percent level will not be reached again during the 1990s and predict that Japan's annual GNP growth will not exceed 3 percent in the foreseeable future. For 1993, the GDP growth was negative, the best estimates for 1994 and 1995 are merely 2 percent. In 1992 in Japan, the electronics market, which grew by 10 percent annually during 1980s, fell by 10.6 percent to $189 billion. It has become fat, slow-footed, and cautious. Japan is finding it is easier and cheaper to copy and improve old technologies than to invent new ones. Furthermore, it is finding that protecting established lines of businesses instead of embracing new technologies is a dead-end strategy, squeezed by bolder and leaner American and East Asian producers.

The 1993 recession had a major impact on Japan. At the end of 1993, Fujitsu Ltd. announced that it was cutting nearly $400 million (12 percent) from its research and development budget. Fujitsu plans to cut its work force from 56,000 to 50,000 and make large-scale cutbacks of new recruits to 300 college graduates per year. In the winter of 1992 1993, 114 corporations announced their decision to cancel outstanding offers to new college graduates. Toshiba plans to cut jobs and close two factories. Pioneer is planning to increase its overseas output from 30 percent to 50 percent by 1996. In Pioneer, as part of a larger restructuring, thirty-five managers over the age of fifty were given the choice of early retirement or dismissal. Nippon Telegraph & Telephone Corporation (NTT) is shedding some 30,000 jobs, mainly through transfers and attrition. The Japan Research Institute estimates that impending deregulation in telecommunications, health care, and other industries could vaporize 4.1 million jobs and $314 billion worth of demand over the next decade.

Although layoffs did occur, no Western style mass job losses ensued. Instead, employers cut working hours, wages, and capital spending rather than fire people. Companies trimmed their payroll the traditional way by paring back overtime and other compensation, not people. Older workers paychecks were in many cases trimmed. Those that took the worst fall during Japan's recession were temporary and part-time workers; Honda Motor Company had 2,000 temporary workers in Japan in 1991; in 1994, it had none (Williams, 1994). Japanese businesses are also freezing hiring; in 1990, Honda hired 2,075 new employees, in 1994, it hired just 249.

Toyota's production fell in 1993 by 9 percent. Japan's car exports fell nearly 16 percent. Nissan has announced that it will close its Zama plant (thus reducing yearly production capability in Japan to 2 million from 2.5 million) and it will cut employment by 5,000 each of the next three years through attrition and by lowering the early retirement age to forty-five. Nissan lost money in 1992. Honda and Mazda each plan to cut 3,000 jobs as well by attrition during the next few years. About 25 percent of currently employed workers are unneeded, auto analysts believe. Those workers will be farmed out to dealerships or part suppliers—which don't need them either but have no choice—or continue to go to their office without work to do. In a scene reminiscent in the American rust belt in the 1980s, Japanese companies are criticized at home for "hollowing out" the industry (sending the best jobs and factory overseas instead of keeping them at home for Japanese workers). Honda has cut development time so much that it could redesign the Accord every three years; but a redesign costs $1 billion. Honda is limiting itself to a four- or five-year cycle to keep costs down. Automakers desperate to stay in the black are lowering standards.

Nippon Steel has reported that it is lowering its quality standards. During 1992, Japanese industrial output fell by more than 8 percent. Yamaha, among many others, decided in 1992 to adopt voluntary retirement programs. At ALPS Electric, 830 accepted such a program offer.   This presents a historic, significant breakdown of the commitment of worker to company. JAL plans to reduce its ground service staff by as many as 200 people. Mitsui Mining and Smelting plans to eliminate 6 percent of employees (300), most of them management. Nippon Trust Bank plans to cut its staff by one third from 2,300 to 1,500 by reduced recruiting and attrition.   NKK plans to reduce its staff by 15 percent (3,200 workers).   Sanyo Electric has slashed the number of headquarters departments to seventeen from thirty-six and reduced staff from 1,700 to 1,350, trimming 3,600 people (10 percent) from the payroll through retirement and implementing a hiring freeze. Ajinomoto cut its product line from 4,000 to 2,500 items.   Ricoh will cut its 14,000 payroll by 28 percent by 1996. What is alarming is that massive layoffs and firings have not occurred in any large numbers yet.

The issue of labor provides two bleak scenarios for Japan. In the first, Japan's corporate giants stumble into the twenty-first century with bloated white-collar payrolls, whereas their downsized, nimble competitors in America and East Asia race around them, grabbing opportunities from them. In the second, Japanese companies discard the lifetime employment practice and Japanese unemployment reaches double-digit proportions. Neither scenario is far fetched; neither is attractive.

Changes which must occur include the migration offshore of manufacturing jobs, the flattening of corporate organizations, specialization in particular markets and products, and the elimination of deadwood resulting from decades of lifetime employment. What is happening and must continue to occur includes a shakeout of electronics companies, a pare-down of product offerings by the Japanese companies, a pull-out of oversaturated markets, a slimming down, a delayering of management, and a delegating of more responsibility to individual executives. A 1993 survey of 250 large companies in Japan by Tokyo's Industrial Labor Research Institute found that nearly 50 percent of the companies surveyed plan to reduce management ranks within the next eighteen months (Neff, 1993). Several sacred cows such as lifetime employment, automatic promotion, and avoidance of individual responsibility cannot any longer be taken for granted. It appears that Japan is pursuing the second scenario.

The lingering recession of the early 1990s in Japan reflects major deficiencies in the economy, and the engine that drove Japan's success is in need of a major overhaul. A single-minded focus on production and process technology worked well for the Japanese for forty years. Now the battle has shifted to white-collar functions, where no such advantages exist and indeed severe disadvantages exist for Japanese companies. Japanese companies must focus on improving the productivity and innovativeness of white-collar workers with the same fervor that they did the manufacturing process. Singleminded attention to market share and neglect of costs have finally caught up with the Japanese. Although IBM and Hitachi have sales revenues of the same order of magnitude, Hitachi's profit is almost one fifth that of IBM, a characteristic common to such comparisons of U.S.-Japanese firms.

Only export-led industries such as electronics, autos, semiconductors, and consumer electronics have been truly successful in global competition. The other 80 percent of the Japanese economy wage competition almost exclusively within the confines of Japan's insular and protective market, which has made it difficult to impossible for foreign companies to challenge Japanese companies in Japan. As a result, these companies have become complacent and unproductive. Japan's high prices, cartelized market structure, and lack of global competition have allowed many mediocre domestic companies to survive. Japanese food labor productivity declined by 50 percent relative to U.S. productivity between 1975 and 1989. Most of Japan's domestic service sector requires or tolerates levels of employment which would be considered unusually high in other countries (e.g., elevator operators, greeters, receptionists, etc.). Japan has the most efficient factory floors and most inefficient offices in the world. This reflects Japan's cultural obsession with the role of human relations in business. Japanese managers, and even CEOs, are expected to drop everything to attend the funeral of an employee's parent. Executives feel that they have to deliver monthly bills to their main customers and subcontractors in person. This is caused by poor white collar performance and a bloated overhead structure.

Between 1984 and 1992, Japanese corporate overhead expenses (sales and general and administrative expenses) increased from 14 to 17 percent of sales. Overhead personnel climbed from 29 percent to nearly 35 percent of the total work force during the same timeframe. Simultaneously, many Japanese manufacturing companies decreased their blue-collar forces while seeing their white-collar sectors increase by between 50 and 100 percent. The focus was on cost of production and bringing costs down quickly to gain market share. The Japan Productivity Center concluded in 1992 that to reach overall United States productivity levels, Japanese manufacturing companies would have to eliminate 39 percent of their head count. Currently, it is estimated that at least 5 to 6 million redundant workers are on Japanese corporate payrolls. The removal of these excess employees, if it could be achieved, would increase the level of Japanese unemployment from 2.5 to 10 percent. The choice is not easy: maintain the lifetime employment system at huge internal costs to the companies or forego it and create considerable social unrest.

It appears the choice has already been made. This process has already started in the form of at-home work and early retirement; cancellation of new recruits, voluntary retirement with incentive programs; implementation of annual salary reviews and performance management, management by objectives (MBO) and merit pay; and greatly expanded salary ranges. Other practices include a freeze on new hiring, incentives for early retirement, encouraging young women to marry and stay home, and redistributing workers. Japanese companies are in the process of eliminating entire layers of senior management, consolidating research labs, and reassigning personnel. The Japanese companies have a saying for this practice: "Close the front door" (not hire new hires) and "open the back door" (attrition and encouraging seniors to leave). The Japanese government is trying to prevent sackings through an employment subsidy fund run by the labor ministry: It pays half the salary of an unwanted worker sent home or to a training course, and in small companies it pays up to two thirds. Previously, instead of sacking workers, Japanese companies cut costs by reducing overtime and bonus payments. This kept lifetime employment possible and as a result kept up consumer spending in previous recessions. This has worked in the past, but now the drag may be too much.

Lifetime employment is costly and inefficient. Long-term planning is leading to too many dead ends. Stability and predictability have bogged the system down. The status quo has been holding back necessary change and stifling creativity. Consensus building and bottoms-up decision making may be great management tools, but they are now slowing things down and costing Japanese companies much of their former competitive edge. Not only are companies with lifetime employment beginning to lay off people, but they are beginning to do so at an ever greater rate. With the fall of the Liberal Democratic Party (LDP), political stability and predictability are gone, as is economic stability. The *keiretsu* system, with its close relationship with suppliers, is less profitable than independents. The tight *keiretsu* ties among assemblers and suppliers allowed for close, integrated planning and guaranteed smaller parts makers a constant stream of business. This arrangement was smooth when sales and the economy grew. When the recession hit and retrenching occurred, it bogged down the system (Schlesinger, Williams, and Forman, 1993).

SCENARIOS FOR TWENTY-FIRST CENTURY JAPAN

Japanese weaknesses include the following:

1. The Japanese education system is better suited to the process of catch-up than to fostering innovative skills. It overemphasizes rote memorization and permits little individual initiative and experimentation.
2. A dual structure of large and small firms leads to control over small firms, which creates extreme difficulties for small and new companies in obtaining venture capital.
3. Drastic changes in the labor market are occurring as Japanese workers get older, the number of women increases sharply, and less than fanatic Westernized work habits take hold. Japanese companies are moving the manual work of manufacturing out of Japan to low-cost countries.
4. Being a follower, even one as good as Japan has been, implies severe disadvantages and major risks which could cause an end or a slowing down of the Japanese miracle. The Japanese government policy of cheap and plentiful capital for large-scale industry encouraged technological innovation; nonetheless, once a developing country has caught up, there are no obvious areas in which application of large-scale capital can produce certainty of rewards.

Infoplan, a Tokyo-based market research consultant company, has identified twenty-one trends that are changing Japan *(Focus Japan,* October 1991, pp. 6-8):

- from group identity to individual identity (greater variety in behavior)
- from role playing to a more assertive self (not as subsumed in a group)
- from nuclear families to diversified families (single households and living alone)
- from traditional expectations to personal preferences
- from building Japan Inc. to supporting society (focus on the person rather than Japan)
- from focused commitment to expanding network (friends take precedence over family)
- from obsession with work to balanced life (there is more to life than work)
- a change in emphasis from the company to the work itself (big is not enough)
- from functional to ambient (personalized to oneself)
- from diminished to heightened sensuality (e.g., use of fragrances)
- from real nature to implied nature (artificially created nature is okay)
- from being healthy to feeling healthy (active, involved, personal feeling of health)
- from targeted information to information environment (complex and personal choice)
- from mass media to personalized media (from TV to magazines)
- from role allotting to role choice (each partner choosing own role)
- from home/career choice to home/career accommodation (having both)
- from world market to global community (integration into world community)
- from economic animal to pleasure-seeking consumer (less work, more play)
- from things to experiences (experiencing new things)
- from luxury purchase to luxury enjoyment (not just display, but enjoyment)
- from famous brands to authentic.

Two potential scenarios for Japan's future are (1) maturity and industrial decline and (2) renewed growth after a readjustment period. In the former case, Japan joins the rest of the industrial countries, beset by an aging population; rising welfare costs; larger government budgets; higher deficits; higher taxes; slower savings and private investment (eventually decreasing to rates of savings similar to levels in other industrial country), which will result in its basic industries losing competitiveness (in one sense this has already occurred, as many of its basic industries have been consolidate and downsized); an inability to innovate and invest; closing export markets; increased competition from the NIEs (newly industrialized economies such as Hong Kong, Singapore, Taiwan, and South Korea, which is already happening); and increased military spending (as a response to threats from Korea and China), which results in low growth and an affluent but static economy. The Japanese, according to this scenario, will spend more, save less, get richer, enjoy life's luxuries more, and become more cosmopolitan, less deferential, and less hierarchal. As the economy matures, a propensity to import increases and its industrial base gives away to services.

The second case—renewed growth after a readjustment phase—is marked by welfare increases, reorganization of the tax structure, political redistricting with lower land and agricultural prices and subsidies, reorganizing and possible privatization of public corporations (this is in process or achieved already), automation of conventional manufacturers to FMS (flexible manufacturing systems), a shift to higher technologies, heavy foreign investment, stimulus from Asian growth, moderate defense expenditures, moderate growth throughout 1990s, and a position as the world economic leader. In this scenario, the relatively unchanged Japanese national priority is wealth creation and an ever-expanding global market share in ever-more-profitable products. The system would remain basically the same that is instead of consumption, there would be more investment. The key determinant for this scenario is not internal to Japan but external: Will the world tolerate forever Japan's mercantile economic imperialism?

To date, all signs are pointing toward the first scenario.

Conclusions

The five stages of technological development (Moritani, 1982) are (1) modification and improvement; (2) technology applications in new product development; (3) high technology; (4) future technologies; and (5) invention or discovery of revolutionary new technological principles. By 1960, Japan had reached international levels in the first stages of technology. From 1965 on, it had begun to achieve dramatic results in applying existing technology to the creation of new products, the second stage. In the 1980s, it began excelling in the third stage.

Japan's weaknesses are in the latter stages—in new technology development. The fourth stage requires basic R&D. Japan has put little effort into these technologies to date. Example of weak Japanese industries are in the fields of chemistry and energy. The difference between Japan's poor performance in chemicals and its leadership in steel is the fundamental difference between the two fields. In steel, there is room for continuous steady improvement in automating and rationalizing the production process to make it more continuous. In contrast, technological development in chemistry tends to come in sudden transformations rather than steady growth, not Japan's strong suit. Such development requires fresh and original thinking and makes it difficult to set clear goals; it is high in risk because it is so unpredictable. In short, changes in chemistry are not well suited to the general work habits and attitudes of the Japanese, who tend to emphasize patient perseverance toward long-term goals. Another weakness lies in fields requiring technological sophistication, in which the technology itself has specialized applications and a corresponding limited market (e.g., industrial chemicals). Japan's weaknesses lie in areas in which the market is small or uncertain or which require a long-term commitment without any prospects for immediate application.

In 1981, U.S. patent records revealed that Japan excelled in only three areas: television, internal combustion engines, and instruments to measure time. By 1991, Japanese firms had received more patents than American companies in those three areas as well as photography, active solid-state devices, thermoelectric and photoelectric batteries, clutches and power stop control, dynamic information storage or retrieval, image analysis, motor vehicles, music and musical instruments, photocopying, recorders, textiles, typewriting machines, and printing and office machinery. During the same time, Japan increased research investment from 2.4 percent of gross domestic product in 1981 to 3.1 percent in 1991.

A study of the growth performance of the world's seventy leading firms in five industries—electrical equipment, business machines and computers, industrial chemicals, pharmaceuticals, and aerospace—shows that corporate R&D intensity, measured in terms of R&D spending as a percentage of sales revenues, is positively and significantly related to relative worldwide corporate growth and thus to shifts in world market shares. The study indicated that corporate-funded R&D matters most. World growth performance is consistent with levels of corporate funding (Franko, 1982). The five leading Japanese firms in the electrical equipment industry had an average corporate-funded R&D to sales ratio nearly double that of the largest U.S. electrical producers throughout the 1970s with results seen in the 1980s reflected in America's near abandonment of consumer electronics.

Japan has reached state-of-the art technology in a variety of industrial segments: iron and steel production, agricultural chemicals, new materials, nuclear energy processing, semiconductors, computer peripherals, office automation, robotics, flexible manufacturing systems, telecommunications, pharmaceuticals, biotechnology, and industrial lasers. These technologies tend to be well known, their technological trajectories are predictable, and product advances are made in continuous or incremental steps. Small adaptations in proprietary designs such as miniaturization often create vast new commercial opportunities. However, progress has been slower in technologies for which the theoretical parameters for problem solving are highly complex (jet aircraft design) and technological trajectories are not readily predictable (software). Japanese firms are not as apt to make seminal inventions that lead to the creation of whole new industries, due in part to their relatively low level of government R&D sponsorship and the narrowly applied nature of much commercial R&D. The pattern of Japan's multinationalism is clustered in a few relatively competitive industries that produce standardized or traditional goods, such as textiles, sundries, metal products, consumer electronics, and basic chemicals. The more competitive the industry is (the more standardized the product is), the greater the incidence of Japan's manufacturing investment in the developing Asian countries (Ozawa, 1979).

Table 9.1 shows a U.S. Department of Commerce assessment of the relative positions of U.S. and Japan in twelve major future technologies; a "+" indicates the United States is ahead, a "•" indicates both are at the same level, and a "-" indicates Japan is ahead in that particular technology. Table 9.2 shows an MITI assessment of the technological capabilities of the two countries.

Japan is in the lead in peripheral areas, but has a well-known weakness in the software sector. Japanese information technology is still low in terms of exports (which account for less than 10 percent of its turnover). In oceanography, Japan is far behind both the Europeans and the Americans. In the space sector, the Japanese program is ambitious but is not cost-effective and is several years behind European countries, and this gap seems difficult to bridge with a space budget of a similar size to that of the French CNES. One therefore concludes that Japan is in a particularly strong position in technologies for mass production but has yet to show strength in either the fourth or fifth stages of technological development. Research efforts in Japan are aimed at ensuring Japanese technological independence (which it is far from achieving), and at enabling Japan gradually to move from products for the general public to more professional markets. In essence, Japan is clearly ahead of the United States in production and product development engineering related to electronics products used by individuals and families, office equipment, and retail machinery. Japan has an overall superiority in production engineering. Japan excels in technologies suited to the general needs of its population, such as production and public welfare technologies, but it is behind in basic technologies, large-scale engineering fields, and seminal research (Kosaka, 1988).

Major fundamental differences exist between closing a technological gap and generating high technology. It is easier for a nation to choose potential future winner industries when it is in a follower position, as Japan has been for most of its technological history. The organizational structure best suited for catch-up innovations is different from that which facilitates radical innovations. Incremental innovations benefit from R&D professionals with a specific knowledge of the firm and its products, a hierarchical and formal structure, and intense loyalty to the firm—all features of the typical Japanese corporation, with its emphasis on permanent employment, seniority-based wages, and rotation of engineers from R&D labs to production. Radical innovation

Table 9.1
Comparing Future Technologies

	R&D	New Products	Trends
Advanced Materials	•	—	—
Advanced Semiconductor Devices	*	—	—
Artificial Intelligence	+	+	•
Biotechnology	+	+	-
Digital Imaging Technology	•	—	—
Flexible Computer Integrated Manufacturing	+	•	•
High-Density Data Storage	•	—	•
High Performance Computing	+	+	•
Medical Devices and Diagnostics	+	+	•
Optoelectronics	•	—	•
Sensor Technology	+	•	•
Super Conductors	•	•	—

Key: + United States rated as ahead

 • Countries relatively equal

 — Japan rated as ahead

Source: U.S. Commerce Department

Table 9.2
MITI Assessment of U.S. and Japanese Technology (Comparative Standings)

	1983		1993	
	Level of Technology	Technology Development Capability	Level of Technology	Technology Development Capability
Data Base	U.S.	U.S.	U.S.	U.S.
Semiconductor Memory Devices	equal	equal	Japan	Japan
Computers	U.S.	equal	equal	equal
VCRs	Japan	Japan	Japan	Japan
D-PBX	U.S.	U.S.	equal	Japan
Micro-Processors	equal	equal	equal	Japan
Laser Printers	U.S.	equal	equal	Japan
Copy Machines	equal	equal	equal	Japan
Assembly Robots	equal	Japan	equal	Japan
CAD/CAM	U.S.	equal	equal	Japan
Communications Satellites	U.S.	equal	equal	equal
Photovoltaics	Japan	equal	Japan	Japan
Aircraft Engines	U.S.	U.S.	U.S.	equal
Skyscrapers	U.S.	U.S.	equal	equal
Advanced Composite Materials	U.S.	U.S.	equal	equal
Fine Ceramics	equal	Japan	Japan	Japan

requires organizations that are informal and collegian and researchers that are cosmopolitan (i.e., who have numerous contacts outside the firm). What is needed to pursue radical innovation successfully for the Japanese firm is the difficult transition from a bureaucratic to an entrepreneurial climate.

Innovation (*inobesbion*), is seen as the means for leaping from the old system into a new plane of being. It implies that the Japanese no longer are satisfied with improving on the past; they desire to be molders of the future. Innovation as a marketing weapon is practically indefensible to the Japanese. A wholly new product around which a wholly new market springs up has no competition. Innovative products often precede customer demand. Radical innovations are characterized by diverse and uncertain performance criteria. For this type of research, a different type of researcher as well as a different type of organization is required. Technological expertise in Japan is less specialized than in America. Employees obtain most of their expertise internally, from the company, rather than from educational institutions. They are rotated often and thus become generalists, with a wide range of work experience, yet aware of the specific processes and product requirements of the company. Everyone in Japanese factories works together to utilize technologies benefiting their companies. It is becoming increasingly difficult for generalists within a company to possess all the relevant knowledge in high-technology fields; specialists may be necessary. But this may pull down the lifetime employment and flexibility of Japanese firms.

For decades, Japan has mined America's great research base and has sent its best and brightest to top American research universities, institutes, and national labs. Japan's R&D infrastructure revolves around commercial interests. It is less interested in replenishing the world's endowment of intellectual capital than in capturing new ideas and techniques and turning them into profitable products. The Japanese are generally quicker and more economical only when moving externally developed technology through the innovation process. Hardly any gap exists when the technology is developed within a firm. American firms tend to invest about twice as much as Japanese firms in preproduction marketing, activities whereas the Japanese expend twice as much as American firms on tooling and manufacturing equipment and facilities.

For years, Japan has tended to be a free rider, capitalizing on external research at a very low cost to itself. Japan is in many areas approaching the limits of existing research and is nearing the frontiers of knowledge and the limits of followership. The increasing reluctance of Western firms to license technology and their greater aggressiveness in pursuing legal redress for perceived infringements on proprietary technology are causing much alarm in Japan. Europe and the United States are beginning to close their laboratories to Japanese researchers because of reciprocal lack of access to Japanese laboratories to foreign researchers (no quid pro quo exists). Under the Super 301 clause, foreign companies such as Mitsubishi can be prevented from importing products into the United States if an American company believes that they have violated its patent rights. The burden of proof falls on Japanese companies to demonstrate that they did not copy (Tatsumo, 1985).

Six characteristics of successful high-technology firms have been identified (Maidique and Hayes, 1984): business focus, adaptability, organizational cohesion, entrepreneurial culture, sense of integrity, and hands-on top management. Two of these attributes are not present in many Japanese organizations. Business focus means to concentrate on a single product or closely related set of product lines; this is diametrically opposed to the large, diversified, traditional Japanese firm. A lack of an entrepreneurial climate also exists in Japan. To have such an entrepreneurial climate entails avoiding strict hierarchical relationships, creating small divisions that allow for quick decision making, and providing a variety of funding channels to potential inventors as well as the opportunity to pursue outside projects. The big culprits are deeply ingrained traditions, the same ones that made Japan an industrial powerhouse: acquiescence to authority, strict seniority, a stable but immobile work force, and little debate. These customs often inspire loyalty among factory hands and teamwork among the engineers who whisk product ideas to market. They can also stunt free-ranging thought in scientists soon after they leave the university. Japan, to remain a technological leader, must rely on ground-breaking scientific work outside its borders and be dependent on the international R&D community.

Top Japanese high-technology firms are large (dominant), diverse, and typically vertically integrated. Large Japanese firms have two major areas of competitive advantage in technology over U.S. firms. First, they have developed ways of embodying technology in products and moving from development through manufacturing to the marketplace quickly, with high quality and with a relatively low purchase price. Second, Japanese firms have extremely effective systems of global technology scanning, developed over decades of playing catch-up. These include global patent scanning, in-house international scientific and technical information systems, and high-level technology scanning systems in their foreign subsidiaries. Several advantages accrue to these Japanese corporations due to their size and diversity: In high-tech where short product life cycles, increasingly expensive R&D, and higher and higher capital investments are the norm, larger firms may be at an advantage. Membership in a *keiretsu* also provides advantages to many high-technology firms. Intra-*keiretsu* trading provides leverage in selling Japanese products within *keiretsu* members, and temporary personnel shortages can be filled by borrowing workers from less successful sister *keiretsu* companies. Low cost capital is available from the lead *keiretsu* bank. Risk sharing and hence longer term objectives and market flexibility naturally result. The *keiretsu* system leads naturally to greater technology transfer between member concerns. This is especially evident between manufacturers and contractors. Before product details are finalized, researchers from these companies are working together, discussing ideas freely to improve the product. *Keiretsu* membership partially insulates a firm from capital markets, and thus management may be able to carry out projects that are very long term in nature. However, data suggest that auto suppliers in the *keiretsu* system are less profitable than independent suppliers.

Large-scale corporations tend to have lower innovating rates than small-scale ones. The Japanese model relies on big producers. Technological know-how is diffused easily from firm to subcontractor and vice versa. Interdependencies between organizations have occurred so that technology transfers from larger to smaller and vice versa take place more readily. The government, the banks, the *keiretsu*, and *sogo shosha* approve of this cooperation. Large firms typically aim for efficiency. They aim to produce incrementally superior goods efficiently; the production of radically different and superior ideas is opposed to this. R&D is more efficiently done in medium to small-sized firms than in large ones. Those that produce ideas are different from those that aim to make production more efficient. Differences in integration and ownership style are particularly important in accessing competition in the high-tech marketplace. Most Japanese firms are giant firms, vertically integrated as well as horizontally integrated into other related fields. Long time horizons and high levels of capital and R&D investment are needed for success in most high-tech environments. In addition, stable corporate ownership leads to patient capital, which places less emphasis on short-term returns and more on long-term survival and growth, less on return on investment as the primary measure of success and more on market share. The Japanese model of competition puts a premium on competition through technical change, high quality products, and product differentiation. It permits and encourages a long-term view with respect to research, training, and investment. Through *keiretsu* relationships with a major bank, low-cost credit is available and the enterprise is freed from short-term pressures to concentrate on long-term objectives. As a result, Japan is particularly strong in technologies for mass production. Research efforts in Japan are aimed at ensuring Japanese technological independence and at enabling Japan gradually to move from products for the general public to more professional markets (Godet, 1987). American scientists are considered world class and contribute to a continuing flow of inventions. Unlike Japan, however, the United States hasn't yet identified the imbalance between pure and applied science as a concern (Sakach, 1987).

Japan's R&D has had a festival mentality (i.e., a herd mentality), in which companies and government establish joint projects to focus on narrowly defined goals. Everyone participating is usually guaranteed gigantic profits if the goal is achieved. The goal is clear and all it takes to reach it is a grand charge with flags waving. Truly creative R&D is not like that. Japanese researchers tend to want projects with clearly defined goals and easily seen results. That is not the type of researcher that Japan will need in the future. Japan's R&D has also had a lack of leeway and a spirit of play. The sweep of vision and human breadth these attitudes give rise to is indispensable to the free exercise of creativity. An orientation towards money-making technology is all well and good but will not foster creativity. In Japan, gambling has long been held in contempt; it is not respectable. The lack of a gambling spirit does not permit an individual to take all the responsibility for failure. This reflects in part the inability of the Japanese to take the initiative lest they make trouble for colleagues and superiors. A strong demand for creativity throughout Japanese society must be developed.

Japan's industrial composition has a reputation for cutthroat competition for market shares. Each firm keeps an eye on its standing compared to all other firms. If the firm falls in the rankings, it vows to fight its way back up. The entire company delights in victory and agonizes over defeat; this produces a sense of rivalry between firms within a given industry. This determination, which springs from the bitterness of defeat, comes to a fever pitch in the development of new technology. The result is a leap-frog game in which a firm darts ahead only to have one of its competitors get a jump on it. The players are absolutely determined not to lose out in the struggle for market share. In the past, Japanese corporations achieved high returns on R&D because they focused on incremental innovations, in which the risks were less.

This strategy required the importation of technology. The cost of relying on technology purchased from abroad may increase significantly as foreign companies anticipate that the sale of technology will strengthen competition from Japanese firms. A decline in availability of imported technology would force Japanese firms to spend more on high-risk radical innovations, which in turn would reduce the profits from R&D for the Japanese firm.

Japan's import promotion strategy is one sided. It promotes low value-added imports, such as raw materials and selected agricultural products, high-tech goods that it does not produce, and the foreign capital, technology, and plant investments needed to create new jobs and produce high-tech goods. On the other hand, government policies have discouraged many companies from importing technology-intensive goods that pose a threat to Japan's infant industries. The high valued-added imports that are promoted are in mature industries in which Japanese companies offer stiff competition. In short, Japan wants the benefits of foreign investments and technology without foreign competition. Selective import promotion threatens to derail international cooperation. Japan risks intensifying trade friction and discouraging foreign companies from opening plants or investing in Japan. The Japanese government seemingly wants foreign money and technology but not foreign products or competition.

Although the Japanese indicate that this is changing, the more things change, the more they remain the same. Japan's old tricks of helping domestic companies withstand harsh winds of international competition persist. For example in the field of medical equipment, American companies have a 52 percent market share worldwide and Japanese companies only have a 7 percent market share (outside of Japan). The Japanese government is determined increase its share; in 1992, the government put up 70 percent of the capital for a $20 million research project to develop a Japanese pacemaker, which has not come on the market. Japanese bureaucrats have organized a Japanese consortium (including Toshiba and Hitachi) to develop the underlying technologies for a rival technology to magnetic source imaging and are spending upward of $100 million a year (Eisenstodt, 1993a). American companies also dominate in heart valves and artificial joints, products which the Ministry of Health wants to circumvent. It appears that MITI wants to promote industrial policy to build a local health care technology industry with government money and with government hurdles strewn in the path of American competitors. Until Japan truly plays fair, the rest of the world will be constantly needling it and threatening it with sanctions.

When Japan was playing catch-up with the United States and Europe, its goals were clear and tasks self-evident. No treacherous places along the road existed. But in the future, Japan must advance down a path along which unimaginable dangers lurk. What Japan needs today is not a uniform crop of gifted students but people with extraordinary talents—human resources with potential for achieving great things. Japan badly needs the unorthodox—those that will rise to the challenge of creativity.

The Japanese encounter the following obstacles in their pursuit of scientific creativity and discovery:

- They are reluctant to explore the unknown alone.
- They prefer to follow the leaders into new fields.
- They delight in perfecting the wheel, not inventing it. To the Japanese, this is the surest way to professional security and economic prosperity. Highly outspoken, independent-minded people who challenge the professional wisdom tend to be ostracized in Japan.
- Japanese college "examination hell" rewards students adept at rote memorization and taking tests but penalizes students with creative, inquisitive minds.
- A lack of leeway, gambler's spirit, and risk-taking exists in Japan. Researchers rarely risk the possibility of failure. If you are different, you are a hindrance; originality is nipped in the bud.
- Japanese universities tend to be backwaters in the scientific communities. Underfunded, research is controlled by rigid hierarchies of elite professors and bureaucrats. Schools tend to be poor quality and own obsolete equipment. Few post-doctoral programs exist in Japanese universities.
- Japan has weak university-industry ties. Professors believe it is beneath their professional dignity to work with people more interested in profits than theory. Few professors work as consultants or serve on corporate boards.
- The American patent system awards patents to first to invent whereas the Japanese system awards to first to file. The American system protects individuals, whereas the Japanese system balances individual rights with broader social and industrial interests.

Some Japanese believe that to produce any significant people capable of scientific innovation, Japan must restructure its education system and social institutions to emphasize individualism and deemphasize Japan's group orientation. The Japanese approach is oriented toward creativity based on the special characteristics of the Japanese people, a delicately balanced marriage of self-assertion and group consciousness (Christopher, 1983). Whether or not the Japanese approach will work is still much up in the air; their track record to date is not favorable.

In the twenty-first century, Japan's key challenge will be to overcome the cultural domination of the West. The Japanese must develop their own blend of individual and group creativity. The West can not continue supplying ideas free of charge in such vital areas as biotechnology and computer science. The Japanese planners are dreaming up programs to foster originality and change centuries old parasitic habits in science, but to date limited success has been achieved. Japanese will continue to excel in process and evolutionary innovation but until such time as structural and cultural changes in their society have been made, the prospect for succeeding, let alone leading, in radical (basic) innovation appears poor.

Types of Innovation

Innovation consists of not merely discrete occurrences but a continuous flow of events. The innovation timepath begins with the fundamental science and ends with the diffusion of the innovation throughout the market. Within this framework are the heart of innovation, the stages of discovery, feasibility (invention), and commercial production (innovation).

Examples of the scientific discovery of the basic principle (pure or fundamental research) include Maxwell's electromagnetism equations and Einstein's famous equation relating energy and matter. Discovery is an event that is most often credited to a single individual and is often done in isolation (Mendel's experiments with pea plants and the codification of the basic laws of genetics). Discovery alone is but the first step. At times, a period of many years is required before the practical application of a discovery (as in daVinci's drawings of helicopters and other modern marvels hundreds of years before their actual invention). Although the discovery is important, it is the application of that discovery rather than the discovery itself which becomes critical to the advancement of civilization. Although discovery is an important step, unless action is taken, the usefulness of the discovery may be lost. It is only when feasibility occurs life is life breathed into an innovation.

The invention step is the first working model resulting from the discovery (technical invention or applied research). Examples include Marconi's wireless, the first transistor by Bell Labs in 1947, or the first controlled fission below the University of Chicago's football stadium in 1942. Invention is the act of insight, a new combination of preexisting knowledge, by which a new and promising technical possibility is recognized and worked out in its essential, most rudimentary form. Most social scientists establish the date of an invention as the earliest conception of the product in substantially its commercial form. Chance is not unimportant. It is, however, often overshadowed by the society's intellectual heritage; that is, invention is often built on other inventions and requires yet other inventions to be fully realizable. The joint determinants of invention are the wants which inventions satisfy and the intellectual insights of which they are made. Many inventions do not immediately enter the stream of commercial or industrial application. In fact, many never get beyond the stage of conception, whereas others are abandoned during the period of development. However marvelous technological invention may be, it does not constitute innovation if it creates no growth or profit in the market economy. Many inventions fail at the commercialization step.

The innovation is the first practical commercial demonstration of the invention. Innovation is the conversion of that invention into a business or other useful application. It is the process by which an invention is designed to meet some anticipated need and developed through a working prototype, then a pilot manufacturing preproduction model and finally mass manufacturing. If no market (or use) exists for a product, innovation will not occur. Unlike invention, innovation is related to potential uses and potential markets. In simplest terms, innovation = invention + exploitation.

Innovation can take any of four forms, radical innovation, continuous innovation, modified innovation, or process innovation. Radical (also called basic or discontinuous) innovation requires the establishment of new behavioral patterns resulting from the introduction of totally new products. Radical technologies tend to create whole new industries and diffuse throughout the industrial base whereas lower order innovations tend to be found in specific segments. Examples of radical innovations include computers, photocopiers, lasers, atomic energy, and radar. A radical innovation is a fundamental change in technology with clear departures from existing practices—an unusually high-risk proposition for both the developing firm and the user. Continuous (also called evolutionary) innovation is the least disruptive type of innovation, involving only the introduction of a modified product. This incremental change is usually the low-risk notion of minor improvements or simple adjustments in current technologies. Examples include product line extensions, new sizes, and new flavors. Modified innovation (also called dynamically continuous) is more disruptive than a continuous innovation, but it stops short of altering behavioral patterns. An example is the creation of a product which incorporates state-of-the-art technology but which has the same basic functions—an electric pencil sharpener or an electric toothbrush.

A fourth form of innovation is process innovation. Process innovations are improvements in the way existing products are being produced or in the development of new ways of producing new products. Process innovations are used within the manufacturing process or during the transference of the good or service. Consequently, considerable interrelationship exists between process and product innovations. Adoption of a process innovation creates higher productivity, lower costs, and higher quality for an already existing good or service. Examples include ship containerization, just-in-time (*kanban*), material resource planning systems, quality circles, TQM (total quality management), computer-aided design (CAD), computer automated manufacturing (CAM), and computer-aided engineering (CAE) systems. Any industry has literally thousands of process innovations every year. In this book, process innovations mean those significant process innovations which are applicable across many, if not all, industry segments. Sometimes whether an innovation is a process innovation or a product innovation is dependent on the perspective of the producing/using firm. CAD/CAM systems were product innovations to computer manufacturers but process innovations to all other manufacturers.

Glossary

amae:	indulgence and dependency on another
amakudari:	"descent from heaven:" government bureaucrats retire and assume senior positions in private sector upon retirement.
atarimae hinshitsu:	quality taken for granted
chu-sho kigyo:	small and medium-size companies
dai kigyo:	large companies
dantai kyoyaku:	Japanese collective agreements
datsusara:	entrepreneurs: literally "salaryman who have broken loose"
doryo:	one's colleagues, those with the same rank
gaiatsu:	foreigners, foreign pressure
gaijin:	outside people, foreigners
gaku:	universities
gambare:	persevere, endure
gemba:	place where action occurs
giri:	reciprocal obligation
gonin-gumi:	five-person product development teams
gyosei shido:	administrative guidance, informal guidelines issued by governmental ministries with quasi-legal status. It is not backed by legal sanctions, but it carries the weight of statutory law in terms of eliciting voluntary compliance by companies.
heijunka:	leveling production at final assembly that makes JIT possible; averaging both the volume and sequence of different model types on the production line.

hiyatoi:	day laborers
hojokin:	low-interest loans that need only be repaid when the project succeeds
honne:	real intention, one's personal feelings
ikusei:	cultivation
ino beshion:	innovation
ipo-ipo:	little-by-little
Jidoka:	A defect detection system which automatically or manually stops the production operation and/or equipment whenever an abnormal or defective condition arises.
jishu kanri:	describes how employees solve problems on the factory floor in cooperation with each other. Each individual aims at self-realization by developing his or her capacity and displaying his or her creativity. All employees respect one another and endeavor to create a lively, comfortable work area. Through their group activity, the employees contribute to the prosperity of the company and society.
joyo-ko:	regular workers employed on a lifetime basis
kaikoku:	open country
kaisha:	Japanese corporation
kaizen:	continuous improvement
kan:	local governments
kanban:	just-in-time system
kata:	institutionaized process that practically describes behavior expected for every situation
keihokutanshoka:	making things lighter, slimmer, shorter, and smaller
keiretsu:	interlocking corporations
Keiten aijin:	fostering spirit of participation
kenkyu kaihatsu:	literally R&D—implies commercialization
kohai:	juniors, inferiors, subordinates
kohei:	fair
ko-in:	immobility of wage earners
kojin shugi:	individualism, selfishness
kokusaika:	internationalization
koza:	chair, professor
kyakkanteki :	objective, literally, guest's point of view
kyoryokukai:	formal association of cooperative part makers
manabu:	to learn

maneru:	to imitate
mibun:	status principle
miryokuteki hinshitsu:	quality that fascinates
muga:	egolessness or self-effacement
mura hachibu:	ostracism, banishment
nemawashi:	laying the ground work for obtaining one's objectives
nenko-joretsu:	seniority principle: salaries for all employees hired at the same time are the same regardless of differences in ability, dedication, or motivation.
ningen kankei:	human relations
omote:	legal self, formal public expression
on:	sense of obligation
oyabun:	relationship with someone of higher social position
ringi:	collective decision-making principle
rinji-ko:	part-time workers
ringi-sho:	decision proposal
ristora:	restructuring
ronin:	masterless, wandering, disenfranchised samurai; workers without a lord; students still trying to get admitted into a good school.
sabetsu:	discrimination
sakoku:	closed country
san:	businesses
satori:	personal enlightenment
sempai:	seniors, superiors
shikata:	way of doing things with special emphasis on the form and order of the process; way something is supposed to be done; expressing and maintaining harmony in society.
shikata ga nai:	there is no way, it is utterly hopeless to try
shogai-fuyo:	employment for full working life
shogyo sok shugyo:	all work is the pursuit of knowledge
shugyo:	transferred knowledge
shukanteki:	subjective, literally, host's point of view
shunki chin-age kyodo bosi-shunto:	spring wage offensive
shusa:	the boss
shushin-koya:	permanent employment of labor
soozoo:	creativity
soto:	out-group

sukima:	small opening that remains when a sliding door does not quite fit its frame; idiom for market niche, unprotected market segment.
takt-time:	the time which should be taken to produce a component
tanohkoh seido:	multiple-skills system under which job classifications will be as flexible as possible and a single worker will be able to handle a variety of different tasks; company as one big household.
tatemae:	face or facade; public airs.
teinen:	compulsory early retirement principle
uchi:	in-group
ura:	private beliefs
wa:	harmony
yugo-ha:	fusion of an idea
zen no junkan:	reinvest funds for tomorrow and generate new profits; this cycle allows companies to flourish and workers' incomes to rise.

References

Abegglen, James C. and George Stalk. (1985). *Kaisha, the Japanese Corporation.* Englewood Cliffs, N. J.: Prentice Hall.

Adam, John A. (1990). "Competing in a Global Economy."*IEEE Spectrum* 27/4: 20–24.

Alston, Jon P. (1986). "Wa, Guanxi, and Inhwa: Managerial Principles in Japan, China, and Korea." *Business Horizons* 32/2 (March/April): 26–31.

Aoki, Masahiko. (1986). "Horizontal vs. Vertical Information Structure of the Firm." *American Economic Review* 76/5 (December): 971–983.

Aoki, Masahiko and Narthan Rosenberg. (1989). "The Japanese Firm as an Innovating Institution," in Takashi Shiraishi and Shigeto Tsuru, eds., *Economic Institutions in a Dynamic Society.* London: Macmillan: 137–154.

Aoki, Reiko. (1990). "Toward an Economic Model of the Japanese Firm." *Journal of Economic Literature* 28/1 (March): 1–27.

Aoki, Reiko. (1988). *Information, Incentives, and Bargaining in the Japanese Economy,* Cambridge: Cambridge University Press.

Aoki, Reiko. (1991). "R&D Competition for Product Innovation: An Endless Race." *American Economic Review* 8/2 (May): 252–256.

Baba, Yasunori. (1989). "The Dynamics of Continuous Innovation in Scale-Intensive Industries." *Strategic Management Journal* 10/1 (January/February): 89–100.

Baba, Yasunori and Ken-ichi Imai. (1992). "Systematic Innovationand Cross-Border Networks: The Case of the Evolution of the VCR system," in Frederic M. Scherer and Mark Perlman, eds., *Entrepreneurship, Technological Innovation and Economic Growth.* Ann Arbor, Mich.: University of Michigan Press.

Baily, Martin Neil and Alok K. Chakrabarti. (1985). "Innovation and U.S. Competitiveness." *Brookings Review* 4/1 (Fall): 14–21.

Berger, Michael. (1987)."Japan's Energetic New Search for Creativity." *International Management* 42 (October): 71–78.

Best, Michael H. (1990). *New Competition.* Cambridge, Mass.: Harvard University Press.

Black, J. Stewart and Mark Mendenhall. (1993). "Resolving Conflicts with the Japanese: Mission Impossible." *Sloan Management Review* (Spring): 49–59.

Boisot, M. (1983). "Convergence Revisited: The Codification and Diffusion of Knowledge in a British and a Japanese Firm."*Journal of Management Studies (UK)* 20/2 (April): 159–190.

Bolton, Michele. (1993). "Imitation versus Innovation." *Organizational Dynamics* 21/3 (Winter): 30–46.

Bowonder, B., and T. Miyake. (1992). "A Model of Corporate Innovation Management: Some Recent High Tech Innovations in Japan." *R&D Management* 2/4: 319–336.

Bowonder, B., and T. Miyake. (1991). "Industrial Competitiveness: An Analysis of the Japanese Electronics Industry." *Science and Public Policy* 18/2 (April): 93–110.

Branscomb, Lewis M. and Fumio Kodama. (1993). *Japanese Innovation Strategies: Technical Support for Business Visions.* Lanham, Md.: University Press of America.

Bylinski, Gene. (1987). "Trying to Transcend CopyCat Science." *Fortune* 115/7 (March 30): 42–47.

Campbell, Nigel. (1985). "Sources of Competitive Rivalry in Japan." *Journal of Product Innovation Management* 4: 224–231.

"Can Japan make Einsteins too?" (1990). *The Economist* (August 11): 81–83.

Chakrabarti, Alok K., Stephen Feinman, and William Fuentevilla. (1982). "The Cross National Comparisons of Patterns of Industrial Innovations." *Columbia Journal of World Business* (Fall): 33–35.

Chakrabarti, Alok K., Stephen Feinman, and William Fuentevilla. (1978). "Industrial Product Innovation: An International Comparison." *Industrial Marketing Management* 7: 231–237.

Choi, Hyung Sup. (1989). "Transition from Imitation to Creation." *Technological Forecasting and Social Change* 36: 209–215.

Christopher, Robert C. (1983). *The Japanese Mind: The Goliath Explained.* New York: Simon & Schuster.

Clark, Rodney. (1984). *Aspects of Japanese Commercial Innovation.* London: The Technical Change Centre.

Cody, Jennifer. (1994). "Many Career Women Venture Out of Japan to Find Advancement." *The Wall Street Journal* (August 29): B1.

Coe, Barbara J. (1990). "Strategy in Retreat: Pricing Drops Out." *Journal of Business and Industrial Marketing* 5/1 (Winter/Spring): 5–25.

Cohen, Stephen S. and John Zysman. (1986). "Manufacturing Innovation and American Industrial Competitiveness."*Science* 239 (March 4): 1110–1115.

Cross, Michael. (1990). "Innovation or Imitation: The State of Japanese Research." *Japan Update* (Summer): 19–21.

Cusamano, Michael A. (1991). *Japan's Software Factories.* New York: Oxford Press.

Cusumano, Michael A. (1994). "The Limits of 'Lean.'" *Sloan Management Review* (Summer): 27–32.

DeMente, Boye. (1990). *The Kata Factor.* Phoenix, Ariz.: Phoenix Book Publishers.

Dore, Ronald. (1989). "Technology in a World of National Frontiers." *World Development* 17/11: 1665–1675.

Drucker, Peter F. (1985). *Innovation and Entrepreneurship.* New York: Harper & Row.

Drucker, Peter F. (1993). *Post Capitalist Society.* New York: Harper & Row.

Dumaine, Brian. (1991). "Closing the Innovation Gap." *Fortune* (December 2): 56–60.

Eisenstodt, Gale. (1993a). "Breaking Up." *Forbes* (May 24): 88–90.

Eisenstodt, Gale. (1993b). "They Say Change, But . . ." *Forbes* (December 20): 62–66.

Fallows, James. (1989a). "Containing Japan." *The Atlantic Monthly* (May): 40–54.

Fallows, James. (1989b). *More Like U.S.: Making America Great Again.* Boston: Houghton Mifflin Company.

Feigenbaum, Edward A. and Pamela McCorduck. (1983). *The Fifth Generation.* Reading, Mass.: Addison-Wesley.

Franko, Lawrence G. (1982). *World Market Share Research Note No. 1: Research and Development Spending Matters.* London: J. Henry Schroder Wagg & Co. Ltd. Strategy Group.

Franko, Lawrence G. (1983). *The Threat of Japanese Multinationals.* New York: John Wiley.

Freeman, Christopher. (1987). *Technology Policy and Economic Performance.* London: Pinter Publishers.

Friedman, David. (1988). *The Misunderstood Miracle.* Ithaca, N.Y. : Cornell University Press.

Frost, Ellen L. (1987). *For Richer, For Poorer.* New York: Council on Foreign Relations.

Fruin, W. Mark. (1992). *The Japanese Enterprise System.* Oxford: Clarendon Press.

Gerstenfeld, A. and L. H. Wortzel. (1977). "Strategies for Innovation in Developing Countries." *Sloan Management Review* 19(1): 57–68.

Giget, Marc. (1988). "The Bonsai Trees of Japanese Industry." *Futures* 20 (April):147–154.

Giraud, Pierre. (1987). "Japan at the Turning Point." *Futures* 19/4 (August): 385–401.

Godet, Michel (1987). "Ten Unfashionable and Controversial Findings on Japan," *Futures* 19/4 (August): 371-383.

Guile, Bruce R. and Harvey Brooks (eds.). (1987). *Technology and Global Industry.* Washington, D.C.: National Academy Press.

Hall, Edward T. and Mildred Reed Hall. (1987). *Hidden Differences.* New York: Anchor Books.

Hamilton, David P. (1994). "Big Fiber-Optic Project is Private Sector's Job, Japan's Reformers Say." *The Wall Street Journal* (August 15): A1,A8.

Harper, Stephen C. (1988). "Now that the Dust Has Settled; Learning from Japanese Management." *Business Horizons* (July/August): 43–51.

Hatvany, Nina and Vladimir Pucik (1981). "Japanese Management: Practices and Productivity." *Organizational Dynamics* (Spring): 1-15.

Healy, Mel. (1983). "Innovative Ireland—Technological, Industrial, and Societal Challenges." *Technovation (Netherlands)* 2/1 (February): 45–53.

Heiduk, Gunter and Kozo Yamamura (eds.). (1990). *Technological Competition and Interdependence.* Seattle,Wash.: University of Washington Press.

Hellwign, Helmut. (1992). "Differences in Competitive Strategies between the United States and Japan." *IEEE Transactions on Engineering Management* 39/1 (February): 77–79.

Herbert, Evan. (1989). "Japanese R&D in the U.S." *Research Technology Management* 32/6: 11–20.

Herbig, Paul A. and Joseph C. Miller. (1991). "The Effect of Culture upon Innovativeness: A Comparison of United States and Japan Sourcing Capabilities." *Journal of International Consumer Marketing* 3/3: 1–57.

Hidaka, Satoshi. (1985). *The Geneology of Creativity.* Tokyo: Diamond Publishing.

Hirono, Ryokichi. (1986). "Japanese Experiences in Technology Transfer." *Management Japan* 19/1 (Spring): 9–19.

Hofstede, Geert. (1984). *Culture's Consequences.* London: Sage.

Hofstede, Geert. (1992). *Culture and Organization.* London: McGraw-Hill Europe.

Holstein, William J. (1991). *The Japanese Power Game.* New York: Plume.

Hooper, Laurence and Jacob M. Schlesinger. (1990). "Is Optical Computing the Next Frontier, or Just a Nutty Idea?" *The Wall Street Journal* CXXII/21 (Tuesday, January 30): A1, A8.

Hull, Frank, Jerald Hage, and Koya Azumi. (1984). "Strategies for Innovation and Productivity in Japan and America." *Technovation* 2: 121–139.

Hull, Frank, and Koya Azumi. (1989). "Teamwork in Japanese and U.S. Labs." *Research Technology Management* (November/December): 21–28.

"Ideas Business." (1989). *The Economist* 313/7634 (December 23): 99–102.

Imai, Ken-ichi. (1992). "The Japanese Pattern of Innovation and Its Evolution," in Nathan Rosenberg, Ralph Landau, and David C. Mowery, eds., *Technology and the Wealth of Nations.* Stanford, Calif.: Stanford University Press.

Imai, Kenichi, Ikujiro Nonaka, and Hirotaka Takeuchi. (1985). "Managing the New Product Development Process: How Japanese Companies Learn and Unlearn," in Kim B. Clark, Robert H. Hayes, and Christoper Lorenz, eds. *The Uneasy Alliance.* Boston, Mass.: Harvard Business School.

Imai, Ken-ichi and Hiroyuki Itami. (1984). "Interpenetration of Organization an Market." *International Journal of Industrial Organization* 2: 285–310.

Imai, Masaaki. (1992). "Comment: Solving Quality Problems Using Common Sense," *International Journal of Quality and Reliability Management* 9/5: 71–75.

Imai, Masaaki. (1990). "Kaizen Wave Circles the Globe." *Tokyo Business Today* 58/5 (May): 44–48.

Imai, Masaaki. (1988). *Kaizen: The Key to Japan's Competitive Success.* New York: McGraw-Hill.

"Innovation in America." (1989). *Business Week* (special issue).

Ishii, Yohei. (1993). "A Neglect of Research May Doom Japan's Future." *Economic Eye* (Spring): 9–13.

Johnson, Chalmers, Laura D'andrea Tyson, and John Zysman. (1989). *Politics and Productivity.* New York: Harper Business Press.

Jorde, Thomas M. and David J. Teece. (1990). "Innovation, Dynamic Competition and Antitrust Policy." *CATO Review of Business and Government* 13/3: 35–45.

Kahn, Herman. (1979). *World Economic Development.* Boulder, Colo.: Westview Press.

Kamath, Rajan R. and Jeffrey K. Liker. (1994), "A Second Look at Japanese Product Development." *Harvard Business Review* (November/December): 154–174.

Kanamori, Hisao. (1987). *Innovation and Industrial Structure.* Tokyo: Japan Economic Journal Press.

Kash, Don E. (1989). *Perpetual Innovation.* New York: Basic Books.

Kennard, R. B. (1991). "From Experience: Japanese Product Development Process," *Journal of Product Innovation Management* 8/3 (September): 184-188.

Kennedy, Martin and Richard Florida. (1989). "Japan's Role in the Post Fordist Society." *Futures* 22: 136–151.

Kennedy, Martin and Richard Florida. (1993). *Beyond Mass Production.* New York: Oxford University Press.

Kilburn,David. (1986). " How Japanese Products Succeed in Japan." *The Journal of the American Chamber of Commerce in Japan* (June): 24–27.

Kingery, D. W. (1991). *Japanese-American Technological Innovation.* Englewood Cliffs, N.J. : Prentice Hall.

Kirkland, Richard. (1992). "What If Japan Triumphs?" *Fortune* (May): 60–67.

Kodama, Fumio. (1991). *Analyzing Japanese High Technology.* New York: Pinter Publishing.

Kosaka, Masataka (ed.). (1988). *Japan's Choices: New Globalism and Cultural Orientations in an Industrial State.* New York: Pinter Publishing.

Kotkin, Joel and Yoriko Kishimoto. (1988). *The Third Century: America's Resurgence in the Asian Era.* New York: Crown Publishing Inc.

Kotler, Philip and L. Fahey. (1982). "The World's Champion Marketers: The Japanese." *Journal of Business Strategy* 2 (Summer): 3–13.

Kotler, Philip, Liam Fahey, and S. Jatusripitak (1985). *The New Competition.* Englewood Cliffs, N.J.: Prentice Hall.

Lazer, William, Shoji Murata, and Hiroshi Kosaka. (1985). "Japanese Marketing: Towards a Better Understanding." *Journal of Marketing* 49 (Spring): 69–81.

Leonard, J.W. and J. Thanopoulous. (1982). "Japanese Management: Reasons for Success," in Sang M. Lee and G. Schwendiman (eds.), *Japanese Management: Cultural and Environmental Considerations.* New York: Praeger.

MacDowell, Joseph. (1984). "Technology Innovation System in Japan." *Journal of Product Innovation and Management* (September): 165–169.

Maidique, Modesto and Robert Hayes. (1984). "The Art of High Technology Management." *Sloan Management Review* (Winter): 17–31.

Makino, Noburu. (1987). *Decline and Prosperity: Corporate Innovation in Japan.* Tokyo: Kodansha International.

Mansfield, Edwin. (1988a). "Industrial Innovation in Japan and the United States." *Science* 241 (September 30): 1769–1774.

Mansfield, Edwin. (1988b). "Industrial R&D in Japan and the United States: A Comparative Study." *American Economic Review Papers and Proceedings* 78/2 (May): 223–234.

Mansfield, Edwin. (1988c). "The Speed and Cost of Industrial Innovation in Japan and the United States: External versus Internal Technology." *Management Science* 34/10 (October): 1157–1167.

Mansfield, Edwin. (1989). "Technological Creativity: Japan and the United States." *Business Horizons* 32/2 (March/April): 48–53.

Marshall, Unger J. (1987). *The Fifth Generation Fallacy.* New York: Oxford University Press.

McCraw, Thomas K. (1986). *America versus Japan.* Boston: Harvard Business School Press.

Melloan, George. (1988). "An American Views Japan's Copycat Culture." *The Wall Street Journal* (Tuesday, July 12): 29.

Methe, David T. (1991). *Technological Competition in Global Industries.* New York: Quorum.

Moffat, Susan. (1991). "Picking Japan's Research Brains." *Fortune* (March 25): 84–90.

Montgomery, David B. (1991). "Understanding the Japanese as Customers, Competitors, and Collaborators." *Japan and the World Economy* 3: 61–91.

Morgan, James C. and J. Jeffrey Morgan. (1991). *Cracking the Japanese Market.* New York: Free Press.

Morishima, Michio. (1982). *Why Has Japan Succeeded: Western Technology and the Japanese Ethos.* Cambridge, England: Cambridge University Press.

Moritani, Masanori. (1982). *Japanese Technology: Best for the Least.* Tokyo: Simul Press.

Murray, Alan and Urban C. Lehner. (1990). "What U.S. Scientists Discover, the Japanese Convert—Into Profit." *The Wall Street Journal* (June 25): A1.

Musselwhite, W. Christopher. (1990). "Time-Based Innovation: the New Competitive Advantage." *Training & Development Journal* (January): 53–55.

Nadler, Leonard. (1984). "What Japan Learned from the U.S.—that We Forgot to Remember." *California Management Review* XXVI/4 (Summer): 46–56.

Neff, Clayton. (1994), *About Face: How I Stumbled onto Japan's Social Revolution.* New York: Kodansha International.

Neff, Robert. (1993). "Japan Inc. Finally Starts Its Diet." *Business Week Enterprise*: 227–229.

Nelson, Richard R. (1992). "U.S. Technological Leadership: Where Did It Come from and Where Did It Go?" in Frederic M. Scherer and Mark Perlman, eds., *Entrepreneurship, Technological Innovation and Economic Growth.* Ann Arbor, Mich.: University of Michigan Press.

Nonaka, Ikujiro. (1988). "Creating Organizational Order out of Chaos: Self Renewal in Japanese Firms." *California Management Review* (Summer): 57–67.

Nonaka, Ikujiro. (1990). "Redundant, Overlapping Organization: A Japanese Approach to Managing the Innovation Process." *California Management Review* (Spring): 27–40.

Ohinata, Yoshinobur. (1994), "Benchmarking: The Japanese Experience." *Long Range Planning* 27/4: 48–53.

Okimoto, Daniel I. (1989). *Between MITI and the Market.* Stanford, Calif.: Stanford University Press.

Okimoto, Daniel I. and Gary R. Saxonhouse. (1987). "Technology and the Future of the Economy," in Kozo Yamamura and Yasukichi Yasuba, eds., *The Political Economy of Japan.* Stanford, Calif.: Stanford University Press.

Okimoto, Daniel I., and Thomas P. Rohlen (eds.). (1988). *Inside the Japanese System.* Stanford, Calif.: Stanford University Press.

Oshima, Keichi. (1984). "Technological Innovation and Industrial Research in Japan." *Research Policy* 13: 285–301.

Ozaki, Robert. (1991). *Human Capitalism.* Tokyo: Kodansha International.

Ozawa, Terutomo. (1979). *Multinationalism, Japanese Style: The Political Economy of Dependency.* Princeton, N.J.: Princeton University Press.

Pavitt, K. (1985). "Patent Statistics as Indicators of Innovative Activities: Possibilities and Problems." *Scientometrics* 7/1–2: 77–99.

Pine, B. Joseph. (1993). *Mass Customization.* Boston, Mass.: Harvard Business School Press.

"Pricing Japanese Success." (1989). *Management Today* (May): 84–89.

Ramo, Simon. (1988). *The Business of Science; Winning and Losing in the High-Tech Age.* New York: McGraw-Hill.

Rapoport, Carla. (1991). "Why Japan Keeps On Winning. " *Fortune* (July): 76–85.

Reich, Robert B. (1987). "The Rise of Techno Nationalism." *The Atlantic Monthly* (May): 63–69.

Riggs, Henry E. (1984). "Innovation : A U.S.-Japan Perspective." Working paper, Stanford University.

Rodrigues, Carl A. (1985). "A Process for Innovators in Developing Countries to Implement New Technology." *Columbia Journal of World Business* 20/3: 21–28.

Rosenberg, Larry J. (1986). "Deciphering the Japanese Cultural Code." *International Marketing Review* (Autumn): 46–56.

Rosenberg, Nathan, Ralph Landau and David C. Mowery. (1992). *Technology and the Wealth of Nations.* Stanford, Calif.: Stanford University Press.

Rosenberg, Nathan and W. Edward Steinmueller. (1988). " Why Are Americans Such Poor Imitators?" *American Economic Review Papers and Proceedings* (May): 229–234.

Rosenberger, Jane. (1992). "Japan's Surplus in Trade Grew by 24% in June." *The Wall Street Journal* (July 14): A13.

Rosenbloom, Richard S. and William J. Abernathy. (1982). "The Climate for Innovation in Industry." *Research Policy* 11: 209–225.

Rothwell, Roy and Hans Wissema. (1986). "Technology, Culture, and Public Policy." *Technovation* 4/2: 91–115.

Sakach, Joseph M. (1987). "Can We Compete?" *Business Marketing* 72/9 (September): 82–96.

Sakakibara, Kiyonori and D. Eleanor Westney. (1992). "Japan's Management of Global Innovation: Technology Management Crossing Borders," in Nathan Rosenberg, Ralph Landau, and David C. Mowery, eds., *Technology and the Wealth of Neations.* Stanford, Calif.: Stanford University Press.

Sasaki, Naota. (1990). *Management and Industrial Structure in Japan.* New York: Pergamon Press.

Scherer, F. M. (1984. *Innovation and Growth: Schumpeterian Perspectives.* Cambridge, Mass.: MIT Press.

Scherer, F. M. (1992). *International High Technology Competition.* Cambridge, Mass.: Harvard University Press.

Scherer, Frederic M., and Mark Perlman (1992). *Entrepreneurship, Technological Innovation and Economic Growth.* Ann Arbor, Mich.: University of Michigan Press.

Schlesinger, Jacob, Michael Wiliams, and Craig Forman (1993). "Japan Inc. Wracked by Recession, Takes Stock of its Methods." *The Wall Street Journal* (September 29): A1, A10.

Song, X. Michael, and Mark E. Parry. (1993a). "How the Japanese Manage R&D Interface." *Research Technology Management* 36/4: 32–38.

Song, X. Michael, and Mark E. Parry. (1993b). "R&D Marketing Integration in Japanese High Technology Firms: Hypotheses and Empirical Evidence." *Journal of the Academy of Marketing Science* 21/2 (Spring): 125–134.

Sullivan, Jeremiah J. (1992). *Invasion of the Salaryman.* Westport, Conn.: Praeger.

Tatsumo, Sheridan. (1985). *Created in Japan.* Tokyo: Kodansha Intl.

Tatsumo, Sheridan. (1986). *Technopolis Strategy.* New York: Prentice Hall.

Taylor, Jared. (1983). *Shadows of the Rising Sun.* New York: William Morrow.

Thornton, Emily. (1993a). "Japan's Struggle to be Creative." *Fortune* (April 19): 129–135.

Thornton, Emily. (1993b). "Japan's Struggle to Restructure." *Fortune* (June 28): 84–88.

Thurow, Lester C. (1992). *Head to Head.* New York: William Morrow.

Thurow, Lester C. (1987). "A Weakness in Process Technology." *Science* (December 18): 1659–1663.

Tokuyama, Jiro. (1987). "Strengths and Weaknesses of Japanese Management." *New Management* 5/2 (Fall): 27–31.

Tsurumi, Yoshihiro. (1976). *The Japanese Are Coming.* New York: Ballinger Press.

"Turning Point." (1993). *The Economist* (March 6): 4–18.

Turpin, Dominique V. (1992). "The Strategic Persistence of the Japanese Firm." *The Journal of Business Strategy* (January-February): 49–55.

Utterback, James M. (1987). "Innovation and Industrial Evolution," in Bruce R. Guile and Harvey Brooks, eds., *Technology and Global Industry.* Washington, D.C.: National Academy Press.

Vogel, Ezra F. (1985). *Japan as Number One.* New York: Harper & Row.

Watanabe, Chihiro. (1991). *The Inducing Power of Japanese Technological Innovation.* London: Pinter Publishing.

Watanabe, Takao. (1987). *DeMystifying Japanese Management.* Tokyo: International Business Studies Association.

Westbrook, Roy and Peter Williamson. (1993). "Mass Customization: Japan's New Frontier." *European Management Journal* 11/1 (March): 38–45.

Westney, D. Eleanor and Kiyonori Sakakibara. (1985). " Japan Based R&D in Global Technology Strategy." *Technology in Society* 7/2,3: 315–330.

"What Makes Yoshio Invent?" (1991). *The Economist* (January 12): 61.

Whitehill, Arthur M. (1991). *Japanese Management: Tradition and Transition.* London: Routledge.

Whittaker, D. H. (1990). *Managing Innovation: A Study of British & Japanese Factories.* Cambridge, England: Cambridge University Press.

Williams, Michael. (1994). " Japan's Labor System Survives Recession." *The Wall Street Journal* (Tuesday, November 8): A18.

Wolferen, Karel Van. (1988). *The Enigma of Japanese Power.* New York: Knopf.

Womack, P., Daniel T. Jones, and Daniel Roos. (1990). *The Machine that Changed the World.* New York: Maxwell Macmillan International.

Worthy, Ford S. (1991). "Japan's Smart Secret Weapon." *Fortune* (August 12): 72–76.

Wyatt, Geoffrey. (1986). *The Economics of Invention: A Study of the Determinants of Inventive Activity.* New York: St. Martin's Press.

Yoder, Stephen Kreider. (1988). "Japan's Scientists Find Pure Research Suffers Under Rigid Life Style." *The Wall Street Journal* (October 31): A1.

Yoder, Stephen Kreider, and E. Lachia. (1988). "U.S. Tries Once Again to Persuade Japan to Overhaul Unfair Patent Procedures." *The Wall Street Journal* (August 26): 8.

Yoshimori, Masaru. (1992). "Sources of Japanese Competitiveness." *Management Japan* 25/1 (Spring):18–24.

Index

About the Author

PAUL HERBIG is a Visiting Professor in the Management and Marketing Department at the Graduate School of International Trade and Business Administration of Texas A&M International University in Laredo, Texas. Prior to entering academia, he worked in marketing management at AT&T, Honeywell, and Texas Instruments. His research interests include reputation and market signaling, industrial trade shows, futuristics, cross-cultural influences on innovation, and Japanese marketing practices. He is the author of *The Innovation Matrix* (Quorum, 1994).